COLLECTED WORKS OF
SIGMUND FREUD

CONTENTS

THREE CONTRIBUTIONS TO THE THEORY OF SEX

DREAM PSYCHOLOGY

THREE CONTRIBUTIONS TO THE THEORY OF SEX

AUTHORIZED TRANSLATION BY

A.A. BRILL, PH.B., M.D.

CLINICAL ASSISTANT, DEPARTMENT OF PSYCHIATRY AND
NEUROLOGY, COLUMBIA UNIVERSITY; ASSISTANT IN MENTAL
DISEASES, BELLEVUE HOSPITAL; ASSISTANT VISITING PHYSICIAN,
HOSPITAL FOR NERVOUS DISEASES

WITH INTRODUCTION BY

JAMES J. PUTNAM, M.D.

INTRODUCTION TO TRANSLATION

The somewhat famous "Three Essays," which Dr. Brill is here bringing to the attention of an English-reading public, occupy—brief as they are—an important position among the achievements of their author, a great investigator and pioneer in an important line. It is not claimed that the facts here gathered are altogether new. The subject of the sexual instinct and its aberrations has long been before the scientific world and the names of many effective toilers in this vast field are known to every student. When one passes beyond the strict domains of science and considers what is reported of the sexual life in folkways and art-lore and the history of primitive culture and in romance, the sources of information are immense. Freud has made considerable additions to this stock of knowledge, but he has done also something of far greater consequence than this. He has worked out, with incredible penetration, the part which this instinct plays in every phase of human life and in the development of human character, and has been able to establish on a firm footing the remarkable thesis that psychoneurotic illnesses never occur with a perfectly normal sexual life. Other sorts of emotions contribute to the result, but some aberration of the sexual life is always present, as the cause of especially insistent emotions and repressions.

The instincts with which every child is born furnish desires or cravings which must be dealt with in some fashion. They may be refined ("sublimated"), so far as is necessary and desirable, into energies of other sorts—as happens readily with the play-instinct—or they may remain as the source of perversions and inversions, and of cravings of new sorts substituted for those of the more primitive kinds under the pressure of a

11

conventional civilization. The symptoms of the functional psychoneuroses represent, after a fashion, some of these distorted attempts to find a substitute for the imperative cravings born of the sexual instincts, and their form often depends, in part at least, on the peculiarities of the sexual life in infancy and early childhood. It is Freud's service to have investigated this inadequately chronicled period of existence with extraordinary acumen. In so doing he made it plain that the "perversions" and "inversions," which reappear later under such striking shapes, belong to the normal sexual life of the young child and are seen, in veiled forms, in almost every case of nervous illness.

It cannot too often be repeated that these discoveries represent no fanciful deductions, but are the outcome of rigidly careful observations which any one who will sufficiently prepare himself can verify. Critics fret over the amount of "sexuality" that Freud finds evidence of in the histories of his patients, and assume that he puts it there. But such criticisms are evidences of misunderstandings and proofs of ignorance.

Freud had learned that the amnesias of hypnosis and of hysteria were not absolute but relative and that in covering the lost memories, much more, of unexpected sort, was often found. Others, too, had gone as far as this, and stopped. But this investigator determined that nothing but the absolute impossibility of going further should make him cease from urging his patients into an inexorable scrutiny of the unconscious regions of their memories and thoughts, such as never had been made before. Every species of forgetfulness, even the forgetfulness of childhood's years, was made to yield its hidden stores of knowledge; dreams, even though apparently absurd, were found to be interpreters of a varied class of thoughts, active, although repressed as out of harmony with the selected life of consciousness; layer after layer, new sets of motives underlying motives were laid bare, and each patient's interest was strongly enlisted in the task of learning to know himself in order more truly and wisely to "sublimate" himself. Gradually other workers joined patiently in this laborious undertaking, which now stands, for those who have taken pains to comprehend it, as by far the most important movement in psychopathology.

It must, however, be recognized that these essays, of which Dr. Brill has given a translation that cannot but be timely, concern a subject which is not only important but unpopular. Few physicians read the works of v. Krafft-Ebing, Magnus Hirschfeld, Moll, and others of like sort. The remarkable volumes of Havelock Ellis were refused publication in his native England. The sentiments which inspired this hostile attitude towards the study of the sexual life are still active, though growing steadily less common. One may easily believe that if the facts which Freud's truth-seeking researches forced him to recognize and to publish had not been of an unpopular sort, his rich and abundant contributions to observational psychology, to the significance of dreams, to the etiology and therapeutics of the psychoneuroses, to the interpretation of mythology, would have won for him, by universal acclaim, the same recognition among all physicians that he has received from a rapidly increasing band of followers and colleagues.

May Dr. Brill's translation help toward this end.

There are two further points on which some comments should be made. The first is this, that those who conscientiously desire to learn all that they can from Freud's remarkable contributions should not be content to read any one of them alone. His various publications, such as "The Selected Papers on Hysteria and Other Psychoneuroses,"[1] "The Interpretation of Dreams,"[2] "The Psychopathology of Everyday Life,"[3] "Wit and its Relation to the Unconscious,"[4] the analysis of the case of the little boy called Hans, the study of Leonardo da Vinci,[4a] and the various short essays in the four Sammlungen kleiner Schriften, not only all hang together, but supplement each other to a remarkable extent. Unless a course of study such as this is undertaken many critics may think various statements and inferences in this volume to be far fetched or find them too obscure for comprehension.

The other point is the following: One frequently hears the psychoanalytic method referred to as if it was customary for those practicing it to exploit the sexual experiences of their patients and nothing more, and the insistence on the details of the sexual life, presented in this book, is likely to emphasize that notion. But the fact is, as every thoughtful inquirer is aware, that the whole progress of civilization, whether in the individual or the race, consists largely in a "sublimation" of infantile instincts, and especially certain portions of the sexual instinct, to other ends than those which they seemed designed to serve. Art and poetry are fed on this fuel and the evolution of character and mental force is largely of the same origin. All the forms which this sublimation, or the abortive attempts at sublimation, may take in any given case, should come out in the course of a thorough psychoanalysis. It is not the sexual life alone, but every interest and every motive, that must be inquired into by the physician who is seeking to obtain all the data about the patient, necessary for his reeducation and his cure. But all the thoughts and emotions and desires and motives which appear in the man or woman of adult years were once crudely represented in the obscure instincts of the infant, and among these instincts those which were concerned directly or indirectly with the sexual emotions, in a wide sense, are certain to be found in every case to have been the most important for the end-result.

JAMES J. PUTNAM.

BOSTON, August 23, 1910.

1   Translated by A.A. Brill, NERVOUS AND MENTAL DISEASE MONOGRAPH SERIES, NO. 4.
2   Translated by A.A. Brill, The Macmillan Co., New York, and Allen & Unwin, London.
3   Translated by A.A. Brill, The Macmillan Co., New York.
4   Translated by A.A. Brill, Moffatt, Yard & Co., New York.
4a Translated by A.A. Brill, Moffatt, Yard & Co., New York.

AUTHOR'S PREFACE TO THE
SECOND EDITION

Although the author is fully aware of the gaps and obscurities contained in this small volume, he has, nevertheless, resisted a temptation to add to it the results obtained from the investigations of the last five years, fearing that thus its unified and documentary character would be destroyed. He accordingly reproduces the original text with but slight modifications, contenting himself with the addition of a few footnotes. For the rest, it is his ardent wish that this book may speedily become antiquated—to the end that the new material brought forward in it may be universally accepted, while the shortcomings it displays may give place to juster views.

VIENNA, December, 1909.

AUTHOR'S PREFACE TO THE THIRD EDITION

After watching for ten years the reception accorded to this book and the effect it has produced, I wish to provide the third edition of it with some prefatory remarks dealing with the misunderstandings of the book and the demands, insusceptible of fulfillment, made against it. Let me emphasize in the first place that whatever is here presented is derived entirely from every-day medical experience which is to be made more profound and scientifically important through the results of psychoanalytic investigation. The "Three Contributions to the Theory of Sex" can contain nothing except what psychoanalysis obliges them to accept or what it succeeds in corroborating. It is therefore excluded that they should ever be developed into a "theory of sex," and it is also quite intelligible that they will assume no attitude at all towards some important problems of the sexual life. This should not however give the impression that these omitted chapters of the great theme were unfamiliar to the author, or that they were neglected by him as something of secondary importance.

The dependence of this work on the psychoanalytic experiences which have determined the writing of it, shows itself not only in the selection but also in the arrangement of the material. A certain succession of stages was observed, the occasional factors are rendered prominent, the constitutional ones are left in the background, and the ontogenetic development receives greater consideration than the phylogenetic. For the occasional factors play the principal rôle in analysis, and are almost completely worked up in it, while the constitutional factors only become evident from behind as elements which have been made functional through experience, and a discussion of these would lead far beyond the working sphere of psychoanalysis.

A similar connection determines the relation between ontogenesis and phylogenesis. Ontogenesis may be considered as a repetition of phylogenesis insofar as the latter has not been varied by a more recent experience. The phylogenetic disposition makes itself visible behind the ontogenetic process. But fundamentally the constitution is really the precipitate of a former experience of the species to which the newer experience of the individual being is added as the sum of the occasional factors.

Beside its thoroughgoing dependence on psychoanalytic investigation I must emphasize as a character of this work of mine its intentional independence of biological investigation. I have carefully avoided the inclusion of the results of scientific investigation in general sex biology or of particular species of animals in this study of human sexual functions which is made possible by the technique of psychoanalysis. My aim was indeed to find out how much of the biology of the sexual life of man can be discovered by means of psychological investigation; I was able to point to additions and agreements which resulted from this examination, but I did not have to become confused if the psychoanalytic methods led in some points to views and results which deviated considerably from those merely based on biology.

I have added many passages in this edition, but I have abstained from calling attention to them, as in former editions, by special marks. The scientific work in our sphere has at present been retarded in its progress, nevertheless some supplements to this work were indispensable if it was to remain in touch with our newer psychoanalytic literature.

VIENNA, October, 1914.

17

I

THE SEXUAL ABERRATIONS[1]

The fact of sexual need in man and animal is expressed in biology by the assumption of a "sexual impulse." This impulse is made analogous to the impulse of taking nourishment, and to hunger. The sexual expression corresponding to hunger not being found colloquilly, science uses the expression "libido."[2]

Popular conception makes definite assumptions concerning the nature and qualities of this sexual impulse. It is supposed to be absent during childhood and to commence about the time of and in connection with the maturing process of puberty; it is supposed that it manifests itself in irresistible attractions exerted by one sex upon the other, and that its aim is sexual union or at least such actions as would lead to union.

But we have every reason to see in these assumptions a very untrustworthy picture of reality. On closer examination they are found to abound in errors, inaccuracies and hasty conclusions.

If we introduce two terms and call the person from whom the sexual attraction emanates the *sexual object*, and the action towards which the impulse strives the *sexual aim*, then the scientifically examined experience shows us many deviations in reference to both sexual object and sexual aim, the relations of which to the accepted standard require thorough investigation.

1. DEVIATION IN REFERENCE TO THE SEXUAL OBJECT

The popular theory of the sexual impulse corresponds closely to the poetic fable of dividing the person into two halves—man and woman—who strive to become reunited through love. It is therefore very surprising to hear that there are men for whom the sexual object is not woman but man, and that there are women for whom it is not man but woman. Such *persons* are called contrary sexuals, or better, inverts; the *condition*, that of inversion. The number of such individuals is considerable though difficult of accurate determination.[3]

A. *Inversion*

The Behavior of Inverts.—The above-mentioned persons behave in many ways quite differently.

(a) They are absolutely inverted; *i.e.*, their sexual object must be always of the same sex, while the opposite sex can never be to them an object of sexual longing, but leaves them indifferent or may even evoke sexual repugnance. As men they are unable, on account of this repugnance, to perform the normal sexual act or miss all pleasure in its performance.

(b) They are amphigenously inverted (psychosexually hermaphroditic); *i.e.*, their sexual object may belong indifferently to either the same or to the other sex. The inversion lacks the character of exclusiveness.

(c) They are occasionally inverted; *i.e.*, under certain external conditions, chief among which are the inaccessibility of the normal sexual object and initiation, they are able to take as the sexual object a person of the same sex and thus find sexual gratification.

The inverted also manifest a manifold behavior in their judgment about the peculiarities of their sexual impulse. Some take the inversion as a matter of course, just as the normal person does regarding his libido, firmly demanding the same rights as the normal. Others, however, strive against the fact of their inversion and perceive in it a morbid compulsion.[4]

Other variations concern the relations of time. The characteristics of the inversion in any individual may date back as far as his memory goes, or they may become manifest to him at a definite period before or after puberty.[5] The character is either retained throughout life, or it occasionally recedes or represents an episode on the road to normal development. A periodical fluctuation between the normal and the inverted sexual object has also been observed. Of special interest are those cases in which the libido changes, taking on the character of inversion after a painful experience with the normal sexual object.

These different categories of variation generally exist independently of one another. In the most extreme cases it can regularly be assumed that the inversion has existed at all times and that the person feels contented with his peculiar state.

Many authors will hesitate to gather into a unit all the cases enumerated here and will prefer to emphasize the differences rather than the common characters of these groups, a view which corresponds with their preferred judgment of inversions. But no matter what divisions may be set up, it cannot be overlooked that all transitions are abundantly met with, so that the formation of a series would seem to impose itself.

Conception of Inversion.—The first attention bestowed upon inversion gave rise to the conception that it was a congenital sign of nervous degeneration. This harmonized with the fact that doctors first met it among the nervous, or among persons giving such an impression. There are two elements which should be considered independently in this conception: the congenitality, and the degeneration.

Degeneration.—This term *degeneration* is open to the objections which may be urged against the promiscuous use of this word in general. It has in fact become customary to designate all morbid manifestations not of traumatic or infectious origin as degenerative. Indeed, Magnan's classification of degenerates makes it possible that the highest general configuration of nervous accomplishment need not exclude the application of the concept of degeneration. Under the circumstances, it is a question what use and what new content the judgment of "degeneration" still possesses. It would seem more appropriate not to speak of degeneration: (1) Where there are not many marked deviations from the normal; (2) where the capacity for working and living do not in general appear markedly impaired.[6]

That the inverted are not degenerates in this qualified sense can be seen from the following facts:

1. The inversion is found among persons who otherwise show no marked deviation from the normal.
2. It is found also among persons whose capabilities are not disturbed, who on the contrary are distinguished by especially high intellectual development and ethical culture.[7]
3. If one disregards the patients of one's own practice and strives to comprehend a wider field of experience, he will in two directions encounter facts which will prevent him from assuming inversions as a degenerative sign.

(a) It must be considered that inversion was a frequent manifestation among the ancient nations at the height of their culture. It was an institution endowed with important functions. (b) It is found to be unusually prevalent among savages and primitive races, whereas the term degeneration is generally limited to higher civilization (I. Bloch). Even among the most civilized nations of Europe, climate and race have a most powerful influence on the distribution of, and attitude toward, inversion.[8]

22

Innateness.—Only for the first and most extreme class of inverts, as can be imagined, has innateness been claimed, and this from their own assurance that at no time in their life has their sexual impulse followed a different course. The fact of the existence of two other classes, especially of the third, is difficult to reconcile with the assumption of its being congenital. Hence, the propensity of those holding this view to separate the group of absolute inverts from the others results in the abandonment of the general conception of inversion. Accordingly in a number of cases the inversion would be of a congenital character, while in others it might originate from other causes.

In contradistinction to this conception is that which assumes inversion to be an *acquired* character of the sexual impulse. It is based on the following facts. (1) In many inverts (even absolute ones) an early affective sexual impression can be demonstrated, as a result of which the homosexual inclination developed. (2) In many others outer influences of a promoting and inhibiting nature can be demonstrated, which in earlier or later life led to a fixation of the inversion—among which are exclusive relations with the same sex, companionship in war, detention in prison, dangers of hetero-sexual intercourse, celibacy, sexual weakness, etc. (3) Hypnotic suggestion may remove the inversion, which would be surprising in that of a congenital character.

In view of all this, the existence of congenital inversion can certainly be questioned. The objection may be made to it that a more accurate examination of those claimed to be congenitally inverted will probably show that the direction of the libido was determined by a definite experience of early childhood, which has not been retained in the conscious memory of the person, but which can be brought back to memory by proper influences (Havelock Ellis). According to that author inversion can be designated only as a frequent variation of the sexual impulse which may be determined by a number of external circumstances of life.

The apparent certainty thus reached is, however, overthrown by the retort that manifestly there are many persons who have experienced even in their early youth those very sexual influences, such as seduction, mutual onanism, without becoming inverts, or without constantly remaining so. Hence, one is forced to assume that the alternatives congenital and acquired are either incomplete or do not cover the circumstances present in inversions.

Explanation of Inversion.—The nature of inversion is explained neither by the assumption that it is congenital nor that it is acquired. In the first case, we need to be told what there is in it of the congenital, unless we are satisfied with the roughest explanation, namely, that a person brings along a congenital sexual impulse connected with a definite sexual object. In the second case it is a question whether the manifold accidental influences suffice to explain the acquisition unless there is something in the individual to meet them half way. The negation of this last factor is inadmissible according to our former conclusions.

The Relation of Bisexuality.—Since the time of Frank Lydston, Kiernan, and Chevalier, a new series of ideas has been introduced for the explanation of the possibility of sexual inversion. This contains a new contradiction to the popular belief which assumes that a human being is either a man or a woman. Science shows cases in which the sexual characteristics appear blurred and thus the sexual distinction is made difficult, especially on an anatomical basis. The genitals of such persons unite the male and female characteristics (hermaphroditism). In rare cases both parts of the sexual apparatus are well developed (true hermaphroditism), but usually both are stunted.[9]

The importance of these abnormalities lies in the fact that they unexpectedly facilitate the understanding of the normal formation. A certain degree of anatomical hermaphroditism really belongs to the normal. In no normally formed male or female are traces of the apparatus of the other sex lacking; these either continue functionless as rudimentary organs, or they are transformed for the purpose of assuming other functions.

The conception which we gather from this long known anatomical fact is the original predisposition to bisexuality, which in the course of development has changed to monosexuality, leaving slight remnants of the stunted sex.

It was natural to transfer this conception to the psychic sphere and to conceive the inversion in its aberrations as an expression of psychic hermaphroditism. In order to bring the question to a decision, it was only necessary to have one other circumstance, viz., a regular concurrence of the inversion with the psychic and somatic signs of hermaphroditism.

But this second expectation was not realized. The relations between the assumed psychical and the demonstrable anatomical androgyny should never be conceived as being so close. There is frequently found in the inverted a diminution of the sexual impulse (H. Ellis) and a slight anatomical stunting of the organs. This, however, is found frequently but by no means regularly or preponderately. Thus we must recognize that inversion and somatic hermaphroditism are totally independent of each other.

Great importance has also been attached to the so-called secondary and tertiary sex characters and their aggregate occurrence in the inverted has been emphasized (H. Ellis). There is much truth in this but it should not be forgotten that the secondary and tertiary sex characteristics very frequently manifest themselves in the other sex, thus indicating androgyny without, however, involving changes in the sexual object in the sense of an inversion.

Psychic hermaphroditism would gain in substantiality if parallel with the inversion of the sexual object there should be at least a change in the other psychic qualities, such as in the impulses and distinguishing traits characteristic of the other sex. But such inversion of character can be expected with some regularity only in inverted women; in men the most perfect psychic manliness may be united with the inversion. If one firmly adheres to the hypothesis of a psychic hermaphroditism, one must add that in certain spheres its manifestations allow the recognition of only a very slight contrary determination. The same also holds true in the somatic androgyny. According to Halban, the appearance of individual stunted organs and secondary sex characters are quite independent of each other.[10]

A spokesman of the masculine inverts stated the bisexual theory in its crudest form in the following words: "It is a female brain in a male body." But we do not know the characteristics of a "female brain." The substitution of the anatomical for the psychological is as frivolous as it is unjustified. The tentative explanation by v. Krafft-Ebing seems to be more precisely formulated than that of Ulrich but does not essentially differ from it. v. Krafft-Ebing thinks that the bisexual predisposition gives to the individual male and female brain centers as well as somatic sexual organs. These centers develop first towards puberty mostly under the influence of the independent sex glands. We can, however, say the same of the male and female "centers" as of the male and female brains; and, moreover, we do not even know whether we can assume for the sexual functions separate brain locations ("centers") such as we may assume for language.

After this discussion, two notions, at all events, persist; first, that a bisexual predisposition is to be presumed for the inversion also, only we do not know of what it consists beyond the anatomical formations; and, second, that we are dealing with disturbances which are experienced by the sexual impulse during its development.[11]

The Sexual Object of Inverts.—The theory of psychic hermaphroditism presupposed that the sexual object of the inverted is the reverse of the normal. The inverted man, like the woman, succumbs to the charms emanating from manly qualities of body and mind; he feels himself like a woman and seeks a man.

But however true this may be for a great number of inverts, it by no means indicates the general character of inversion. There is no doubt that a great part of the male inverted have retained the psychic character of virility, that proportionately they show but little of the secondary characters of the other sex, and that they really look for real feminine psychic features in their sexual object. If that were not so it would be incomprehensible why masculine prostitution, in offering itself to inverts, copies in all its exterior, today as in antiquity, the dress and attitudes of woman. This imitation would otherwise be an insult to the ideal of the inverts. Among the Greeks, where the most manly men were found among inverts, it is quite obvious that it was not the masculine character of the boy which kindled the love of man, but it was his physical resemblance to woman as well as his feminine psychic qualities, such as shyness, demureness, and the need of instruction and help. As soon as the boy himself became a man he ceased to be a sexual object for men and in turn became a lover of boys. The sexual object in this case as in many others is therefore not of the like sex, but it unites both sex characters, a compromise between the impulses striving for the man and for the woman, but firmly conditioned by the masculinity of body (the genitals).[12]

The conditions in the woman are more definite; here the active inverts, with special frequency, show the somatic and psychic characters of man and desire femininity in their sexual object; though even here greater variation will be found on more intimate investigation.

The Sexual Aim of Inverts.—The important fact to bear in mind is that no uniformity of the sexual aim can be attributed to inversion. Intercourse per anum in men by no means goes with inversion; masturbation is just as frequently the exclusive aim; and the limitation of the sexual aim to mere effusion of feelings is here even more frequent than in heterosexual love. In women, too, the sexual aims of the inverted are manifold, among which contact with the mucous membrane of the mouth seems to be preferred.

Conclusion.—Though from the material on hand we are by no means in a position satisfactorily to explain the origin of inversion, we can say that through this investigation we have obtained an insight which can become of greater significance to us than the solution of the above problem. Our attention is called to the fact that we have assumed a too close connection between the sexual impulse and the sexual object. The experience gained from the so called abnormal cases teaches us that a connection exists between the sexual impulse and the sexual object which we are in danger of overlooking in the uniformity of normal states where the impulse seems to bring with it the object. We are thus instructed to separate this connection between the impulse and the object. The sexual impulse is probably entirely independent of its object and is not originated by the stimuli proceeding from the object.

B. *The Sexually Immature and Animals as Sexual Objects*

Whereas those sexual inverts whose sexual object does not belong to the normally adapted sex, appear to the observer as a collective number of perhaps otherwise normal individuals, the persons who choose for their sexual object the sexually immature (children) are apparently from the first sporadic aberrations. Only exceptionally are children the exclusive sexual objects. They are mostly drawn into this rôle by a faint-hearted and impotent individual who makes use of such substitutes, or when an impulsive urgent desire cannot at the time secure the proper object. Still it throws some light on the nature of the sexual impulse, that it should suffer such great variation and depreciation of its object, a thing which hunger, adhering more energetically to its object, would allow only in the most extreme cases. The same may be said of sexual relations with animals—a thing not at all rare among farmers—where the sexual attraction goes beyond the limits of the species.

For esthetic reasons one would fain attribute this and other excessive aberrations of the sexual impulse to the insane, but this cannot be done.

Experience teaches that among the latter no disturbances of the sexual impulse can be found other than those observed among the sane, or among whole races and classes. Thus we find with gruesome frequency sexual abuse of children by teachers and servants merely because they have the best opportunities for it. The insane present the aforesaid aberration only in a somewhat intensified form; or what is of special significance is the fact that the aberration becomes exclusive and takes the place of the normal sexual gratification.

This very remarkable relation of sexual variations ranging from the normal to the insane gives material for reflection. It seems to me that the fact to be explained would show that the impulses of the sexual life belong to those which even normally are most poorly controlled by the higher psychic activities. He who is in any way psychically abnormal, be it in social or ethical conditions, is, according to my experience, regularly so in his sexual life. But many are abnormal in their sexual life who in every other respect correspond to the average; they have followed the human cultural development, but sexuality remained as their weak point.

As a general result of these discussions we come to see that, under numerous conditions and among a surprising number of individuals, the nature and value of the sexual object steps into the background. There is something else in the sexual impulse which is the essential and constant.[13]

2. DEVIATION IN REFERENCE TO THE SEXUAL AIM

The union of the genitals in the characteristic act of copulation is taken as the normal sexual aim. It serves to loosen the sexual tension and temporarily to quench the sexual desire (gratification analogous to satisfaction of hunger). Yet even in the most normal sexual process those additions are distinguishable, the development of which leads to the aberrations described as *perversions*. Thus certain intermediary relations to the sexual object connected with copulation, such as touching and looking, are recognized as preliminary to the sexual aim. These activities are on the one hand themselves connected with pleasure and on the other hand they enhance the excitement which persists until the definite sexual aim is reached. One definite kind of contiguity, consisting of mutual approximation of the mucous membranes of the lips in the form of a kiss, has received among the most civilized nations a sexual value, though the parts of the body concerned do not belong to the sexual apparatus but form the entrance to the digestive tract. This therefore supplies the factors which allow us to bring the perversions into relation with the normal sexual life, and which are available also for their classification. The perversions are either *(a)* anatomical *transgressions* of the bodily regions destined for sexual union, or *(b)* a *lingering* at the intermediary relations to the sexual object which should normally be rapidly passed on the way to the definite sexual aim.

(a) Anatomical Transgression

Overestimation of the Sexual Object.—The psychic estimation in which the sexual object as a goal of the sexual impulse shares is only in the rarest cases limited to the genitals; generally it embraces the whole body and tends to include all sensations emanating from the sexual object. The same overestimation spreads over the psychic sphere and manifests itself as a logical blinding (diminished judgment) in the face of the psychic attainments and perfections of the sexual object, as well as a blind obedience to the judgments issuing from the latter. The full faith of love thus becomes an important, if not the primordial source of authority.[14]

It is this sexual overvaluation, which so ill agrees with the restriction of the sexual aim to the union of the genitals only, that assists other parts of the body to participate as sexual aims.[15] In the development of this most manifold anatomical overestimation there is an unmistakable desire towards variation, a thing denominated by Hoche as "excitement-hunger" (Reiz-hunger).[16]

Sexual Utilization of the Mucous Membrane of the Lips and Mouth.—The significance of the factor of sexual overestimation can be best studied in the man, in whom alone the sexual life is accessible to investigation, whereas in the woman it is veiled in impenetrable darkness, partly in consequence of cultural stunting and partly on account of the conventional reticence and dishonesty of women.

The employment of the mouth as a sexual organ is considered as a perversion if the lips (tongue) of the one are brought into contact with the genitals of the other, but not when the mucous membrane of the lips of both touch each other. In the latter exception we find the connection with the normal. He who abhors the former as perversions, though these since antiquity have been common practices among mankind, yields to a distinct *feeling of loathing* which protects him from adopting such sexual aims. The limit of such loathing is frequently purely conventional; he who kisses fervently the lips of a pretty girl will perhaps be able to use her tooth brush only with a sense of loathing, though there is no reason to assume that his own oral cavity for which he entertains no loathing is cleaner than that of the girl. Our attention is here called to the factor of loathing which stands in the way of the libidinous overestimation of the sexual aim, but which may in turn be vanquished by the libido. In the loathing we may observe one of the forces which have brought about the restrictions of the sexual aim. As a rule these forces halt at the genitals; there is, however, no doubt that even the genitals of the other sex themselves may be an object of loathing. Such behavior is characteristic of all hysterics, especially women. The force of the sexual impulse prefers to occupy itself with the overcoming of this loathing (see below).

Sexual Utilization of the Anal Opening.—It is even more obvious than in the former case that it is the loathing which stamps as a perversion the use of the anus as a sexual aim. But it should not be interpreted as espousing a cause when I observe that the basis of this loathing— namely, that this part of the body serves for the excretion and comes in

31

contact with the loathsome excrement—is not more plausible than the basis which hysterical girls have for the disgust which they entertain for the male genital because it serves for urination.

The sexual rôle of the mucous membrane of the anus is by no means limited to intercourse between men; its preference has nothing characteristic of the inverted feeling. On the contrary, it seems that the *pedicatio* of the man owes its rôle to the analogy with the act in the woman, whereas among inverts it is mutual masturbation which is the most common sexual aim.

The Significance of Other Parts of the Body.—Sexual infringement on the other parts of the body, in all its variations, offers nothing new; it adds nothing to our knowledge of the sexual impulse which herein only announces its intention to dominate the sexual object in every way. Besides the sexual overvaluation, a second and generally unknown factor may be mentioned among the anatomical transgressions. Certain parts of the body, like the mucous membrane of the mouth and anus, which repeatedly appear in such practices, lay claim as it were to be considered and treated as genitals. We shall hear how this claim is justified by the development of the sexual impulse, and how it is fulfilled in the symptomatology of certain morbid conditions.

Unfit Substitutes for the Sexual Object. Fetichism.—We are especially impressed by those cases in which for the normal sexual object another is substituted which is related to it but which is totally unfit for the normal sexual aim. According to the scheme of the introduction we should have done better to mention this most interesting group of aberrations of the sexual impulse among the deviations in reference to the sexual object, but we have deferred mention of these until we became acquainted with the factor of sexual overestimation, upon which these manifestations, connected with the relinquishing of the sexual aim, depend.

The substitute for the sexual object is generally a part of the body but little adapted for sexual purposes, such as the foot, or hair, or an inanimate object which is in demonstrable relation with the sexual person, and preferably with the sexuality of the same (fragments of clothing, white underwear). This substitution is not unjustly compared with the fetich in which the savage sees the embodiment of his god.

The transition to the cases of fetichism, with a renunciation of a normal or of a perverted sexual aim, is formed by cases in which a fetichistic determination is demanded in the sexual object if the sexual aim is to be attained (definite color of hair, clothing, even physical blemishes). No other variation of the sexual impulse verging on the pathological claims our interest as much as this one, owing to the peculiarity occasioned by its manifestations. A certain diminution in the striving for the normal sexual aim may be presupposed in all these cases (executive weakness of the sexual apparatus).[17] The connection with the normal is occasioned by the psychologically necessary overestimation of the sexual object, which inevitably encroaches upon everything associatively related to it (sexual object). A certain degree of such fetichism therefore regularly belong to the normal, especially during those stages of wooing when the normal sexual aim seems inaccessible or its realization deferred.

"Get me a handkerchief from her bosom—a garter of my love."

—FAUST.

The case becomes pathological only when the striving for the fetich fixes itself beyond such determinations and takes the place of the normal sexual aim; or again, when the fetich disengages itself from the person concerned and itself becomes a sexual object. These are the general determinations for the transition of mere variations of the sexual impulse into pathological aberrations.

The persistent influence of a sexual impress mostly received in early childhood often shows itself in the selection of a fetich, as Binet first asserted, and as was later proven by many illustrations,—a thing which may be placed parallel to the proverbial attachment to a first love in the normal ("On revient toujours à ses premiers amours"). Such a connection is especially seen in cases with only fetichistic determinations of the sexual object. The significance of early sexual impressions will be met again in other places.

In other cases it was mostly a symbolic thought association, unconscious to the person concerned, which led to the replacing of the object by means of a fetich. The paths of these connections can not always be definitely demonstrated. The foot is a very primitive sexual symbol already found in myths.[18] Fur is used as a fetich probably on account of its association with the hairiness of the mons veneris. Such symbolism seems often to depend on sexual experiences in childhood.[19]

(b) Fixation of Precursory Sexual Aims

The Appearance of New Intentions.—All the outer and inner determinations which impede or hold at a distance the attainment of the normal sexual aim, such as impotence, costliness of the sexual object, and dangers of the sexual act, will conceivably strengthen the inclination to linger at the preparatory acts and to form them into new sexual aims which may take the place of the normal. On closer investigation it is always seen that the ostensibly most peculiar of these new intentions have already been indicated in the normal sexual act.

Touching and Looking.—At least a certain amount of touching is indispensable for a person in order to attain the normal sexual aim. It is also generally known that the touching of the skin of the sexual object causes much pleasure and produces a supply of new excitement. Hence, the lingering at the touching can hardly be considered a perversion if the sexual act is proceeded with.

The same holds true in the end with looking which is analogous to touching. The manner in which the libidinous excitement is frequently awakened is by the optical impression, and selection takes account of this circumstance—if this teleological mode of thinking be permitted—by making the sexual object a thing of beauty. The covering of the body, which keeps abreast with civilization, serves to arouse sexual inquisitiveness, which always strives to restore for itself the sexual object by uncovering the hidden parts. This can be turned into the artistic ("sublimation") if the interest is turned from the genitals to the form of the body.[20] The tendency to linger at this intermediary sexual aim of the sexually accentuated looking is found to a certain degree in most normals; indeed it gives them the possibility of directing a certain amount of their libido to a higher artistic aim. On the other hand, the fondness for looking becomes a perversion (a) when it limits itself entirely to the genitals; (b) when it becomes connected with the overcoming of loathing (voyeurs and onlookers at the functions of excretion); and (c) when instead of preparing for the normal sexual aim it suppresses it. The latter, if I may draw conclusions from a single analysis, is in a most pronounced way true of exhibitionists, who expose their genitals so as in turn to bring to view the genitals of others.

In the perversion which consists in striving to look and be looked at we are confronted with a very remarkable character which will occupy us even more intensively in the following aberration. The sexual aim is here present in twofold formation, in an *active* and a *passive* form.

The force which is opposed to the peeping mania and through which it is eventually abolished is *shame* (like the former loathing).

Sadism and Masochism.—The desire to cause pain to the sexual object and its opposite, the most frequent and most significant of all perversions, was designated in its two forms by v. Krafft-Ebing as sadism or the

35

active form, and masochism or the passive form. Other authors prefer the narrower term algolagnia which emphasizes the pleasure in pain and cruelty, whereas the terms selected by v. Krafft-Ebing place the pleasure secured in all kinds of humility and submission in the foreground.

The roots of active algolagnia, sadism, can be readily demonstrable in the normal. The sexuality of most men shows a taint of *aggression*, it is a propensity to subdue, the biological significance of which lies in the necessity of overcoming the resistance of the sexual object by actions other than mere *courting*. Sadism would then correspond to an aggressive component of the sexual impulse which has become independent and exaggerated and has been brought to the foreground by displacement.

The conception of sadism fluctuates in the usage of language from a mere active or impetuous attitude towards the sexual object to the exclusive attachment of the gratification to the subjection and maltreatment of the object. Strictly speaking only the last extreme case has a claim to the name of perversion.

Similarly, the designation of masochism comprises all passive attitude to the sexual life and to the sexual object; in its most extreme form the gratification is connected with suffering of physical or mental pain at the hands of the sexual object. Masochism as a perversion seems to be still more remote from the normal sexual life by forming a contrast to it; it may be doubted whether it ever appears as a primary form or whether it does not more regularly originate through transformation from sadism. It can often be recognized that the masochism is nothing but a continuation of the sadism turning against one's own person in which the latter at first takes the place of the sexual object. Analysis of extreme cases of masochistic perversions show that there is a coöperation of a large series of factors which exaggerate and fix the original passive sexual attitude (castration complex, conscience).

The pain which is here overcome ranks with the loathing and shame which were the resistances opposed to the libido.

Sadism and masochism occupy a special place among the perversions, for the contrast of activity and passivity lying at their bases belong to the common traits of the sexual life.

That cruelty and sexual impulse are most intimately connected is beyond doubt taught by the history of civilization, but in the explanation of this connection no one has gone beyond the accentuation of the aggressive factors of the libido. The aggression which is mixed with the sexual impulse is according to some authors a remnant of cannibalistic lust, a participation on the part of the domination apparatus (Bemächtigungsapparatus), which served also for the gratification of the great wants of the other, ontogenetically the older impulse.[21] It has also been claimed that every pain contains in itself the possibility of a pleasurable sensation. Let us be satisfied with the impression that the explanation of this perversion is by no means satisfactory and that it is possible that many psychic efforts unite themselves into one effect.

The most striking peculiarity of this perversion lies in the fact that its active and passive forms are regularly encountered together in the same person. He who experiences pleasure by causing pain to others in sexual relations is also able to experience the pain emanating from sexual relations as pleasure. A sadist is simultaneously a masochist, though either the active or the passive side of the perversion may be more strongly developed and thus represent his preponderate sexual activity.[22]

We thus see that certain perverted propensities regularly appear in *contrasting pairs*, a thing which, in view of the material to be produced later, must claim great theoretical value. It is furthermore clear that the existence of the contrast, sadism and masochism, can not readily be attributed to the mixture of aggression. On the other hand one may be tempted to connect such simultaneously existing contrasts with the united contrast of male and female in bisexuality, the significance of which is reduced in psychoanalysis to the contrast of activity and passivity.

3. GENERAL STATEMENTS APPLICABLE TO ALL PERVERSIONS

Variation and Disease.—The physicians who at first studied the *perversions* in pronounced cases and under peculiar conditions were naturally inclined to attribute to them the character of a morbid or degenerate sign similar to the *inversions*. This view, however, is easier to refute in this than in the former case. Everyday experience has shown that most of these transgressions, at least the milder ones, are seldom wanting as components in the sexual life of normals who look upon them as upon other intimacies. Wherever the conditions are favorable such a perversion may for a long time be substituted by a normal person for the normal sexual aim or it may be placed near it. In no normal person does the normal sexual aim lack some designable perverse element, and this universality suffices in itself to prove the inexpediency of an opprobrious application of the name perversion. In the realm of the sexual life one is sure to meet with exceptional difficulties which are at present really unsolvable, if one wishes to draw a sharp line between the mere variations within physiological limits and morbid symptoms.

Nevertheless, the quality of the new sexual aim in some of these perversions is such as to require special notice. Some of the perversions are in content so distant from the normal that we cannot help calling them "morbid," especially those in which the sexual impulse, in overcoming the resistances (shame, loathing, fear, and pain) has brought about surprising results (licking of feces and violation of cadavers). Yet even in these cases one ought not to feel certain of regularly finding among the perpetrators persons of pronounced abnormalities or insane minds. We can not lose sight of the fact that persons who otherwise behave normally are recorded as sick in the realm of the sexual life where they are dominated by the most unbridled of all impulses. On the other hand, a manifest abnormality in any other relation in life generally shows an undercurrent of abnormal sexual behavior.

In the majority of cases we are able to find the morbid character of the perversion not in the content of the new sexual aim but in its relation to the normal. It is morbid if the perversion does not appear beside the normal (sexual aim and sexual object), where favorable circumstances promote it and unfavorable impede the normal, or if it has under all circumstances repressed and supplanted the normal; *the exclusiveness* and *fixation* of the perversion justifies us in considering it a morbid symptom.

The Psychic Participation in the Perversions.—Perhaps it is precisely in the most abominable perversions that we must recognize the most prolific psychic participation for the transformation of the sexual impulse. In these cases a piece of psychic work has been accomplished in which, in spite of its gruesome success, the value of an idealization of the impulse can not be disputed. The omnipotence of love nowhere perhaps shows itself stronger than in this one of her aberrations. The highest and the lowest everywhere in sexuality hang most intimately together. ("From heaven through the world to hell.")

Two Results.—In the study of perversions we have gained an insight into the fact that the sexual impulse has to struggle against certain psychic forces, resistances, among which shame and loathing are most prominent. We may presume that these forces are employed to confine the impulse within the accepted normal limits, and if they have become developed in the individual before the sexual impulse has attained its full strength, it is really they which have directed it in the course of development.[23]

We have furthermore remarked that some of the examined perversions can be comprehended only by assuming the union of many motives. If they are amenable to analysis—disintegration—they must be of a composite nature. This may give us a hint that the sexual impulse itself may not be something simple, that it may on the contrary be composed of many components which detach themselves to form perversions. Our clinical observation thus calls our attention to *fusions* which have lost their expression in the uniform normal behavior.

4. THE SEXUAL IMPULSE IN NEUROTICS

Psychoanalysis.—A proper contribution to the knowledge of the sexual impulse in persons who are at least related to the normal can be gained only from one source, and is accessible only by one definite path. There is only one way to obtain a thorough and unerring solution of problems in the sexual life of so-called psychoneurotics (hysteria, obsessions, the wrongly-named neurasthenia, and surely also dementia præcox, and paranoia), and that is by subjecting them to the psychoanalytic investigations propounded by J. Breuer and myself in 1893, which we called the "cathartic" treatment.

I must repeat what I have said in my published work, that these psychoneuroses, as far as my experience goes, are based on sexual motive powers. I do not mean that the energy of the sexual impulse merely contributes to the forces supporting the morbid manifestations (symptoms), but I wish distinctly to maintain that this supplies the only constant and the most important source of energy in the neurosis, so that the sexual life of such persons manifests itself either exclusively, preponderately, or partially in these symptoms. As I have already stated in different places, the symptoms are the sexual activities of the patient. The proof for this assertion I have obtained from the psychoanalysis of hysterics and other neurotics during a period of twenty years, the results of which I hope to give later in a detailed account.

Psychoanalysis removes the symptoms of hysteria on the supposition that they are the substitutes—the transcriptions as it were—for a series of emotionally accentuated psychic processes, wishes, and desires, to which a passage for their discharge through the conscious psychic activities has been cut off by a special process (repression). These thought formations which are restrained in the state of the unconscious strive for expression, that is, for *discharge*, in conformity to their affective value, and find such in hysteria through a process of *conversion* into somatic phenomena—the hysterical symptoms. If, *lege artis*, and with the aid of a special technique, retrogressive transformations of the symptoms into the affectful and conscious thoughts can be effected, it then becomes possible to get the most accurate information about the nature and origin of these previously unconscious psychic formations.

Results of Psychoanalysis.—In this manner it has been discovered that the symptoms represent the equivalent for the strivings which received their strength from the source of the sexual impulse. This fully concurs with what we know of the character of hysterics, which we have taken as models for all psycho-neurotics, before they have become diseased, and with what we know concerning the causes of the disease. The hysterical character evinces a part of sexual repression which reaches beyond the normal limits, an exaggeration of the resistances against the sexual impulse which we know as shame and loathing. It is an instinctive flight from intellectual occupation with the sexual problem, the consequence of which in pronounced cases is a complete sexual ignorance, which is preserved till the age of sexual maturity is attained.[24]

This feature, so characteristic of hysteria, is not seldom concealed in crude observation by the existence of the second constitutional factor of hysteria, namely, the enormous development of the sexual craving. But the psychological analysis will always reveal it and solves the very contradictory enigma of hysteria by proving the existence of the contrasting pair, an immense sexual desire and a very exaggerated sexual rejection.

The provocation of the disease in hysterically predisposed persons is brought about if in consequence of their progressive maturity or external conditions of life they are earnestly confronted with the real sexual demand. Between the pressure of the craving and the opposition of the sexual rejection an outlet for the disease results, which does not remove

41

the conflict but seeks to elude it by transforming the libidinous strivings into symptoms. It is an exception only in appearance if a hysterical person, say a man, becomes subject to some banal emotional disturbance, to a conflict in the center of which there is no sexual interest. Psychoanalysis will regularly show that it is the sexual components of the conflict which make the disease possible by withdrawing the psychic processes from normal adjustment.

Neurosis and Perversion.—A great part of the opposition to my assertion is explained by the fact that the sexuality from which I deduce the psychoneurotic symptoms is thought of as coincident with the normal sexual impulse. But psychoanalysis teaches us better than this. It shows that the symptoms do not by any means result at the expense only of the so called normal sexual impulse (at least not exclusively or preponderately), but they represent the converted expression of impulses which in a broader sense might be designated as *perverse* if they could manifest themselves directly in phantasies and acts without deviating from consciousness. The symptoms are therefore partially formed at the cost of abnormal sexuality. *The neurosis is, so to say, the negative of the perversion.*[25]

The sexual impulse of the psychoneurotic shows all the aberrations which we have studied as variations of the normal and as manifestations of morbid sexual life.

(a) In all the neurotics without exception we find feelings of inversion in the unconscious psychic life, fixation of libido on persons of the same sex. It is impossible, without a deep and searching discussion, adequately to appreciate the significance of this factor for the formation of the picture of the disease; I can only assert that the unconscious propensity to inversion is never wanting and is particularly of immense service in explaining male hysteria.[26]

(b) All the inclinations to anatomical transgression can be demonstrated in psychoneurotics in the unconscious and as symptom-creators. Of special frequency and intensity are those which impart to the mouth and the mucous membrane of the anus the rôle of genitals.

(c) The partial desires which usually appear in contrasting pairs play a very prominent rôle among the symptom-creators in the psychoneuroses. We have learned to know them as carriers of new sexual aims, such as peeping mania, exhibitionism, and the actively and passively formed impulses of cruelty. The contribution of the last is indispensable for the understanding of the morbid nature of the symptoms; it almost regularly controls some portion of the social behavior of the patient. The transformation of love into hatred, of tenderness into hostility, which is characteristic of a large number of neurotic cases and apparently of all cases of paranoia, takes place by means of the union of cruelty with the libido.

The interest in these deductions will be more heightened by certain peculiarities of the diagnosis of facts.

Alpha. There is nothing in the unconscious streams of thought of the neuroses which would correspond to an inclination towards fetichism; a circumstance which throws light on the psychological peculiarity of this well understood perversion.

Beta. Wherever any such impulse is found in the unconscious which can be paired with a contrasting one, it can regularly be demonstrated that the latter, too, is effective. Every active perversion is here accompanied by its passive counterpart. He who in the unconscious is an exhibitionist is at the same time a voyeur, he who suffers from sadistic feelings as a result of repression will also show another reinforcement of the symptoms from the source of masochistic tendencies. The perfect concurrence with the behavior of the corresponding positive perversions is certainly very noteworthy. In the picture of the disease, however, the preponderant rôle is played by either one or the other of the opposing tendencies.

Gamma. In a pronounced case of psychoneurosis we seldom find the development of one single perverted impulse; usually there are many and regularly there are traces of all perversions. The individual impulse, however, on account of its intensity, is independent of the development of the others, but the study of the positive perversions gives us the accurate counterpart to it.

PARTIAL IMPULSES AND EROGENOUS ZONES

Keeping in mind what we have learned from the examination of the positive and negative perversions, it becomes quite obvious that they can be referred to a number of "partial impulses," which are not, however, primary but are subject to further analysis. By an "impulse" we can understand in the first place nothing but the psychic representative of a continually flowing internal somatic source of excitement, in contradistinction to the "stimulus" which is produced by isolated excitements coming from without. The impulse is thus one of the concepts marking the limits between the psychic and the physical. The simplest and most obvious assumption concerning the nature of the impulses would be that in themselves they possess no quality but are only taken into account as a measure of the demand for effort in the psychic life. What distinguishes the impulses from one another and furnishes them with specific attributes is their relation to their somatic *sources* and to their *aims*. The source of the impulse is an exciting process in an organ, and the immediate aim of the impulse lies in the elimination of this organic stimulus.

Another preliminary assumption in the theory of the impulse which we cannot relinquish, states that the bodily organs furnish two kinds of excitements which are determined by differences of a chemical nature. One of these forms of excitement we designate as the specifically sexual and the concerned organ as the *erogenous zone*, while the sexual element emanating from it is the partial impulse.[27]

44

In the perversions which claim sexual significance for the oral cavity and the anal opening the part played by the erogenous zone is quite obvious. It behaves in every way like a part of the sexual apparatus. In hysteria these parts of the body, as well as the tracts of mucous membrane proceeding from them, become the seat of new sensations and innervating changes in a manner similar to the real genitals when under the excitement of normal sexual processes.

The significance of the erogenous zones in the psychoneuroses, as additional apparatus and substitutes for the genitals, appears to be most prominent in hysteria though that does not signify that it is of lesser validity in the other morbid forms. It is not so recognizable in compulsion neurosis and paranoia because here the symptom formation takes place in regions of the psychic apparatus which lie at a great distance from the central locations for bodily control. The more remarkable thing in the compulsion neurosis is the significance of the impulses which create new sexual aims and appear independently of the erogenous zones. Nevertheless, the eye corresponds to an erogenous zone in the looking and exhibition mania, while the skin takes on the same part in the pain and cruelty components of the sexual impulse. The skin, which in special parts of the body becomes differentiated as sensory organs and modified by the mucous membrane, is the erogenous zone, κατ ex ogen.[28]

EXPLANATION OF THE MANIFEST PREPONDERANCE OF SEXUAL PERVERSIONS IN THE PSYCHONEUROSES

The sexuality of psychoneurotics has perhaps been placed in a false light by the above discussions. It appears that the sexual behavior of the psychoneurotic approaches in predisposition to the pervert and deviates by just so much from the normal. Nevertheless, it is very possible that the constitutional disposition of these patients besides containing an immense amount of sexual repression and a predominant force of sexual impulse also possesses an unusual tendency to perversions in the broadest sense.

45

However, an examination of milder cases shows that the last assumption is not an absolute requisite, or at least that in pronouncing judgment on the morbid effects one ought to discount the effect of one of the factors. In most psychoneurotics the disease first appears after puberty following the demands of the normal sexual life. Against these the repression above all directs itself. Or the disease comes on later, owing to the fact that the libido is unable to attain normal sexual gratification. In both cases the libido behaves like a stream the principal bed of which is dammed; it fills the collateral roads which until now perhaps have been empty. Thus the manifestly great (though to be sure negative) tendency to perversion in psychoneurotics may be collaterally conditioned; at any rate, it is certainly collaterally increased. The fact of the matter is that the sexual repression has to be added as an inner factor to such external ones as restriction of freedom, inaccessibility to the normal sexual object, dangers of the normal sexual act, etc., which cause the origin of perversions in individuals who might have otherwise remained normal.

In individual cases of neurosis the behavior may be different; now the congenital force of the tendency to perversion may be more decisive and at other times more influence may be exerted by the collateral increase of the same through the deviation of the libido from the normal sexual aim and object. It would be unjust to construe a contrast where a cooperation exists. The greatest results will always be brought about by a neurosis if constitution and experience cooperate in the same direction. A pronounced constitution may perhaps be able to dispense with the assistance of daily impressions, while a profound disturbance in life may perhaps bring on a neurosis even in an average constitution. These views similarly hold true in the etiological significance of the congenital and the accidental experiences in other spheres.

If, however, preference is given to the assumption that an especially formed tendency to perversions is characteristic of the psychoneurotic constitution, there is a prospect of being able to distinguish a multiformity of such constitutions in accordance with the congenital preponderance of this or that erogenous zone, or of this or that partial impulse. Whether there is a special relationship between the predisposition to perversions and the selection of the morbid picture has not, like many other things in this realm, been investigated.

REFERENCE TO THE INFANTILISM OF SEXUALITY

By demonstrating the perverted feelings as symptomatic formations in psychoneurotics, we have enormously increased the number of persons who can be added to the perverts. This is not only because neurotics represent a very large proportion of humanity, but we must consider also that the neuroses in all their gradations run in an uninterrupted series to the normal state. Moebius was quite justified in saying that we are all somewhat hysterical. Hence, the very wide dissemination of perversions urged us to assume that the predisposition to perversions is no rare peculiarity but must form a part of the normally accepted constitution.

We have heard that it is a question whether perversions should be referred to congenital determinations or whether they originate from accidental experiences, just as Binet showed in fetichisms. Now we are forced to the conclusion that there is indeed something congenital at the basis of perversions, but it is something *which is congenital in all persons*, which as a predisposition may fluctuate in intensity and is brought into prominence by influences of life. We deal here with congenital roots in the constitution of the sexual impulse which in one series of cases develop into real carriers of sexual activity (perverts); while in other cases they undergo an insufficient suppression (repression), so that as morbid symptoms they are enabled to attract to themselves in a round-about way a considerable part of the sexual energy; while again in favorable cases between the two extremes they originate the normal sexual life through effective restrictions and other elaborations.

But we must also remember that the assumed constitution which shows the roots of all perversions will be demonstrable only in the child, though all impulses can be manifested in it only in moderate intensity. If we are led to suppose that neurotics conserve the infantile state of their sexuality or return to it, our interest must then turn to the sexual life of the child, and we will then follow the play of influences which control the processes of development of the infantile sexuality up to its termination in a perversion, a neurosis or a normal sexual life.

1   The facts contained in the first "Contribution" have been gathered from the familiar publications of Krafft-Ebing, Moll, Moebius, Havelock Ellis, Schrenk-Notzing, Löwenfeld, Eulenberg, J. Bloch, and M. Hirschfeld, and from the later works published in the "Jahrbuch für sexuelle Zwischenstufen." As these publications also mention the other literature bearing on this subject I may forbear giving detailed references.

   The conclusions reached through the investigation of sexual inverts are all based on the reports of J. Sadger and on my own experience.

2   For general use the word "libido" is best translated by "craving." (Prof. James J. Putnam, Journal of Abnormal Psychology, Vol. IV, 6.)

3   For the difficulties entailed in the attempt to ascertain the proportional number of inverts compare the work of M. Hirschfeld in the Jahrbuch für sexuelle Zwischenstufen, 1904. Cf. also Brill, The Conception of Homosexuality, Journal of the A.M.A., August 2, 1913.

4   Such a striving against the compulsion to inversion favors cures by suggestion of psychoanalysis.

5   Many have justly emphasized the fact that the autobiographic statements of inverts, as to the time of the appearance of their tendency to inversion, are untrustworthy as they may have repressed from memory any evidences of heterosexual feelings.

   Psychoanalysis has confirmed this suspicion in all cases of inversion accessible, and has decidedly changed their anamnesis by filling up the infantile amnesias.

6   With what reserve the diagnosis of degeneration should be made and what slight practical significance can be attributed to it can be gathered from the discussions of Moebius (Ueber Entartung; Grenzfragen des Nerven-und

Seelenlebens, No. III, 1900). He says: "If we review the wide sphere of degeneration upon which we have here turned some light we can conclude without further ado that it is really of little value to diagnose degeneration."

7   We must agree with the spokesman of "Uranism" that some of the most prominent men known have been inverts and perhaps absolute inverts.

8   In the conception of inversion the pathological features have been Separated from the anthropological. For this credit is due to I. Bloch (Beiträge zur Ätiologie der Psychopathia Sexualis, 2 Teile, 1902-3), who has also brought into prominence the existence of inversion in the old civilized nations.

9   Compare the last detailed discussion of somatic hermaphroditism (Taruffi, Hermaphroditismus und Zeugungsunfähigkeit, German edit. by R. Teuscher, 1903), and the works of Neugebauer in many volumes of the Jahrbuch für sexuelle Zwischenstufen.

10   J. Halban, "Die Entstehung der Geschlechtscharaktere," Arch. für Gynäkologie, Bd. 70, 1903. See also there the literature on the subject.

11   According to a report in Vol. 6 of the Jahrbuch f. sexuelle Zwischenstufen, E. Gley is supposed to have been the first to mention bisexuality as an explanation of inversion. He published a paper (Les Abérrations de l'instinct Sexuel) in the Revue Philosophique as early as January, 1884. It is moreover noteworthy that the majority of authors who trace the inversion to bisexuality assume this factor not only for the inverts but also for those who have developed normally, and justly interpret the inversion as a result of a disturbance in development. Among these authors are Chevalier (Inversion Sexuelle, 1893), and v. Krafft-Ebing ("Zur Erklärung der konträren Sexualempfindung," Jahrbücher f. Psychiatrie u. Nervenheilkunde, XIII), who states that there are a number of observations "from which at least the virtual and continued existence of this second center (of the underlying sex) results." A Dr. Arduin (Die Frauenfrage und die sexuellen Zwischenstufen, 2d vol. of the Jahrbuch f. sexuelle Zwischenstufen, 1900) states that "in every man there exist male and female elements." See also the same Jahrbuch, Bd. I, 1899 ("Die objektive Diagnose der Homosexualitat," by M. Hirschfeld, pp. 8-9). In the determination of sex, as far as heterosexual persons are concerned, some are disproportionately more strongly developed than others. G. Herman is firm in his belief "that in every woman there are male, and in every man there are female germs and qualities" (Genesis, das Gesetz der Zeugung, 9 Bd., Libido und Manie, 1903). As recently as 1906 W. Fliess (Der Ablauf des

Lebens) has claimed ownership of the idea of bisexuality (in the sense of double sex). Psychoanalytic investigation very strongly opposes the attempt to separate homosexuals from other persons as a group of a special nature. By also studying sexual excitations other than the manifestly open ones it discovers that all men are capable of homosexual object selection and actually accomplish this in the unconscious. Indeed the attachments of libidinous feelings to persons of the same sex play no small rôle as factors in normal psychic life, and as causative factors of disease they play a greater rôle than those belonging to the opposite sex. According to psychoanalysis, it rather seems that it is the independence of the object, selection of the sex of the object, the same free disposal over male and female objects, as observed in childhood, in primitive states and in prehistoric times, which forms the origin from which the normal as well as the inversion types developed, following restrictions in this or that direction. In the psychoanalytic sense the exclusive sexual interest of the man for the woman is also a problem requiring an explanation, and is not something that is self-evident and explainable on the basis of chemical attraction. The determination as to the definite sexual behavior does not occur until after puberty and is the result of a series of as yet not observable factors, some of which are of a constitutional, while some are of an accidental nature. Certainly some of these factors can turn out to be so enormous that by their character they influence the result. In general, however, the multiplicity of the determining factors is reflected by the manifoldness of the outcomes in the manifest sexual behavior of the person. In the inversion types it can be ascertained that they are altogether controlled by an archaic constitution and by primitive psychic mechanisms. The importance of the *narcissistic object selection* and the *clinging* to the erotic significance of the *anal* zone seem to be their most essential characteristics. But one gains nothing by separating the most extreme inversion types from the others on the basis of such constitutional peculiarities. What is found in the latter as seemingly an adequate determinant can also be demonstrated only in lesser force in the constitution of transitional types and in manifestly normal persons. The differences in the results may be of a qualitative nature, but analysis shows that the differences in the determinants are only quantitative. As a remarkable factor among the accidental influences of the object selection, we found the sexual rejection or the early sexual intimidation, and our attention was also called to the fact that the existence of both parents plays an important rôle in the child's life. The disappearance of a strong father in childhood not infrequently favors the inversion. Finally, one might demand that the inversion of the sexual object should notionally be strictly separated from the mixing of the sex characteristics in the subject. A certain amount of independence is unmistakable also in this relation.

12   Although psychoanalysis has not yet given us a full explanation for the origin of inversion, it has revealed the psychic mechanism of its genesis and has essentially enriched the problems in question. In all the cases examined we have ascertained that the later inverts go through in their childhood a phase of very intense but short-lived fixation on the woman (usually on the mother) and after overcoming it they identify themselves with the woman and take themselves as the sexual object; that is, proceeding on a narcissistic basis, they look for young men resembling themselves in persons whom they wish to love as their mother has loved them. We have, moreover, frequently found that alleged inverts are by no means indifferent to the charms of women, but the excitation evoked by the woman is always transferred to a male object. They thus repeat through life the mechanism which gave origin to their inversion. Their obsessive striving for the man proves to be determined by their restless flight from the woman.

13   The most pronounced difference between the sexual life (Liebesleben) of antiquity and ours lies in the fact that the ancients placed the emphasis on the impulse itself, while we put it on its object. The ancients extolled the impulse and were ready to ennoble through it even an inferior object, while we disparage the activity of the impulse as such and only countenance it on account of the merits of the object.

14   I must mention here that the blind obedience evinced by the hypnotized subject to the hypnotist causes me to think that the nature of hypnosis is to be found in the unconscious fixation of the libido on the person of the hypnotizer (by means of the masochistic component of the sexual impulse).

Ferenczi connects this character of suggestibility with the "parent complex" (Jahrbuch für Psychoanalytische und psychopathologische Forschungen, I, 1909).

15   Moreover, it is to be noted that sexual overvaluation does not become pronounced in all mechanisms of object selection, and that we shall later learn to know another and more direct explanation for the sexual rôle of the other parts of the body.

16   Further investigations lead to the conclusion that I. Bloch has overestimated the factor of excitement-hunger (Reizhunger). The various roads upon which the libido moves behave to each other from the very beginning like communicating pipes; the factor of collateral streaming must also be considered.

17   This weakness corresponds to the constitutional predisposition. The early sexual intimidation which pushes the person away from the normal sexual aim and urges him to seek a substitute, has been demonstrated by psychoanalysis, as an accidental determinant.

18   The shoe or slipper is accordingly a symbol for the female genitals.

19   Psychoanalysis has filled up the gap in the understanding of fetichisms by showing that the selection of the fetich depends on a coprophilic smell-desire which has been lost by repression. Feet and hair are strong smelling objects which are raised to fetiches after the renouncing of the now unpleasant sensation of smell. Accordingly, only the filthy and ill-smelling foot is the sexual object in the perversion which corresponds to the foot fetichism. Another contribution to the explanation of the fetichistic preference of the foot is found in the Infantile Sexual Theories (see later). The foot replaces the penis which is so much missed in the woman. In some cases of foot fetichism it could be shown that the desire for looking originally directed to the genitals, which wished to reach its object from below, was stopped on the way by prohibition and repression, and therefore adhered to the foot or shoe as a fetich. In conformity with infantile expectation, the female genital was hereby imagined as a male genital.

20   I have no doubt that the conception of the "beautiful" is rooted in the soil of sexual excitement and originally signified the sexual excitant. The more remarkable, therefore, is the fact that the genitals, the sight of which provokes the greatest sexual excitement, can really never be considered "beautiful."

21   Cf. here the later communication on the pregenital phases of the sexual development, in which this view is confirmed. See below, "Ambivalence."

22   Instead of substantiating this statement by many examples I will merely cite Havelock Ellis (The Sexual Impulse, 1903): "All known cases of sadism and masochism, even those cited by v. Krafft-Ebing, always show (as has already been shown by Colin, Scott, and Féré) traces of both groups of manifestations in the same individual."

23   On the other hand the restricting forces of the sexual evolution—disgust, shame, morality—must also be looked upon as historic precipitates of the

outer inhibitions which the sexual impulse experienced in the psychogenesis of humanity. One can observe that they appear in their time during the development of the individual almost spontaneously at the call of education and influence.

24 Studien über Hysterie, 1895, J. Breuer tells of the patient on whom he first practiced the cathartic method: "The sexual factor was surprisingly undeveloped."

25 The well-known fancies of perverts which under favorable conditions are changed into contrivances, the delusional fears of paranoiacs which are in a hostile manner projected on others, and the unconscious fancies of hysterics which are discovered in their symptoms by psychoanalysis, agree as to content in the minutest details.

26 A psychoneurosis very often associates itself with a manifest inversion in which the heterosexual feeling becomes subjected to complete repression.—It is but just to state that the necessity of a general recognition of the tendency to inversion in psychoneurotics was first imparted to me personally by Wilh. Fliess, of Berlin, after I had myself discovered it in some cases.

27 It is not easy to justify here this assumption which was taken from a definite class of neurotic diseases. On the other hand, it would be impossible to assert anything definite concerning the impulses if one did not take the trouble of mentioning these presuppositions.

28 One should here think of Moll's assertion, who divides the sexual impulse into the impulses of contrectation and detumescence. Contrectation signifies a desire to touch the skin.

II

THE INFANTILE SEXUALITY

It is a part of popular belief about the sexual impulse that it is absent in childhood and that it first appears in the period of life known as puberty. This, though a common error, is serious in its consequences and is chiefly due to our present ignorance of the fundamental principles of the sexual life. A comprehensive study of the sexual manifestations of childhood would probably reveal to us the existence of the essential features of the sexual impulse, and would make us acquainted with its development and its composition from various sources.

The Neglect of the Infantile.—It is remarkable that those writers who endeavor to explain the qualities and reactions of the adult individual have given so much more attention to the ancestral period than to the period of the individual's own existence—that is, they have attributed more influence to heredity than to childhood. As a matter of fact, it might well be supposed that the influence of the latter period would be easier to understand, and that it would be entitled to more consideration than heredity.[1] To be sure, one occasionally finds in medical literature notes on the premature sexual activities of small children, about erections and masturbation and even actions resembling coitus, but these are referred to merely as exceptional occurrences, as curiosities, or as deterring examples of premature perversity. No author has to my knowledge recognized the normality of the sexual impulse in childhood, and in the numerous writings on the development of the child the chapter on "Sexual Development" is usually passed over.[2]

Infantile Amnesia.—This remarkable negligence is due partly to conventional considerations, which influence the writers on account of their own bringing up, and partly to a psychic phenomenon which has thus far remained unexplained. I refer to the peculiar amnesia which veils from most people (not from all!) the first years of their childhood, usually the first six or eight years. So far it has not occurred to us that this amnesia ought to surprise us, though we have good reasons for surprise. For we are informed that in those years from which we later obtain nothing except a few incomprehensible memory fragments, we have vividly reacted to impressions, that we have manifested pain and pleasure like any human being, that we have evinced love, jealousy, and other passions as they then affected us; indeed we are told that we have uttered remarks which proved to grown-ups that we possessed understanding and a budding power of judgment. Still we know nothing of all this when we become older. Why does our memory lag behind all our other psychic activities? We really have reason to believe that at no time of life are we more capable of impressions and reproductions than during the years of childhood.[3]

On the other hand we must assume, or we may convince ourselves through psychological observations on others, that the very impressions which we have forgotten have nevertheless left the deepest traces in our psychic life, and acted as determinants for our whole future development. We conclude therefore that we do not deal with a real forgetting of infantile impressions but rather with an amnesia similar to that observed in neurotics for later experiences, the nature of which consists in their being detained from consciousness (repression). But what forces bring about this repression of the infantile impressions? He who can solve this riddle will also explain hysterical amnesia.

We shall not, however, hesitate to assert that the existence of the infantile amnesia gives us a new point of comparison between the psychic states of the child and those of the psychoneurotic. We have already encountered another point of comparison when confronted by the fact that the sexuality of the psychoneurotic preserves the infantile character or has returned to it. May there not be an ultimate connection between the infantile and the hysterical amnesias?

The connection between the infantile and the hysterical amnesias is really more than a mere play of wit. The hysterical amnesia which serves the repression can only be explained by the fact that the individual already possesses a sum of recollections which have been withdrawn from conscious disposal and which by associative connection now seize that which is acted upon by the repelling forces of the repression emanating from consciousness.[4] We may say that without infantile amnesia there would be no hysterical amnesia.

I believe that the infantile amnesia which causes the individual to look upon his childhood as if it were a *prehistoric* time and conceals from him the beginning of his own sexual life—that this amnesia is responsible for the fact that one does not usually attribute any value to the infantile period in the development of the sexual life. One single observer cannot fill the gap which has been thus produced in our knowledge. As early as 1896 I had already emphasized the significance of childhood for the origin of certain important phenomena connected with the sexual life, and since then I have not ceased to put into the foreground the importance of the infantile factor for sexuality.

THE SEXUAL LATENCY PERIOD OF CHILDHOOD AND ITS INTERRUPTIONS

The extraordinary frequent discoveries of apparently abnormal and exceptional sexual manifestations in childhood, as well as the discovery of infantile reminiscences in neurotics, which were hitherto unconscious, allow us to sketch the following picture of the sexual behavior of childhood.[5]

It seems certain that the newborn child brings with it the germs of sexual feelings which continue to develop for some time and then succumb to a progressive suppression, which is in turn broken through by the proper advances of the sexual development and which can be checked by individual idiosyncrasies. Nothing is known concerning the laws and periodicity of this oscillating course of development. It seems, however, that the sexual life of the child mostly manifests itself in the third or fourth year in some form accessible to observation.[6]

The Sexual Inhibition.—It is during this period of total or at least partial latency that the psychic forces develop which later act as inhibitions on the sexual life, and narrow its direction like dams. These psychic forces are loathing, shame, and moral and esthetic ideal demands. We may gain the impression that the erection of these dams in the civilized child is the work of education; and surely education contributes much to it. In reality, however, this development is organically determined and can occasionally be produced without the help of education. Indeed education remains properly within its assigned realm only if it strictly follows the path of the organic determinant and impresses it somewhat cleaner and deeper.

Reaction Formation and Sublimation.—What are the means that accomplish these very important constructions so significant for the later personal culture and normality? They are probably brought about at the cost of the infantile sexuality itself, the influx of which has not stopped even in this latency period—the energy of which indeed has been turned away either wholly or partially from sexual utilization and conducted to other aims. The historians of civilization seem to be unanimous in the opinion that such deviation of sexual motive powers from sexual aims to new aims, a process which merits the name of *sublimation*, has furnished powerful components for all cultural accomplishments. We will therefore

57

add that the same process acts in the development of every individual, and that it begins to act in the sexual latency period.[7]

We can also venture an opinion about the mechanisms of such sublimation. The sexual feelings of these infantile years on the one hand could not be utilizable, since the procreating functions are postponed,— this is the chief character of the latency period; on the other hand, they would in themselves be perverse, as they would emanate from erogenous zones and would be born of impulses which in the individual's course of development could only evoke a feeling of displeasure. They therefore awaken contrary forces (feelings of reaction), which in order to suppress such displeasure, build up the above mentioned psychic dams: loathing, shame, and morality.[8]

The Interruptions of the Latency Period.—Without deluding ourselves as to the hypothetical nature and deficient clearness of our understanding regarding the infantile period of latency and delay, we will return to reality and state that such a utilization of the infantile sexuality represents an ideal bringing up from which the development of the individual usually deviates in some measure and often very considerably. A portion of the sexual manifestation which has withdrawn from sublimation occasionally breaks through, or a sexual activity remains throughout the whole duration of the latency period until the reinforced breaking through of the sexual impulse in puberty. In so far as they have paid any attention to infantile sexuality the educators behave as if they shared our views concerning the formation of the moral forces of defence at the cost of sexuality, and as if they knew that sexual activity makes the child uneducable; for the educators consider all sexual manifestations of the child as an "evil" in the face of which little can be accomplished. We have, however, every reason for directing our attention to those phenomena so much feared by the educators, for we expect to find in them the solution of the primitive formation of the sexual impulse.

THE MANIFESTATIONS OF THE INFANTILE SEXUALITY

For reasons which we shall discuss later we will take as a model of the infantile sexual manifestations thumbsucking (pleasure-sucking), to which the Hungarian pediatrist, Lindner, has devoted an excellent essay.[9]

Thumbsucking.—Thumbsucking, which manifests itself in the nursing baby and which may be continued till maturity or throughout life, consists in a rhythmic repetition of sucking contact with the mouth (the lips), wherein the purpose of taking nourishment is excluded. A part of the lip itself, the tongue, which is another preferable skin region within reach, and even the big toe—may be taken as objects for sucking. Simultaneously, there is also a desire to grasp things, which manifests itself in a rhythmical pulling of the ear lobe and which may cause the child to grasp a part of another person (generally the ear) for the same purpose. The pleasure-sucking is connected with an entire exhaustion of attention and leads to sleep or even to a motor reaction in the form of an orgasm.[10] Pleasure-sucking is often combined with a rubbing contact with certain sensitive parts of the body, such as the breast and external genitals. It is by this road that many children go from thumb-sucking to masturbation.

Lindner himself has recognized the sexual nature of this action and openly emphasized it. In the nursery thumbsucking is often treated in the same way as any other sexual "naughtiness" of the child. A very strong objection was raised against this view by many pediatrists and neurologists which in part is certainly due to the confusion of the terms "sexual" and "genital." This contradiction raises the difficult question, which cannot be rejected, namely, in what general traits do we wish to recognize the sexual manifestations of the child. I believe that the association of the manifestations into which we gained an insight through psychoanalytic investigation justify us in claiming thumbsucking as a sexual activity and in studying through it the essential features of the infantile sexual activity.

Autoerotism.—It is our duty here to arrange this state of affairs differently. Let us insist that the most striking character of this sexual activity is that the impulse is not directed against other persons but that it gratifies itself on its own body; to use the happy term invented by Havelock Ellis, we will say that it is autoerotic.[11]

It is, moreover, clear that the action of the thumbsucking child is determined by the fact that it seeks a pleasure which has already been experienced and is now remembered. Through the rhythmic sucking on a portion of the skin or mucous membrane it finds the gratification in the simplest way. It is also easy to conjecture on what occasions the child first experienced this pleasure which it now strives to renew. The first and most important activity in the child's life, the sucking from the mother's breast (or its substitute), must have acquainted it with this pleasure. We would say that the child's lips behaved like an *erogenous zone*, and that the excitement through the warm stream of milk was really the cause of the pleasurable sensation. To be sure, the gratification of the erogenous zone was at first united with the gratification of taking nourishment. He who sees a satiated child sink back from the mother's breast, and fall asleep with reddened cheeks and blissful smile, will have to admit that this picture remains as typical of the expression of sexual gratification in later life. But the desire for repetition of the sexual gratification is separated from the desire for taking nourishment; a separation which becomes unavoidable with the appearance of the teeth when the nourishment is no longer sucked in but chewed. The child does not make use of a strange object for sucking but prefers its own skin because it is more convenient, because it thus makes itself independent of the outer world which it cannot yet control, and because in this way it creates for itself, as it were, a second, even if an inferior, erogenous zone. The inferiority of this second region urges it later to seek the same parts, the lips of another person. ("It is a pity that I cannot kiss myself," might be attributed to it.)

Not all children suck their thumbs. It may be assumed that it is found only in children in whom the erogenous significance of the lip-zone is

60

constitutionally reënforced. Children in whom this is retained are habitual kissers as adults and show a tendency to perverse kissing, or as men they have a marked desire for drinking and smoking. But if repression comes into play they experience disgust for eating and evince hysterical vomiting. By virtue of the community of the lip-zone the repression encroaches upon the impulse of nourishment. Many of my female patients showing disturbances in eating, such as hysterical globus, choking sensations, and vomiting, have been energetic thumbsuckers during infancy.

In the thumbsucking or pleasure-sucking we have already been able to observe the three essential characters of an infantile sexual manifestation. The latter has its origin in conjunction with a bodily function which is very important for life, it does not yet know any sexual object, it is *autoerotic* and its sexual aim is under the control of an *erogenous zone*. Let us assume for the present that these characters also hold true for most of the other activities of the infantile sexual impulse.

THE SEXUAL AIM OF THE INFANTILE SEXUALITY

The Characters of the Erogenous Zones.—From the example of thumbsucking we may gather a great many points useful for the distinguishing of an erogenous zone. It is a portion of skin or mucous membrane in which the stimuli produce a feeling of pleasure of definite quality. There is no doubt that the pleasure-producing stimuli are governed by special determinants which we do not know. The rhythmic characters must play some part in them and this strongly suggests an analogy to tickling. It does not, however, appear so certain whether the character of the pleasurable feeling evoked by the stimulus can be designated as "peculiar," and in what part of this peculiarity the sexual factor exists. Psychology is still groping in the dark when it concerns matters of pleasure and pain, and the most cautious assumption is therefore the most advisable. We may perhaps later come upon reasons which seem to support the peculiar quality of the sensation of pleasure.

The erogenous quality may adhere most notably to definite regions of the body. As is shown by the example of thumbsucking, there are predestined erogenous zones. But the same example also shows that any other region of skin or mucous membrane may assume the function of an erogenous zone; it must therefore carry along a certain adaptability. The production of the sensation of pleasure therefore depends more on the quality of the stimulus than on the nature of the bodily region. The thumbsucking child looks around on his body and selects any portion of it for pleasure-sucking, and becoming accustomed to it, he then prefers it. If he accidentally strikes upon a predestined region, such as breast, nipple or genitals, it naturally has the preference. A quite analogous tendency to displacement is again found in the symptomatology of hysteria. In this neurosis the repression mostly concerns the genital zones proper; these in turn transmit their excitation to the other erogenous zones, usually dormant in mature life, which then behave exactly like genitals. But besides this, just as in thumbsucking, any other region of the body may become endowed with the excitation of the genitals and raised to an erogenous zone. Erogenous and hysterogenous zones show the same characters.[12]

The Infantile Sexual Aim.—The sexual aim of the infantile impulse consists in the production of gratification through the proper excitation of this or that selected erogenous zone. In order to leave a desire for its repetition this gratification must have been previously experienced, and we may be sure that nature has devised definite means so as not to leave this occurrence to mere chance. The arrangement which has fulfilled this purpose for the lip-zone we have already discussed; it is the simultaneous connection of this part of the body with the taking of nourishment. We shall also meet other similar mechanisms as sources of sexuality. The state of desire for repetition of gratification can be recognized through a peculiar feeling of tension which in itself is rather of a painful character, and through a centrally-determined feeling of itching or sensitiveness which is projected into the peripheral erogenous zone. The sexual aim may therefore be formulated as follows: the chief object is to substitute for the projected feeling of sensitiveness in the erogenous zone that outer stimulus which removes the feeling of sensitiveness by evoking the feeling of gratification. This external stimulus consists usually in a manipulation which is analogous to sucking.

It is in full accord with our physiological knowledge if the desire happens to be awakened also peripherally through an actual change in the erogenous zone. The action is puzzling only to some extent as one stimulus for its suppression seems to want another applied to the same place.

THE MASTURBATIC SEXUAL MANIFESTATIONS[13]

It is a matter of great satisfaction to know that there is nothing further of greater importance to learn about the sexual activity of the child after the impulse of one erogenous zone has become comprehensible to us. The most pronounced differences are found in the action necessary for the gratification, which consists in sucking for the lip zone and which must be replaced by other muscular actions according to the situation and nature of the other zones.

The Activity of the Anal Zone.—Like the lip zone the anal zone is, through its position, adapted to conduct the sexuality to the other functions of the body. It should be assumed that the erogenous significance of this region of the body was originally very large. Through psychoanalysis one finds, not without surprise, the many transformations that are normally undertaken with the usual excitations emanating from here, and that this zone often retains for life a considerable fragment of genital irritability.[14] The intestinal catarrhs so frequent during infancy produce intensive irritations in this zone, and we often hear it said that intestinal catarrh at this delicate age causes "nervousness." In later neurotic diseases they exert a definite influence on the symptomatic expression of the neurosis, placing at its disposal the whole sum of intestinal disturbances. Considering the erogenous significance of the anal zone which has been retained at least in transformation, one should not laugh at the hemorrhoidal influences to which the old medical literature attached so much weight in the explanation of neurotic states.

Children utilizing the erogenous sensitiveness of the anal zone can be recognized by their holding back of fecal masses until through accumulation there result violent muscular contractions; the passage of these masses through the anus is apt to produce a marked irritation of the mucus membrane. Besides the pain this must produce also a sensation of pleasure. One of the surest premonitions of later eccentricity or nervousness is when an infant obstinately refuses to empty his bowel when placed on the chamber by the nurse and reserves this function at its own pleasure. It does not concern him that he will soil his bed; all he cares for is not to lose the subsidiary pleasure while defecating. The educators have again the right inkling when they designate children who withhold these functions as bad. The content of the bowel which is an exciting object to the sexually sensitive surface of mucous membrane behaves like the precursor of another organ which does not become active until after the phase of childhood. In addition it has other important meanings to the nursling. It is evidently treated as an additional part of the body, it represents the first "donation," the disposal of which expresses the pliability while the retention of it can express the spite of the little being towards its environment. From the idea of "donation" he later gains the meaning of the "babe" which according to one of the infantile sexual theories is acquired through eating and is born through the bowel.

The retention of fecal masses, which is at first intentional in order to utilize them, as it were, for masturbatic excitation of the anal zone, is at least one of the roots of constipation so frequent in neuropaths. The whole significance of the anal zone is mirrored in the fact that there are but few neurotics who have not their special scatologic customs, ceremonies, etc., which they retain with cautious secrecy.

Real masturbatic irritation of the anal zone by means of the fingers, evoked through either centrally or peripherally supported itching, is not at all rare in older children.

The Activity of the Genital Zone.—Among the erogenous zones of the child's body there is one which certainly does not play the main rôle, and which cannot be the carrier of earliest sexual feeling—which, however, is destined for great things in later life. In both male and female it is connected with the voiding of urine (penis, clitoris), and in the former it is enclosed in a sack of mucous membrane, probably in order not to miss the irritations caused by the secretions which may arouse the sexual excitement at an early age. The sexual activities of this erogenous zone, which belongs to the real genitals, are the beginning of the later normal sexual life.

Owing to the anatomical position, the overflowing of secretions, the washing and rubbing of the body, and to certain accidental excitements (the wandering of intestinal worms in the girl), it happens that the pleasurable feeling which these parts of the body are capable of producing makes itself noticeable to the child even during the sucking age, and thus awakens desire for its repetition. When we review all the actual arrangements, and bear in mind that the measures for cleanliness have the same effect as the uncleanliness itself, we can then scarcely mistake nature's intention, which is to establish the future primacy of these erogenous zones for the sexual activity through the infantile onanism from which hardly an individual escapes. The action of removing the stimulus and setting free the gratification consists in a rubbing contiguity with the hand or in a certain previously-formed pressure reflex effected by the closure of the thighs. The latter procedure seems to be the more primitive and is by far the more common in girls. The preference for the hand in boys already indicates what an important part of the male sexual activity will be accomplished in the future by the impulse to mastery (Bemächtigungstrieb).[15] It can only help towards clearness if I state that the infantile masturbation should be divided into three phases. The first phase belongs to the nursing period, the second to the short flourishing period of sexual activity at about the fourth year, only the third corresponds to the one which is often considered exclusively as onanism of puberty.

The infantile onanism seems to disappear after a brief time, but it may continue uninterruptedly till puberty and thus represent the first marked deviation from the development desirable for civilized man. At some time during childhood after the nursing period, the sexual impulse of the genitals reawakens and continues active for some time until it is again suppressed, or it may continue without interruption. The possible relations are very diverse and can only be elucidated through a more precise analysis of individual cases. The details, however, of this *second* infantile sexual activity leave behind the profoundest (unconscious) impressions in the persons's memory; if the individual remains healthy they determine his character and if he becomes sick after puberty they determine the symptomatology of his neurosis.[16] In the latter case it is found that this sexual period is forgotten and the conscious reminiscences pointing to them are displaced; I have already mentioned that I would like to connect the normal infantile amnesia with this infantile sexual activity. By psychoanalytic investigation it is possible to bring to consciousness the forgotten material, and thereby to remove a compulsion which emanates from the unconscious psychic material.

The Return of the Infantile Masturbation.—The sexual excitation of the nursing period returns during the designated years of childhood as a centrally determined tickling sensation demanding onanistic gratification, or as a pollution-like process which, analogous to the pollution of maturity, may attain gratification without the aid of any action. The latter case is more frequent in girls and in the second half of childhood; its determinants are not well understood, but it often, though not regularly, seems to have as a basis a period of early active onanism. The symptomatology of this sexual manifestation is poor; the genital apparatus is still undeveloped and all signs are therefore displayed by the urinary apparatus which is, so to say, the guardian of the genital apparatus. Most of the so-called bladder disturbances of this period are of a sexual nature; whenever the enuresis nocturna does not represent an epileptic attack it corresponds to a pollution.

The return of the sexual activity is determined by inner and outer causes which can be conjectured from the formation of the symptoms of neurotic diseases and definitely revealed by psychoanalytic investigations. The internal causes will be discussed later, the accidental outer causes attain at this time a great and permanent significance. As the first outer cause we have the influence of seduction which prematurely treats the child as a sexual object; under conditions favoring impressions this teaches the child the gratification of the genital zones, and thus usually forces it to repeat this gratification in onanism. Such influences can come from adults or other children. I cannot admit that I overestimated its frequency or its significance in my contributions to the etiology of hysteria,[17] though I did not know then that normal individuals may have the same experiences in their childhood, and hence placed a higher value on seductions than on the factors found in the sexual constitution and development.[18] It is quite obvious that no seduction is necessary to awaken the sexual life of the child, that such an awakening may come on spontaneously from inner sources.

Polymorphous-perverse Disposition.—It is instructive to know that under the influence of seduction the child may become polymorphous-perverse and may be misled into all sorts of transgressions. This goes to show that it carries along the adaptation for them in its disposition. The formation of such perversions meets but slight resistance because the psychic dams against sexual transgressions, such as shame, loathing and morality—which depend on the age of the child—are not yet erected or are only in the process of formation. In this respect the child perhaps does not behave differently from the average uncultured woman in whom the same polymorphous-perverse disposition exists. Such a woman may remain sexually normal under usual conditions, but under the guidance of a clever seducer she will find pleasure in every perversion and will retain the same as her sexual activity. The same polymorphous or infantile disposition fits the prostitute for her professional activity, and in the enormous number of prostitutes and of women to whom we must attribute an adaptation for prostitution, even if they do not follow this calling, it is absolutely impossible not to recognize in their uniform disposition for all perversions the universal and primitive human.

Partial Impulses.—For the rest, the influence of seduction does not aid us in unravelling the original relations of the sexual impulse, but rather confuses our understanding of the same, inasmuch as it prematurely supplies the child with the sexual object at a time when the infantile sexual impulse does not yet evince any desire for it. We must admit, however, that the infantile sexual life, though mainly under the control of erogenous zones, also shows components in which from the very beginning other persons are regarded as sexual objects. Among these we have the impulses for looking and showing off, and for cruelty, which manifest themselves somewhat independently of the erogenous zones and which only later enter into intimate relationship with the sexual life; but along with the erogenous sexual activity they are noticeable even in the infantile years as separate and independent strivings. The little child is above all shameless, and during its early years it evinces definite pleasure in displaying its body and especially its sexual organs. A counterpart to this desire which is to be considered as perverse, the curiosity to see other persons' genitals, probably appears first in the later years of childhood when the hindrance of the feeling of shame has already reached a certain development. Under the influence of seduction the looking perversion may attain great importance for the sexual life of the child. Still, from my investigations of the childhood years of normal and neurotic patients, I must conclude that the impulse for looking can appear in the child as a spontaneous sexual manifestation. Small children, whose attention has once been directed to their own genitals—usually by masturbation—are wont to progress in this direction without outside interference, and to develop a vivid interest in the genitals of their playmates. As the occasion for the gratification of such curiosity is generally afforded during the gratification of both excrementitious needs, such children become *voyeurs* and are zealous spectators at the voiding of urine and feces of others, After this tendency has been repressed, the curiosity to see the genitals of others (one's own or those of the other sex) remains as a tormenting desire which in some neurotic cases furnishes the strongest motive power for the formation of symptoms.

The cruelty component of the sexual impulse develops in the child with still greater independence of those sexual activities which are connected with erogenous zones. Cruelty is especially near the childish character, since the inhibition which restrains the impulse to mastery before it causes pain to others—that is, the capacity for sympathy—develops comparatively late. As we know, a thorough psychological analysis of this impulse has not as yet been successfully accomplished; we may assume that the cruel feelings emanate from the impulse to mastery and appear at a period in the sexual life before the genitals have taken on their later rôle. It then dominates a phase of the sexual life, which we shall later describe as the pregenital organization. Children who are distinguished for evincing especial cruelty to animals and playmates may be justly suspected of intensive and premature sexual activity in the erogenous zones; and in a simultaneous prematurity of all sexual impulses, the erogenous sexual activity surely seems to be primary. The absence of the barrier of sympathy carries with it the danger that the connections between cruelty and the erogenous impulses formed in childhood cannot be broken in later life.

An erogenous source of the passive impulse for cruelty (masochism) is found in the painful irritation of the gluteal region which is familiar to all educators since the confessions of J.J. Rousseau. This has justly caused them to demand that physical punishment, which usually concerns this part of the body, should be withheld from all children in whom the libido might be forced into collateral roads by the later demands of cultural education.[19]

THE INFANTILE SEXUAL INVESTIGATION

Inquisitiveness.—At the same time when the sexual life of the child reaches its first bloom, from the age of three to the age of five, it also evinces the beginning of that activity which is ascribed to the impulse for knowledge and investigation. The desire for knowledge can neither be added to the elementary components of the impulses nor can it be altogether subordinated under sexuality. Its activity corresponds on the one hand to a sublimating mode of acquisition and on the other hand it labors with the energy of the desire for looking. Its relations to the sexual life, however, are of particular importance, for we have learned from psychoanalysis that the inquisitiveness of children is attracted to the sexual problems unusually early and in an unexpectedly intensive manner, indeed it perhaps may first be awakened by the sexual problems.

The Riddle of the Sphinx.—It is not theoretical but practical interests which start the work of the investigation activity in the child. The threat to the conditions of his existence through the actual or expected arrival of a new child, the fear of the loss in care and love which is connected with this event, cause the child to become thoughtful and sagacious. Corresponding with the history of this awakening, the first problem with which it occupies itself is not the question as to the difference between the sexes, but the riddle: from where do children come? In a distorted form, which can easily be unraveled, this is the same riddle which was given by the Theban Sphinx. The fact of the two sexes is usually first accepted by the child without struggle and hesitation. It is quite natural for the male child to presuppose in all persons it knows a genital like his own, and to find it impossible to harmonize the lack of it with his conception of others.

The Castration Complex.—This conviction is energetically adhered to by the boy and tenaciously defended against the contradictions which soon result, and are only given up after severe internal struggles (castration complex). The substitutive formations of this lost penis of the woman play a great part in the formation of many perversions.

The assumption of the same (male) genital in all persons is the first of the remarkable and consequential infantile sexual theories. It is of little help to the child when biological science agrees with his preconceptions and recognizes the feminine clitoris as the real substitute for the penis. The little girl does not react with similar refusals when she sees the differently formed genital of the boy. She is immediately prepared to recognize it, and soon becomes envious of the penis; this envy reaches its highest point in the consequentially important wish that she also should be a boy.

Birth Theories.—Many people can remember distinctly how intensely they interested themselves, in the prepubescent period, in the question where children came from. The anatomical solutions at that time read very differently; the children come out of the breast or are cut out of the body, or the navel opens itself to let them out. Outside of analysis one only seldom remembers the investigation corresponding to the early childhood years; it had long merged into repression but its results were thoroughly uniform. One gets children by eating something special (as in the fairy tale) and they are born through the bowel like a passage. These infantile theories recall the structures in the animal kingdom, especially do they recall the cloaca of the types which stand lower than the mammals.

Sadistic Conception of the Sexual Act.—If children of so delicate an age become spectators of the sexual act between grown-ups, for which an occasion is furnished by the conviction of the grown-ups that little children cannot understand anything sexual, they cannot help conceiving the sexual act as a kind of maltreating or overpowering, that is, it impresses them in a sadistic sense. Psychoanalysis also teaches us that such an early childhood impression contributes much to the disposition for a later sadistic displacement of the sexual aim. Besides this children also occupy themselves with the problem of what the sexual act consists in or, as they grasp it, of what marriage consists, and seek the solution of the mystery mostly in an association to which the functions of urination and defecation give occasion.

The Typical Failure of the Infantile Sexual Investigation.—It can be stated in general about the infantile sexual theories that they are reproductions of the child's own sexual constitution, and that despite their grotesque mistakes they evince more understanding of the sexual processes than is credited to their creators. Children also perceive the pregnancy of the mother and know how to interpret it correctly; the stork fable is very often related before auditors who confront it with a deep, but mostly mute suspicion. But as two elements remain unknown to the infantile sexual investigation, namely, the rôle of the propagating semen and the female genital opening—precisely the same points in which the infantile organization is still backward—the effort of the infantile investigator regularly remains fruitless, and ends in a renunciation which not infrequently leaves a lasting injury to the desire for knowledge. The sexual investigation of these early childhood years is always conducted alone, it signifies the first step towards independent orientation in the world, and causes a marked estrangement between the child and the persons of his environment who formerly enjoyed its full confidence.

72

The Phases of Development of the Sexual Organization.—As characteristics of the infantile sexuality we have hitherto emphasized the fact that it is essentially autoerotic (it finds its object in its own body), and that its individual partial impulses, which on the whole are unconnected and independent of one another, are striving for the acquisition of pleasure. The end of this development forms the so-called normal sexual life of the adult in which the acquisition of pleasure has been put into the service of the function of propagation, and the partial impulses, under the primacy of one single erogenous zone, have formed a firm organization for the attainment of the sexual aim in a strange sexual object.

Pregenital Organizations.—The study, with the help of psychoanalysis, of the inhibitions and disturbances in this course of development now permits us to recognize additions and primary stages of such organization of the partial impulses which likewise furnish a sort of sexual regime. These phases of the sexual organization normally will pass over smoothly and will only be recognizable by slight indications. Only in pathological cases do they become active and discernible to coarse observation.

Organizations of the sexual life in which the genital zones have not yet assumed the dominating rôle we would call the *pregenital* phase. So far we have become acquainted with two of them which recall reversions to early animal states.

One of the first of such pregenital sexual organizations is the *oral*, or if we wish, the cannibalistic. Here the sexual activity is not yet separated from the taking of nourishment, and the contrasts within the same not yet differentiated. The object of the one activity is also that of the other, the sexual aim consists in the *incorporating* into one's own body of the object, it is the prototype of that which later plays such an important psychic rôle as *identification*. As a remnant of this fictitious phase of organization forced on us by pathology we can consider thumbsucking.

73

Here the sexual activity became separated from the nourishment activity and the strange object was given up in favor of one from his own body.

A second pregenital phase is the sadistic-anal organization. Here the contrasts which run through the whole sexual life are already developed, but cannot yet be designated as *masculine* and *feminine*, but must be called *active* and *passive*. The activity is supplied by the musculature of the body through the mastery impulse; the erogenous mucous membrane of the bowel manifests itself above all as an organ with a passive sexual aim, for both strivings there are objects present, which however do not merge together. Besides them there are other partial impulses which are active in an autoerotic manner. The sexual polarity and the strange object can thus already be demonstrated in this phase. The organization and subordination under the function of propagation are still lacking.

Ambivalence.—This form of the sexual organization could be retained throughout life and continue to draw to itself a large part of the sexual activity. The prevalence of sadism and the rôle of the cloaca of the anal zone stamps it with an exquisitely archaic impression. As another characteristic belonging to it we can mention the fact that the contrasting pair of impulses are developed in almost the same manner, a behavior which was designated by Bleuler with the happy name of *ambivalence*.

The assumption of the pregenital organizations of the sexual life is based on the analysis of the neuroses and hardly deserves any consideration without a knowledge of the same. We may expect that continued analytic efforts will furnish us with still more disclosures concerning the structure and development of the normal sexual function.

To complete the picture of the infantile sexual life one must add that frequently or regularly an object selection takes place even in childhood which is as characteristic as the one we have represented for the phase of development of puberty. This object selection proceeds in such a manner that all the sexual strivings proceed in the direction of one person in whom they wish to attain their aim. This is then the nearest approach to the definitive formation of the sexual life after puberty, that is possible in childhood. It differs from the latter only in the fact that the collection of the partial impulses and their subordination to the primacy of the genitals is very imperfectly or not at all accomplished in childhood. The establishment of this primacy in the service of propagation is therefore the last phase through which the sexual organization passes.

The Two Periods of Object Selection.—That the object selection takes place in two periods, or in two shifts, can be spoken of as a typical occurrence. The first shift has its origin between the age of three and five years, and is brought to a stop or to retrogression by the latency period; it is characterized by the infantile nature of its sexual aims. The second shift starts with puberty and determines the definitive formation of the sexual life.

The fact of the double object selection which is essentially due to the effect of the latency period, becomes most significant for the disturbance of this terminal state. The results of the infantile object selection reach into the later period; they are either preserved as such or are even refreshed at the time of puberty. But due to the development of the repression which takes place between the two phases they turn out as unutilizable. The sexual aims have become softened and now represent what we can designate as the *tender* streams of the sexual life. Only psychoanalytic investigation can demonstrate that behind this tenderness, such as honoring and esteeming, there is concealed the old sexual strivings of the infantile partial impulses which have now become useless. The object selection of the pubescent period must renounce the infantile objects and begin anew as a sensuous stream. The fact that the two streams do not meet often enough has as a result that one of the ideals of the sexual life, namely, the union of all desires in one object, can not be attained.

THE SOURCES OF THE INFANTILE SEXUALITY

In our effort to follow up the origins of the sexual impulse, we have thus far found that the sexual excitement originates (*a*) as an imitation of a gratification which has been experienced in conjunction with other organic processes; (*b*) through the appropriate peripheral stimulation of erogenous zones; (*c*) and as an expression of some "impulse," like the looking and cruelty impulses, the origin of which we do not yet fully understand. The psychoanalytic investigation of later life which leads back to childhood and the contemporary observation of the child itself coöperate to reveal to us still other regularly-flowing sources of the sexual excitement. The observation of childhood has the disadvantage of treating easily misunderstood material, while psychoanalysis is made difficult by the fact that it can reach its objects and conclusions only by great detours; still the united efforts of both methods achieve a sufficient degree of positive understanding.

In investigating the erogenous zones we have already found that these skin regions merely show the special exaggeration of a form of sensitiveness which is to a certain degree found over the whole surface of the skin. It will therefore not surprise us to learn that certain forms of general sensitiveness in the skin can be ascribed to very distinct erogenous action. Among these we will above all mention the temperature sensitiveness; this will perhaps prepare us for the understanding of the therapeutic effects of warm baths.

Mechanical Excitation.—We must, moreover, describe here the production of sexual excitation by means of rhythmic mechanical shaking of the body. There are three kinds of exciting influences: those acting on the sensory apparatus of the vestibular nerves, those acting on the skin, and those acting on the deep parts, such as the muscles and joints. The sexual excitation produced by these influences seems to be of a pleasurable nature—it is worth emphasizing that for some time we shall continue to use indiscriminately the terms "sexual excitement" and "gratification" leaving the search for an explanation of the terms to a later time—and that the pleasure is produced by mechanical stimulation is proved by the fact that children are so fond of play involving passive motion, like swinging or flying in the air, and repeatedly demand its repetition.[20] As we know, rocking is regularly used in putting restless children to sleep. The shaking sensation experienced in wagons and railroad trains exerts such a fascinating influence on older children, that all boys, at least at one time in their lives, want to become conductors and drivers. They are wont to ascribe to railroad activities an extraordinary and mysterious interest, and during the age of phantastic activity (shortly before puberty) they utilize these as a nucleus for exquisite sexual symbolisms. The desire to connect railroad travelling with sexuality apparently originates from the pleasurable character of the sensation of motion. When the repression later sets in and changes so many of the childish likes into their opposites, these same persons as adolescents and adults then react to the rocking and rolling with nausea and become terribly exhausted by a railroad journey, or they show a tendency to attacks of anxiety during the journey, and by becoming obsessed with railroad phobia they protect themselves against a repetition of the painful experiences.

This also fits in with the not as yet understood fact that the concurrence of fear with mechanical shaking produces the severest hysterical forms of traumatic neurosis. It may at least be assumed that inasmuch as even a slight intensity of these influences becomes a source of sexual excitement, the action of an excessive amount of the same will produce a profound disorder in the sexual mechanism.

Muscular Activity.—It is well known that the child has need for strong muscular activity, from the gratification of which it draws extraordinary pleasure. Whether this pleasure has anything to do with sexuality, whether it includes in itself sexual satisfaction? or can be the occasion of sexual excitement; all this may be refuted by critical consideration, which will probably be directed also to the position taken above that the pleasure in the sensations of passive movement are of sexual character or that they are sexually exciting. The fact remains, however, that a number of persons report that they experienced the first signs of excitement in their genitals during fighting or wrestling with playmates, in which situation, besides the general muscular exertion, there is an intensive contact with the opponent's skin which also becomes effective. The desire for muscular contest with a definite person, like the desire for word contest in later years, is a good sign that the object selection has been directed toward this person. "Was sich liebt, das neckt sich."[21] In the promotion of sexual excitement through muscular activity we might recognize one of the sources of the sadistic impulse. The infantile connection between fighting and sexual excitement acts in many persons as a determinant for the future preferred course of their sexual impulse.[22]

Affective Processes.—The other sources of sexual excitement in the child are open to less doubt. Through contemporary observations, as well as through later investigations, it is easy to ascertain that all more intensive affective processes, even excitements of a terrifying nature, encroach upon sexuality; this can at all events furnish us with a contribution to the understanding of the pathogenic action of such emotions. In the school child, fear of a coming examination or exertion expended in the solution of a difficult task can become significant for the breaking through of sexual manifestations as well as for his relations to the school, inasmuch as under such excitements a sensation often occurs urging him to touch the genitals, or leading to a pollution-like process with all its disagreeable consequences. The behavior of children at school, which is so often mysterious to the teacher, ought surely to be considered in relation with their germinating sexuality. The sexually-exciting influence of some painful affects, such as fear, shuddering, and horror, is felt by a great many people throughout life and readily explains why so many seek opportunities to experience such sensations, provided that certain accessory circumstances (as under imaginary circumstances in reading, or in the theater) suppress the earnestness of the painful feeling.

If we might assume that the same erogenous action also reaches the intensive painful feelings, especially if the pain be toned down or held at a distance by a subsidiary determination, this relation would then contain the main roots of the masochistic-sadistic impulse, into the manifold composition of which we are gaining a gradual insight.

Intellectual Work.—Finally, is is evident that mental application or the concentration of attention on an intellectual accomplishment will result, especially often in youthful persons, but in older persons as well, in a simultaneous sexual excitement, which may be looked upon as the only justified basis for the otherwise so doubtful etiology of nervous disturbances from mental "overwork."

If we now, in conclusion, review the evidences and indications of the sources of the infantile sexual excitement, which have been reported neither completely nor exhaustively, we may lay down the following general laws as suggested or established. It seems to be provided in the most generous manner that the process of sexual excitement—the nature of which certainly remains quite mysterious to us—should be set in motion. The factor making this provision in a more or less direct way is the excitation of the sensible surfaces of the skin and sensory organs, while the most immediate exciting influences are exerted on certain parts which are designated as erogenous zones. The criterion in all these sources of sexual excitement is really the quality of the stimuli, though the factor of intensity (in pain) is not entirely unimportant. But in addition to this there are arrangements in the organism which induce sexual excitement as a subsidiary action in a large number of inner processes as soon as the intensity of these processes has risen above certain quantitative limits. What we have designated as the partial impulses of sexuality are either directly derived from these inner sources of sexual excitation or composed of contributions from such sources and from erogenous zones.

It is possible that nothing of any considerable significance occurs in the organism that does not contribute its components to the excitement of the sexual impulse.

It seems to me at present impossible to shed more light and certainty on these general propositions, and for this I hold two factors responsible; first, the novelty of this manner of investigation, and secondly, the fact that the nature of the sexual excitement is entirely unfamiliar to us. Nevertheless, I will not forbear speaking about two points which promise to open wide prospects in the future.

Diverse Sexual Constitutions.—(a) We have considered above the possibility of establishing the manifold character of congenital sexual constitutions through the diverse formation of the erogenous zones; we may now attempt to do the same in dealing with the indirect sources of sexual excitement. We may assume that, although these different sources furnish contributions in all individuals, they are not all equally strong in all persons; and that a further contribution to the differentiation of the diverse sexual constitution will be found in the preferred developments of the individual sources of sexual excitement.

The Paths of Opposite Influences.—(b) Since we are now dropping the figurative manner of expression hitherto employed, by which we spoke of *sources* of sexual excitement, we may now assume that all the connecting ways leading from other functions to sexuality must also be passable in the reverse direction. For example, if the lip zone, the common possession of both functions, is responsible for the fact that the sexual gratification originates during the taking of nourishment, the same factor offers also an explanation for the disturbances in the taking of nourishment if the erogenous functions of the common zone are disturbed. As soon as we know that concentration of attention may produce sexual excitement, it is quite natural to assume that acting on the same path, but in a contrary direction, the state of sexual excitement will be able to influence the availability of the voluntary attention. A good part of the symptomatology of the neuroses which I trace to disturbance of sexual processes manifests itself in disturbances of the other non-sexual bodily functions, and this hitherto incomprehensible action becomes less mysterious if it only represents the counterpart of the influences controlling the production of the sexual excitement.

However the same paths through which sexual disturbances encroach upon the other functions of the body must in health be supposed to serve another important function. It must be through these paths that the attraction of the sexual motive-powers to other than sexual aims, the sublimation of sexuality, is accomplished. We must conclude with the admission that very little is definitely known concerning the paths beyond the fact that they exist, and that they are probably passable in both directions.

1   For it is really impossible to have a correct knowledge of the part belonging to heredity without first understanding the part belonging to the infantile.

2   This assertion on revision seemed even to myself so bold that I decided to test its correctness by again reviewing the literature. The result of this second review did not warrant any change in my original statement. The scientific elaboration of the physical as well as the psychic phenomena of the infantile sexuality is still in its initial stages. One author (S. Bell, "A Preliminary Study of the Emotions of Love Between the Sexes," American Journal of Psychology, XIII, 1902) says: "I know of no scientist who has given a careful analysis of the emotion as it is seen in the adolescent." The only attention given to somatic sexual manifestations occurring before the age of puberty was in connection with degenerative manifestations, and these were referred to as a sign of degeneration. A chapter on the sexual life of children is not to be found in all the representative psychologies of this age which I have read. Among these works I can mention the following: Preyer; Baldwin (The Development of the Mind in the Child and in the Race, 1898); Pérez (L'enfant de 3-7 ans, 1894); Strümpel (Die pädagogische Pathologie, 1899); Karl Groos (Das Seelenleben des Kindes, 1904); Th. Heller (Grundriss

der Heilpädagogic, 1904); Sully (Observations Concerning Childhood, 1897). The best impression of the present situation of this sphere can be obtained from the journal Die Kinderfehler (issued since 1896). On the other hand one gains the impression that the existence of love in childhood is in no need of demonstration. Pérez (l.c.) speaks for it; K. Groos (Die Spiele der Menschen, 1899) states that some children are very early subject to sexual emotions, and show a desire to touch the other sex (p. 336); S. Bell observed the earliest appearance of sex-love in a child during the middle part of its third year. See also Havelock Ellis, The Sexual Impulse, Appendix II.

The above-mentioned judgment concerning the literature of infantile sexuality no longer holds true since the appearance of the great and important work of G. Stanley Hall (Adolescence, Its Psychology and its Relation to Physiology, Anthropology, Sociology, Sex, Crime, Religion, and Education, 2 vols., New York, 1908). The recent book of A. Moll, Das Sexualleben des Kindes, Berlin, 1909, offers no occasion for such a modification. See, on the other hand, Bleuler, Sexuelle abnormitäten der Kinder (Jahrbuch der Schweizerischen Gesellschaft für Schulgesundheitspflege, IX, 1908). A book by Mrs. Dr. H.v. Hug-Hellmuth, Aus dem Seelenleben des Kindes (1913), has taken full account of the neglected sexual factors. [Translated in Monograph Series.]

3   I have attempted to solve the problems presented by the earliest infantile recollections in a paper, "Über Deckerinnerungen" (Monatsschrift für Psychiatrie und Neurologie, VI, 1899). Cf. also The Psychopathology of Everyday Life, The Macmillan Co., New York, and Unwin, London.

4   One cannot understand the mechanism of repression when one takes into consideration only one of the two cooperating processes. As a comparison one may think of the way the tourist is despatched to the top of the great pyramid of Gizeh; he is pushed from one side and pulled from the other.

5   The use of the latter material is justified by the fact that the years of childhood of those who are later neurotics need not necessarily differ from those who are later normal except in intensity and distinctness.

6   An anatomic analogy to the behavior of the infantile sexual function formulated by me is perhaps given by Bayer (Deutsches Archiv für klinische Medizin, Bd. 73) who claims that the internal genitals (uterus) are regularly larger in newborn than in older children. However, Halban's conception, that after birth there is also an involution of the other parts of the sexual apparatus, has not been verified. According to Halban (Zeitschrift für Geburtshilfe u.

Gynäkologie, LIII, 1904) this process of involution ends after a few weeks of extra-uterine life.

7   The expression "sexual latency period" (sexuelle latenz-periode) I have borrowed from W. Fliess.

8   In the case here discussed the sublimation of the sexual motive powers proceed on the road of reaction formations. But in general it is necessary to separate from each other sublimation and reaction formation as two diverse processes. Sublimation may also result through other and simpler mechanisms.

9   Jahrbuch für Kinderheilkunde, N.F., XIV, 1879.

10   This already shows what holds true for the whole life, namely, that sexual gratification is the best hypnotic. Most nervous insomnias are traced to lack of sexual gratification. It is also known that unscrupulous nurses calm crying children to sleep by stroking their genitals.

11   Ellis spoils, however, the sense of his invented term by comprising under the phenomena of autoerotism the whole of hysteria and masturbation in its full extent.

12   Further reflection and observation lead me to attribute the quality of erogenity to all parts of the body and inner organs. See later on narcism.

13   Compare here the very comprehensive but confusing literature on onanism, *e.g.*, Rohleder, Die Masturbation, 1899. Cf. also the pamphlet, "Die Onanie," which contains the discussion of the Vienna Psychoanalytic Society, Wiesbaden, 1912.

14   Compare here the essay on "Charakter und Analerotic" in the Sammlung kleiner Schriften zur Neurosenlehre, Zweite Folge, 1909. Cf. also Brill, Psychanalysis, Chap. XIII, Anal Eroticism and Character, W.B. Saunders, Philadelphia.

15   Unusual techniques in the performance of onanism seem to point to the influence of a prohibition against onanism which has been overcome.

16   Why neurotics, when conscience stricken, regularly connect it with their onanistic activity, as was only recently recognized by Bleuler, is a problem which still awaits an exhaustive analysis.

17   Freud, Selected Papers on Hysteria and Other Psychoneuroses, 3d edition, translated by A.A. Brill, N.Y. Nerv. and Ment. Dis. Pub. Co. Nervous and Mental Disease Monograph, Series No. 4.

18   Havelock Ellis, in an appendix to his study on the Sexual Impulse, 1903, gives a number of autobiographic reports of normal persons treating their first sexual feelings in childhood and the causes of the same. These reports naturally show the deficiency due to infantile amnesia; they do not cover the

prehistoric time in the sexual life and therefore must be supplemented by psychoanalysis of individuals who became neurotic. Notwithstanding this these reports are valuable in more than one respect, and information of a similar nature has urged me to modify my etiological assumption as mentioned in the text.

19 The above-mentioned assertions concerning the infantile sexuality were justified in 1905, in the main through the results of psychoanalytic investigations in adults. Direct observation of the child could not at the time be utilized to its full extent and resulted only in individual indications and valuable confirmations. Since then it has become possible through the analysis of some cases of nervous disease in the delicate age of childhood to gain a direct understanding of the infantile psychosexuality (Jahrbuch für psychoanalytische und psychopathologische Forschungen, Bd. 1, 2, 1909). I can point with satisfaction to the fact that direct observation has fully confirmed the conclusion drawn from psychoanalysis, and thus furnishes good evidence for the reliability of the latter method of investigation.

Moreover, the "Analysis of a Phobia in a Five-year-old Boy" (Jahrbuch, Bd. 1) has taught us something new for which psychoanalysis had not prepared us, to wit, that sexual symbolism, the representation of the sexual by non-sexual objects and relations—reaches back into the years when the child is first learning to master the language. My attention has also been directed to a deficiency in the above-cited statement which for the sake of clearness described any conceivable separation between the two phases of autoerotism and object love as a temporal separation. From the cited analysis (as well as from the above-mentioned work of Bell) we learn that children from three to five are capable of evincing a very strong object-selection which is accompanied by strong affects.

20 Some persons can recall that the contact of the moving air in swinging caused them direct sexual pleasure in the genitals.

21 "Those who love each other tease each other."

22 The analyses of neurotic disturbances of walking and of agoraphobia remove all doubt as to the sexual nature of the pleasure of motion. As everybody knows modern cultural education utilizes sports to a great extent in order to turn away the youth from sexual activity; it would be more proper to say that it replaces the sexual pleasure by motion pleasure, and forces the sexual activity back upon one of its autoerotic components.

III

THE TRANSFORMATION OF PUBERTY

With the beginning of puberty the changes set in which transform the infantile sexual life into its definite normal form. Hitherto the sexual impulse has been preponderantly autoerotic; it now finds the sexual object. Thus far it has manifested itself in single impulses and in erogenous zones seeking a certain pleasure as a single sexual aim. A new sexual aim now appears for the production of which all partial impulses coöperate, while the erogenous zones subordinate themselves to the primacy of the genital zone.[1] As the new sexual aim assigns very different functions to the two sexes their sexual developments now part company. The sexual development of the man is more consistent and easier to understand, while in the woman there even appears a form of regression. The normality of the sexual life is guaranteed only by the exact concurrence of the two streams directed to the sexual object and sexual aim. It is like the piercing of a tunnel from opposite sides.

The new sexual aim in the man consists in the discharging of the sexual products; it is not contradictory to the former sexual aim, that of obtaining pleasure; on the contrary, the highest amount of pleasure is connected with this final act in the sexual process. The sexual impulse now enters into the service of the function of propagation; it becomes, so to say, altruistic. If this transformation is to succeed its process must be adjusted to the original dispositions and all the peculiarities of the impulses.

Just as on every other occasion where new connections and compositions are to be formed in complicated mechanisms, here, too, there is a possibility for morbid disturbance if the new order of things does not get itself established. All morbid disturbances of the sexual life may justly be considered as inhibitions of development.

THE PRIMACY OF THE GENITAL ZONES AND THE FORE-PLEASURE

From the course of development as described we can clearly see the issue and the end aim. The intermediary transitions are still quite obscure and many a riddle will have to be solved in them.

The most striking process of puberty has been selected as its most characteristic; it is the manifest growth of the external genitals which have shown a relative inhibition of growth during the latency period of childhood. Simultaneously the inner genitals develop to such an extent as to be able to furnish sexual products or to receive them for the purpose of forming a new living being. A most complicated apparatus is thus formed which waits to be claimed.

This apparatus can be set in motion by stimuli, and observation teaches that the stimuli can affect it in three ways: from the outer world through the familiar erogenous zones; from the inner organic world by ways still to be investigated; and from the psychic life, which merely represents a depository of external impressions and a receptacle of inner excitations. The same result follows in all three cases, namely, a state which can be designated as "sexual excitation" and which manifests itself in psychic and somatic signs. The psychic sign consists in a peculiar feeling of tension of a most urgent character, and among the manifold somatic signs the many changes in the genitals stand first. They have a definite meaning, that of readiness; they constitute a preparation for the sexual act (the erection of the penis and the glandular activity of the vagina).

The Sexual Tension—The character of the tension of sexual excitation is connected with a problem the solution of which is as difficult as it would be important for the conception of the sexual process. Despite all divergence of opinion regarding it in psychology, I must firmly maintain that a feeling of tension must carry with it the character of displeasure. For me it is conclusive that such a feeling carries with it the impulse to alter the psychic situation, and acts incitingly, which is quite contrary to the nature of perceived pleasure. But if we ascribe the tension of the sexual excitation to the feelings of displeasure we encounter the fact that it is undoubtedly pleasurably perceived. The tension produced by sexual excitation is everywhere accompanied by pleasure; even in the preparatory changes of the genitals there is a distinct feeling of satisfaction. What relation is there between this unpleasant tension and this feeling of pleasure?

Everything relating to the problem of pleasure and pain touches one of the weakest spots of present-day psychology. We shall try if possible to learn something from the determinations of the case in question and to avoid encroaching on the problem as a whole. Let us first glance at the manner in which the erogenous zones adjust themselves to the new order of things. An important rôle devolves upon them in the preparation of the sexual excitation. The eye which is very remote from the sexual object is most often in position, during the relations of object wooing, to become attracted by that particular quality of excitation, the motive of which we designate as beauty in the sexual object. The excellencies of the sexual object are therefore also called "attractions." This attraction is on the one hand already connected with pleasure, and on the other hand it either results in an increase of the sexual excitation or in an evocation of the same where it is still wanting. The effect is the same if the excitation of another erogenous zone, *e.g.*, the touching hand, is added to it. There is on the one hand the feeling of pleasure which soon becomes enhanced by the pleasure from the preparatory changes, and on the other hand there is a further increase of the sexual tension which soon changes into a most distinct feeling of displeasure if it cannot proceed to more pleasure. Another case will perhaps be clearer; let us, for example, take the case where an erogenous zone, like a woman's breast, is excited by touching in a person who is not sexually excited at the time. This touching in itself evokes a feeling of pleasure, but it is also best adapted to awaken sexual excitement which demands still more pleasure. How it happens that the perceived pleasure evokes the desire for greater pleasure, that is the real problem.

Fore-pleasure Mechanism.—But the rôle which devolves upon the erogenous zones is clear. What applies to one applies to all. They are all utilized to furnish a certain amount of pleasure through their own proper excitation, which increases the tension, and which is in turn destined to produce the necessary motor energy in order to bring to a conclusion the sexual act. The last part but one of this act is again a suitable excitation of an erogenous zone; *i.e.*, the genital zone proper of the glans penis is excited by the object most fit for it, the mucous membrane of the vagina, and through the pleasure furnished by this excitation it now produces reflexly the motor energy which conveys to the surface the sexual substance. This last pleasure is highest in its intensity, and differs from the earliest ones in its mechanism. It is altogether produced through discharge, it is altogether gratification pleasure and the tension of the libido temporarily dies away with it.

It does not seem to me unjustified to fix by name the distinction in the nature of these pleasures, the one through the excitation of the erogenous zones, and the other through the discharge of the sexual substance. In contradistinction to the end-pleasure, or pleasure of gratification of sexual activity, we can properly designate the first as *fore-pleasure*. The fore-pleasure is then the same as that furnished by the infantile sexual impulse, though on a reduced scale; while the *end-pleasure* is new and is probably connected with determinations which first appear at puberty. The formula for the new function of the erogenous zones reads as follows: they are utilized for the purpose of making possible the production of the greater pleasure of gratification by means of the fore-pleasure which is gained from them as in infantile life.

I have recently been able to elucidate another example from a quite different realm of the psychic life, in which likewise a greater feeling of pleasure is achieved by means of a lesser feeling of pleasure which thereby acts as an alluring premium. We had there also the opportunity of entering more deeply into the nature of pleasure.[2]

Dangers of the Fore-pleasure.—However the connection of fore-pleasure with the infantile life is strengthened by the pathogenic rôle which may devolve upon it. In the mechanism through which the fore-pleasure is expressed there exists an obvious danger to the attainment of the normal sexual aim. This occurs if it happens that there is too much fore-pleasure and too little tension in any part of the preparatory sexual process. The motive power for the further continuation of the sexual process then escapes, the whole road becomes shortened, and the preparatory action in question takes the place of the normal sexual aim. Experience shows that such a hurtful condition is determined by the fact that the erogenous zone concerned or the corresponding partial impulse has already contributed an unusual amount of pleasure in infantile life. If other factors favoring fixation are added a compulsion readily results for the later life which prevents the fore-pleasure from arranging itself into a new combination. Indeed, the mechanism of many perversions is of such a nature; they merely represent a lingering at a preparatory act of the sexual process.

The failure of the function of the sexual mechanism through the fault of the fore-pleasure is generally avoided if the primacy of the genital zones has also already been sketched out in infantile life. The preparations of the second half of childhood (from the eighth year to puberty) really seem to favor this. During these years the genital zones behave almost as at the age of maturity; they are the seat of exciting sensations and of preparatory changes if any kind of pleasure is experienced through the gratification of other erogenous zones; although this effect remains aimless, *i.e.*, it contributes nothing towards the continuation of the sexual process. Besides the pleasure of gratification a certain amount of sexual tension appears even in infancy, though it is less constant and less abundant. We can now understand also why in the discussion of the sources of sexuality we had a perfectly good reason for saying that the process in question acts as sexual gratification as well as sexual excitement. We note that on our way towards the truth we have at first enormously exaggerated the distinctions between the infantile and the mature sexual life, and we therefore supplement what has been said with a correction. The infantile manifestations of sexuality determine not only the deviations from the normal sexual life but also the normal formations of the same.

THE PROBLEM OF SEXUAL EXCITEMENT

It remains entirely unexplained whence the sexual tension comes which originates simultaneously with the gratification of erogenous zones and what is its nature. The obvious supposition that this tension originates in some way from the pleasure itself is not only improbable in itself but untenable, inasmuch as during the greatest pleasure which is connected with the voiding of sexual substance there is no production of tension but rather a removal of all tension. Hence, pleasure and sexual tension can be only indirectly connected.

The Rôle of the Sexual Substance.—Aside from the fact that only the discharge of the sexual substance can normally put an end to the sexual excitement, there are other essential facts which bring the sexual tension into relation with the sexual products. In a life of continence the sexual activity is wont to discharge the sexual substance at night during pleasurable dream hallucinations of a sexual act, this discharge coming at changing but not at entirely capricious intervals; and the following interpretation of this process—the nocturnal pollution—can hardly be rejected, viz., that the sexual tension which brings about a substitute for the sexual act by the short hallucinatory road is a function of the accumulated semen in the reservoirs for the sexual products. Experiences with the exhaustibility of the sexual mechanism speak for the same thing. Where there is no stock of semen it is not only impossible to accomplish the sexual act, but there is also a lack of excitability in the erogenous zones, the suitable excitation of which can evoke no pleasure. We thus discover incidentally that a certain amount of sexual tension is itself necessary for the excitability of the erogenous zones.

One would thus be forced to the assumption, which if I am not mistaken is quite generally adopted, that the accumulation of sexual substance produces and maintains the sexual tension. The pressure of these products on the walls of their receptacles acts as an excitant on the spinal center, the state of which is then perceived by the higher centers which then produce in consciousness the familiar feeling of tension. If the excitation of erogenous zones increases the sexual tension, it can only be due to the fact that the erogenous zones are connected with these centers by previously formed anatomical connections. They increase there the tone of the excitation, and with sufficient sexual tension they set in motion the sexual act, and with insufficient tension they merely stimulate a production of the sexual substance.

The weakness of the theory which one finds adopted, *e.g.*, in v. Krafft-Ebing's description of the sexual process, lies in the fact that it has been formed for the sexual activity of the mature man and pays too little heed to three kinds of relations which should also have been elucidated. We refer to the relations as found in the child, in the woman, and in the castrated male. In none of the three cases can we speak of an accumulation of sexual products in the same sense as in the man, which naturally renders difficult the general application of this scheme; still it may be admitted without any further ado that ways can be found to justify the subordination of even these cases. Nevertheless one should be cautious about burdening the factor of accumulation of sexual products with actions which it seems incapable of supporting.

Overestimation of the Internal Genitals.—That sexual excitement can be independent to a considerable extent of the production of sexual substance seems to be shown by observations on castrated males, in whom the libido sometimes escapes the injury caused by the operation, although the opposite behavior, which is really the motive for the operation, is usually the rule. It is therefore not at all surprising, as C. Rieger puts it, that the loss of the male germ glands in maturer age should exert no new influence on the psychic life of the individual. The germ glands are really not the sexuality, and the experience with castrated males only verifies what we had long before learned from the removal of the ovaries, namely that it is impossible to do away with the sexual character by removing the germ glands. To be sure, castration performed at a tender age, before puberty, comes nearer to this aim, but it would seem in this case that besides the loss of the sexual glands we must also consider the inhibition of development and other factors which are connected with that loss.

Chemical Theories.—The truth remains, however, that we are unable to give any information about the nature of the sexual excitement for the reason that we do not know with what organ or organs sexuality is connected, since we have seen that the sexual glands have been overestimated in this significance. Since surprising discoveries have taught us the important rôle of the thyroid gland in sexuality, we may assume that the knowledge of the essential factors of sexuality are still withheld from us. One who feels the need of filling up the large gap in our knowledge with a preliminary assumption may formulate for himself the following theory based on the active substances found in the thyroid. Through the appropriate excitement of erogenous zones, as well as through other conditions under which sexual excitement originates, a material which is universally distributed in the organism becomes disintegrated, the decomposing products of which supply a specific stimulus to the organs of reproduction or to the spinal center connected with them. Such a transformation of a toxic stimulus in a particular organic stimulus we are already familiar with from other toxic products introduced into the body from without. To treat, if only hypothetically, the complexities of the pure toxic and the physiologic stimulations which result in the sexual processes is not now our appropriate task. To be sure, I attach no value to this special assumption and I shall be quite ready to give it up in favor of another, provided its original character, the emphasis on the sexual chemism, were preserved. For this apparently arbitrary statement is supported by a fact which, though little heeded, is most noteworthy. The neuroses which can be traced only to disturbances of the sexual life show the greatest clinical resemblance to the phenomena of intoxication and abstinence which result from the habitual introduction of pleasure-producing poisonous substances (alkaloids.)

THE THEORY OF THE LIBIDO

These assumptions concerning the chemical basis of the sexual excitement are in full accord with the auxiliary conception which we formed for the purpose of mastering the psychic manifestations of the sexual life. We have determined the concept of *libido* as that of a force of variable quantity which has the capacity of measuring processes and transformations in the spheres of sexual excitement. This libido we distinguished from the energy which is to be generally adjudged to the psychic processes with reference to its special origin and thus we attribute to it also a qualitative character. In separating libidinous from other psychic energy we give expression to the assumption that the sexual processes of the organism are differentiated from the nutritional processes through a special chemism. The analyses of perversions and psychoneuroses have taught us that this sexual excitement is furnished not only from the so-called sexual parts alone but from all organs of the body. We thus formulate for ourselves the concept of a libido-quantum whose psychic representative we designate as the ego-libido; the production, increase, distribution and displacement of this ego-libido will offer the possible explanation for the observed psycho-sexual phenomena.

But this ego-libido becomes conveniently accessible to psychoanalytic study only when the psychic energy is employed on sexual objects, that is when it becomes object libido. Then we see it as it concentrates and fixes itself on objects, or as it leaves those objects and passes over to others from which positions it directs the individual's sexual activity, that is, it leads to partial and temporary extinction of the libido. Psychoanalysis of the so-called transference neuroses (hysteria and compulsion neurosis) offers us here a reliable insight.

Concerning the fates of the object libido we also state that it is withdrawn from the object, that it is preserved floating in special states of tension and is finally taken back into the ego, so that it again becomes ego-libido. In contradistinction to the object-libido we also call the ego-libido narcissistic libido. From psychoanalysis we look over the boundary which we are not permitted to pass into the activity of the narcissistic libido and thus form an idea of the relations between the two. The narcissistic or ego-libido appears to us as the great reservoir from which the energy for the investment of the object is sent out and into which it is drawn back again, while the narcissistic libido investment of the ego appears to us as the realized primitive state in the first childhood, which only becomes hidden by the later emissions of the libido, and is retained at the bottom behind them.

The task of a theory of libido of neurotic and psychotic disturbances would have for its object to express in terms of the libido-economy all observed phenomena and disclosed processes. It is easy to divine that the greater significance would attach thereby to the destinies of the ego-libido, especially where it would be the question of explaining the deeper psychotic disturbances. The difficulty then lies in the fact that the means of our investigation, psychoanalysis, at present gives us definite information only concerning the transformation of the object-libido, but cannot distinguish without further study the ego-libido from the other effective energies in the ego.[3]

DIFFERENTIATION BETWEEN MAN AND WOMAN

It is known that the sharp differentiation of the male and female character originates at puberty, and it is the resulting difference which, more than any other factor, decisively influences the later development of personality. To be sure, the male and female dispositions are easily recognizable even in infantile life; thus the development of sexual inhibitions (shame, loathing, sympathy, etc.) ensues earlier and with less resistance in the little girl than in the little boy. The tendency to sexual repression certainly seems much greater, and where partial impulses of sexuality are noticed they show a preference for the passive form. But, the autoerotic activity of the erogenous zones is the same in both sexes, and it is this agreement that removes the possibility of a sex differentiation in childhood as it appears after puberty. In respect to the autoerotic and masturbatic sexual manifestations, it may be asserted that the sexuality of the little girl has entirely a male character. Indeed, if one could give a more definite content to the terms "masculine and feminine," one might advance the opinion that *the libido is regularly and lawfully of a masculine nature, whether in the man or in the woman; and if we consider its object, this may be either the man or the woman.*[4]

Since becoming acquainted with the aspect of bisexuality I hold this factor as here decisive, and I believe that without taking into account the factor of bisexuality it will hardly be possible to understand the actually observed sexual manifestations in man and woman.

The Leading Zones in Man and Woman.—Further than this I can only add the following. The chief erogenous zone in the female child is the clitoris, which is homologous to the male penis. All I have been able to discover concerning masturbation in little girls concerned the clitoris and not those other external genitals which are so important for the later sexual functions. With few exceptions I myself doubt whether the female child can be seduced to anything but clitoris masturbation. The frequent spontaneous discharges of sexual excitement in little girls manifest themselves in a twitching of the clitoris, and its frequent erections enable the girl to understand correctly even without any instruction the sexual manifestations of the other sex; they simply transfer to the boys the sensations of their own sexual processes.

If one wishes to understand how the little girl becomes a woman, he must follow up the further destinies of this clitoris excitation. Puberty, which brings to the boy a great advance of libido, distinguishes itself in the girl by a new wave of repression which especially concerns the clitoris sexuality. It is a part of the male sexual life that sinks into repression. The reënforcement of the sexual inhibitions produced in the woman by the repression of puberty causes a stimulus in the libido of the man and forces it to increase its capacity; with the height of the libido there is a rise in the overestimation of the sexual, which can be present in its full force only when the woman refuses and denies her sexuality. If the sexual act is finally submitted to and the clitoris becomes excited its rôle is then to conduct the excitement to the adjacent female parts, and in this it acts like a chip of pine wood which is utilized to set fire to the harder wood. It often takes some time for this transference to be accomplished; during which the young wife remains anesthetic. This anesthesia may become permanent if the clitoris zone refuses to give up its excitability; a condition brought on by abundant activities in infantile life. It is known that anesthesia in women is often only apparent and local. They are anesthetic at the vaginal entrance but not at all unexcitable through the clitoris or even through other zones. Besides these erogenous causes of anesthesia there are also psychic causes likewise determined by the repression.

If the transference of the erogenous excitability from the clitoris to the vagina has succeeded, the woman has thus changed her leading zone for the future sexual activity; the man on the other hand retains his from childhood. The main determinants for the woman's preference for the neuroses, especially for hysteria, lie in this change of the leading zone as well as in the repression of puberty. These determinants are therefore most intimately connected with the nature of femininity.

THE OBJECT-FINDING

While the primacy of the genital zones is being established through the processes of puberty, and the erected penis in the man imperiously points towards the new sexual aim, *i.e.*, towards the penetration of a cavity which excites the genital zone, the object-finding, for which also preparations have been made since early childhood, becomes consummated on the psychic side. While the very incipient sexual gratifications are still connected with the taking of nourishment, the sexual impulse has a sexual object outside its own body in his mother's breast. This object it loses later, perhaps at the very time when it becomes possible for the child to form a general picture of the person to whom the organ granting him the gratification belongs. The sexual impulse later regularly becomes autoerotic, and only after overcoming the latency period is there a resumption of the original relation. It is not without good reason that the suckling of the child at its mother's breast has become a model for every amour. The object-finding is really a re-finding.[5]

The Sexual Object of the Nursing Period.—However, even after the separation of the sexual activity from the taking of nourishment, there still remains from this first and most important of all sexual relations an important share, which prepares the object selection and assists in reestablishing the lost happiness. Throughout the latency period the child learns to love other persons who assist it in its helplessness and gratify its

97

wants; all this follows the model and is a continuation of the child's infantile relations to his wet nurse. One may perhaps hesitate to identify the tender feelings and esteem of the child for his foster-parents with sexual love; I believe, however, that a more thorough psychological investigation will establish this identity beyond any doubt. The intercourse between the child and its foster-parents is for the former an inexhaustible source of sexual excitation and gratification of erogenous zones, especially since the parents—or as a rule the mother—supplies the child with feelings which originate from her own sexual life; she pats it, kisses it, and rocks it, plainly taking it as a substitute for a full-valued sexual object.[6] The mother would probably be terrified if it were explained to her that all her tenderness awakens the sexual impulse of her child and prepares its future intensity. She considers her actions as asexually "pure" love, for she carefully avoids causing more irritation to the genitals of the child than is indispensable in caring for the body. But as we know the sexual impulse is not awakened by the excitation of genital zones alone. What we call tenderness will some day surely manifest its influence on the genital zones also. If the mother better understood the high significance of the sexual impulse for the whole psychic life and for all ethical and psychic activities, the enlightenment would spare her all reproaches. By teaching the child to love she only fulfills her function; for the child should become a fit man with energetic sexual needs, and accomplish in life all that the impulse urges the man to do. Of course, too much parental tenderness becomes harmful because it accelerates the sexual maturity, and also because it "spoils" the child and makes it unfit to temporarily renounce love or be satisfied with a smaller amount of love in later life. One of the surest premonitions of later nervousness is the fact that the child shows itself insatiable in its demands for parental tenderness; on the other hand, neuropathic parents, who usually display a boundless tenderness, often with their caressing awaken in the child a disposition for neurotic diseases. This example at least shows that neuropathic parents have nearer ways than inheritance by which they can transfer their disturbances to their children.

Infantile Fear.—The children themselves behave from their early childhood as if their attachment to their foster-parents were of the nature of sexual love. The fear of children is originally nothing but an expression for the fact that they miss the beloved person. They therefore meet every stranger with fear, they are afraid of the dark because they cannot see the beloved person, and are calmed if they can grasp that person's hand. The effect of childish fears and of the terrifying stories told by nurses is overestimated if one blames the latter for producing the fear in children. Children who are predisposed to fear absorb these stories, which make no impression whatever upon others; and only such children are predisposed to fear whose sexual impulse is excessive or prematurely developed, or has become exigent through pampering. The child behaves here like the adult, that is, it changes its libido into fear when it cannot bring it to gratification, and the grown-up who becomes neurotic on account of ungratified libido behaves in his anxiety like a child; he fears when he is alone, *i.e.*, without a person of whose love he believes himself sure, and who can calm his fears by means of the most childish measures.[7]

Incest Barriers.—If the tenderness of the parents for the child has luckily failed to awaken the sexual impulse of the child prematurely, *i.e.*, before the physical determinations for puberty appear, and if that awakening has not gone so far as to cause an unmistakable breaking through of the psychic excitement into the genital system, it can then fulfill its task and direct the child at the age of maturity in the selection of the sexual object. It would, of course, be most natural for the child to select as the sexual object that person whom it has loved since childhood with, so to speak, a suppressed libido.[8] But owing to the delay of sexual maturity time has been gained for the erection beside the sexual inhibitions of the incest barrier, that moral prescription which explicitly excludes from the object selection the beloved person of infancy or blood relation. The observance of this barrier is above all a demand of cultural society which must guard against the absorption by the family of those interests which it needs for the production of higher social units. Society, therefore, uses every means to loosen those family ties in every individual, especially in the boy, which are authoritative in childhood only.[9]

The object selection, however, is first accomplished in the imagination, and the sexual life of the maturing youth has hardly any escape except indulgence in phantasies or ideas which are not destined to be brought to execution. In the phantasies of all persons the infantile inclinations, now reënforced by somatic emphasis, reappear, and among them one finds in regular frequency and in the first place the sexual feeling of the child for the parents. This has usually already been differentiated by the sexual attraction, the attraction of the son for the mother and of the daughter for the father.[10] Simultaneously with the overcoming and rejection of these distinctly incestuous phantasies there occurs one of the most important as well as one of the most painful psychic accomplishments of puberty; it is the breaking away from the parental authority, through which alone is formed that opposition between the new and old generations which is so important for cultural progress. Many persons are detained at each of the stations in the course of development through which the individual must pass; and accordingly there are persons who never overcome the parental authority and never, or very imperfectly, withdraw their affection from their parents. They are mostly girls, who, to the delight of their parents, retain their full infantile love far beyond puberty, and it is instructive to find that in their married life these girls are incapable of fulfilling their duties to their husbands. They make cold wives and remain sexually anesthetic. This shows that the apparently non-sexual love for the parents and the sexual love are nourished from the same source, *i.e.*, that the first merely corresponds to an infantile fixation of the libido.

The nearer we come to the deeper disturbances of the psychosexual development the more easily we can recognize the evident significance of the incestuous object-selection. As a result of sexual rejection there remains in the unconscious of the psychoneurotic a great part or the whole of the psychosexual activity for object finding. Girls with an excessive need for affection and an equal horror for the real demands of the sexual life experience an uncontrollable temptation on the one hand to realize in life the ideal of the asexual love and on the other hand to conceal their libido under an affection which they may manifest without self reproach; this they do by clinging for life to the infantile attraction for their parents or brothers or sisters which has been repressed in puberty. With the help of the symptoms and other morbid manifestations, psychoanalysis can trace their unconscious thoughts and translate them into the conscious, and thus easily show to such persons that they are in love with their consanguinous relations in the popular meaning of the term. Likewise when a once healthy person falls sick after an unhappy love affair, the mechanism of the disease can distinctly be explained as a return of his libido to the persons preferred in his infancy.

The After Effects of the Infantile Object Selection.—Even those who have happily eluded the incestuous fixation of their libido have not completely escaped its influence. It is a distinct echo of this phase of development that the first serious love of the young man is often for a mature woman and that of the girl for an older man equipped with authority—*i.e.*, for persons who can revive in them the picture of the mother and father. Generally speaking object selection unquestionably takes place by following more freely these prototypes. The man seeks above all the memory picture of his mother as it has dominated him since the beginning of childhood; this is quite consistent with the fact that the mother, if still living, strives against this, her renewal, and meets it with hostility. In view of this significance of the infantile relation to the parents for the later selection of the sexual object, it is easy to

101

understand that every disturbance of this infantile relation brings to a head the most serious results for the sexual life after puberty. Jealousy of the lover, too, never lacks the infantile sources or at least the infantile reinforcement. Quarrels between parents and unhappy marital relations between the same determine the severest predispositions for disturbed sexual development or neurotic diseases in the children.

The infantile desire for the parents is, to be sure, the most important, but not the only trace revived in puberty which points the way to the object selection. Other dispositions of the same origin permit the man, still supported by his infancy, to develop more than one single sexual series and to form different determinations for the object selection.[11]

Prevention of Inversion.—One of the tasks imposed in the object selection consists in not missing the opposite sex. This, as we know, is not solved without some difficulty. The first feelings after puberty often enough go astray, though not with any permanent injury. Dessoir has called attention to the normality of the enthusiastic friendships formed by boys and girls with their own sex. The greatest force which guards against a permanent inversion of the sexual object is surely the attraction exerted by the opposite sex characters on each other. For this we can give no explanation in connection with this discussion. This factor, however, does not in itself suffice to exclude the inversion; besides this there are surely many other supporting factors. Above all, there is the authoritative inhibition of society; experience shows that where the inversion is not considered a crime it fully corresponds to the sexual inclinations of many persons. Moreover, it may be assumed that in the man the infantile memories of the mother's tenderness, as well as that of other females who cared for him as a child, energetically assist in directing his selection to the woman, while the early sexual intimidation experienced through the father and the attitude of rivalry existing between them deflects the boy from the same sex. Both factors also hold true in the case of the girl whose sexual activity is under the special care of the mother. This results in a hostile relation to the same sex which decisively influences the object selection in the normal sense. The bringing up of boys by male persons (slaves in the ancient times) seems to favor homosexuality; the frequency of inversion in the present day nobility is probably explained by their employment of male servants, and by the scant care that mothers of that class give to their children. It happens in some hysterics that one of the parents has disappeared (through death, divorce, or estrangement), thus permitting the remaining parent to absorb all the love of the child, and in this way establishing the determinations for the sex of the person to be selected later as the sexual object; thus a permanent inversion is made possible.

SUMMARY

It is now time to attempt a summing-up. We have started from the aberrations of the sexual impulse in reference to its object and aim and have encountered the question whether these originate from a congenital predisposition, or whether they are acquired in consequence of influences from life. The answer to this question was reached through an examination of the relations of the sexual life of psychoneurotics, a numerous group not very remote from the normal. This examination has been made through psychoanalytic investigations. We have thus found that a tendency to all perversions might be demonstrated in these persons in the form of unconscious forces revealing themselves as symptom creators and we could say that the neurosis is, as it were, the negative of the perversion. In view of the now recognized great diffusion of tendencies to perversion the idea forced itself upon us that the disposition to perversions is the primitive and universal disposition of the human sexual impulse, from which the normal sexual behavior develops in consequence of organic changes and psychic inhibitions in the course of maturity. We hoped to be able to demonstrate the original disposition in the infantile life; among the forces restraining the direction of the sexual impulse we have mentioned shame, loathing and sympathy, and the social constructions of morality and authority. We have thus been forced to perceive in every fixed aberration from the normal sexual life a fragment of inhibited development and infantilism. The significance of the variations of the original dispositions had to be put into the foreground, but between them and the influences of life we had to assume a relation of coöperation and not of opposition. On the other hand, as the original disposition must have been a complex one, the sexual impulse itself appeared to us as something composed of many factors, which in the perversions becomes separated, as it were, into its components. The perversions, thus prove themselves to be on the one hand inhibitions, and on the other dissociations from the normal development. Both conceptions became united in the assumption that the sexual impulse of the adult due to the composition of the diverse feelings of the infantile life became formed into one unit, one striving, with one single aim.

We also added an explanation for the preponderance of perversive tendencies in the psychoneurotics by recognizing in these tendencies collateral fillings of side branches caused by the shifting of the main river bed through repression, and we then turned our examination to the sexual life of the infantile period.[12] We found it regrettable that the existence of a sexual life in infancy has been disputed, and that the sexual manifestations which have been often observed in children have been described as abnormal occurrences. It rather seemed to us that the child brings along into the world germs of sexual activity and that even while taking nourishment it at the same time also enjoys a sexual gratification which it then seeks again to procure for itself through the familiar activity of "thumbsucking." The sexual activity of the child, however, does not develop in the same measure as its other functions, but merges first into the so-called latency period from the age of three to the age of five years. The production of sexual excitation by no means ceases at this period but continues and furnishes a stock of energy, the greater part of which is utilized for aims other than sexual; namely, on the one hand for the delivery of sexual components for social feelings, and on the other hand (by means of repression and reaction formation) for the erection of the future sexual barriers. Accordingly, the forces which are destined to hold the sexual impulse in certain tracks are built up in infancy at the expense of the greater part of the perverse sexual feelings and with the assistance of education. Another part of the infantile sexual manifestations escapes this utilization and may manifest itself as sexual activity. It can then be discovered that the sexual excitation of the child flows from diverse sources. Above all gratifications originate through the adapted sensible excitation of so-called erogenous zones. For these probably any skin region or sensory organ may serve; but there are certain distinguished erogenous zones the excitation of which by certain organic mechanisms is assured from the beginning. Moreover, sexual excitation originates in the organism, as it were, as a by-product in a great number of processes, as soon as they attain a certain intensity; this especially takes place in all strong emotional excitements even if they be of a painful nature. The excitations from all these sources do not yet unite, but they pursue their aim individually—this aim consisting merely in the gaining of a certain pleasure. The sexual impulse of childhood is therefore objectless or *autoerotic*.

Still during infancy the erogenous zone of the genitals begins to make itself noticeable, either by the fact that like any other erogenous zone it furnishes gratification through a suitable sensible stimulus, or because in some incomprehensible way the gratification from other sources causes at the same time the sexual excitement which has a special connection with the genital zone. We found cause to regret that a sufficient explanation of the relations between sexual gratification and sexual excitement, as well as between the activity of the genital zone and the remaining sources of sexuality, was not to be attained.

We were unable to state what amount of sexual activity in childhood might be designated as normal to the extent of being incapable of further development. The character of the sexual manifestation showed itself to be preponderantly masturbatic. We, moreover, verified from experience the belief that the external influences of seduction, might produce premature breaches in the latency period leading as far as the suppression of the same, and that the sexual impulse of the child really shows itself to be polymorphous-perverse; furthermore, that every such premature sexual activity impairs the educability of the child.

Despite the incompleteness of our examinations of the infantile sexual life we were subsequently forced to attempt to study the serious changes produced by the appearance of puberty. We selected two of the same as criteria, namely, the subordination of all other sources of the sexual feeling to the primacy of the genital zones, and the process of object finding. Both of them are already developed in childhood. The first is accomplished through the mechanism of utilizing the fore-pleasure, whereby all other independent sexual acts which are connected with pleasure and excitement become preparatory acts for the new sexual aim, the voiding of the sexual products, the attainment of which under enormous pleasure puts an end to the sexual feeling. At the same time we had to consider the differentiation of the sexual nature of man and woman, and we found that in order to become a woman a new repression is required which abolishes a piece of infantile masculinity, and prepares the woman for the change of the leading genital zones. Lastly, we found the object selection, tracing it through infancy to its revival in puberty; we also found indications of sexual inclinations on the part of the child for the parents and foster-parents, which, however, were turned away from these persons to others resembling them by the incest barriers which had been erected in the meantime. Let us finally add that during the transition period of puberty the somatic and psychic processes of development proceed side by side, but separately, until with the breaking through of an intense psychic love-stimulus for the innervation of the genitals, the normally demanded unification of the erotic function is established.

The Factors Disturbing the Development.—As we have already shown by different examples, every step on this long road of development may become a point of fixation and every joint in this complicated structure may afford opportunity for a dissociation of the sexual impulse. It still remains for us to review the various inner and outer factors which disturb the development, and to mention the part of the mechanism affected by the disturbance emanating from them. The factors which we mention here in a series cannot, of course, all be in themselves of equal validity and we must expect to meet with difficulties in the assigning to the individual factors their due importance.

Constitution and Heredity.—In the first place, we must mention here the congenital *variation of the sexual constitution*, upon which the greatest weight probably falls, but the existence of which, as may be easily understood, can be established only through its later manifestations and even then not always with great certainty. We understand by it a preponderance of one or another of the manifold sources of the sexual excitement, and we believe that such a difference of disposition must always come to expression in the final result, even if it should remain within normal limits. Of course, we can also imagine certain variations of the original disposition that even without further aid must necessarily lead to the formation of an abnormal sexual life. One can call these "degenerative" and consider them as an expression of hereditary deterioration. In this connection I have to report a remarkable fact. In more than half of the severe cases of hysteria, compulsion neuroses, etc., which I have treated by psychotherapy, I have succeeded in positively demonstrating that their fathers have gone through an attack of syphilis before marriage; they have either suffered from tabes or general paresis, or there was a definite history of lues. I expressly add that the children who were later neurotic showed absolutely no signs of hereditary lues, so that the abnormal sexual constitution was to be considered as the last off-shoot of the luetic heredity. As far as it is now from my thoughts to put down a

107

descent from syphilitic parents as a regular and indispensable etiological determination of the neuropathic constitution, I nevertheless maintain that the coincidence observed by me is not accidental and not without significance.

The hereditary relations of the positive perverts are not so well known because they know how to avoid inquiry. Still there is reason to believe that the same holds true in the perversions as in the neuroses. We often find perversions and psychoneuroses in the different sexes of the same family, so distributed that the male members, or one of them, is a positive pervert, while the females, following the repressive tendencies of their sex, are negative perverts or hysterics. This is a good example of the substantial relations between the two disturbances which I have discovered.

Further Elaboration.—It cannot, however, be maintained that the structure of the sexual life is rendered finally complete by the addition of the diverse components of the sexual constitution. On the contrary, qualifications continue to appear and new possibilities result, depending upon the fate experienced by the sexual streams originating from the individual sources. This *further elaboration* is evidently the final and decisive one while the constitution described as uniform may lead to three final issues. If all the dispositions assumed to be abnormal retain their relative proportion, and are strengthened with maturity, the ultimate result can only be a perverse sexual life. The analysis of such abnormally constituted dispositions has not yet been thoroughly undertaken, but we already know cases that can be readily explained in the light of these theories. Authors believe, for example, that a whole series of fixation perversions must necessarily have had as their basis a congenital weakness of the sexual impulse. The statement seems to me untenable in this form, but it becomes ingenious if it refers to a constitutional weakness of one factor in the sexual impulse, namely, the genital zone, which later in the interests of propagation accepts as a function the sum of the individual sexual

108

activities. In this case the summation which is demanded in puberty must fail and the strongest of the other sexual components continues its activity as a perversion.[13]

Repression.—Another issue results if in the course of development certain powerful components experience a *repression*—which we must carefully note is not a suspension. The excitations in question are produced as usual but are prevented from attaining their aim by psychic hindrances, and are driven off into many other paths until they express themselves in a symptom. The result can be an almost normal sexual life—usually a limited one—but supplemented by psychoneurotic disease. It is these cases that become so familiar to us through the psychoanalytic investigation of neurotics. The sexual life of such persons begins like that of perverts, a considerable part of their childhood is filled up with perverse sexual activity which occasionally extends far beyond the period of maturity, but owing to inner reasons a repressive change then results—usually before puberty, but now and then even much later—and from this point on without any extinction of the old feelings there appears a neurosis instead of a perversion. One may recall here the saying, "Junge Hure, alte Betschwester,"—only here youth has turned out to be much too short. The relieving of the perversion by the neurosis in the life of the same person, as well as the above mentioned distribution of perversion and hysteria in different persons of the same family, must be placed side by side with the fact that the neurosis is the negative of the perversion.

Sublimation.—The third issue in abnormal constitutional dispositions is made possible by the process of "sublimation," through which the powerful excitations from individual sources of sexuality are discharged and utilized in other spheres, so that a considerable increase of psychic capacity results from an, in itself dangerous, predisposition. This forms one the sources of artistic activity, and, according as such sublimation is complete or incomplete, the analysis of the character of highly gifted, especially of artistically disposed persons, will show any proportionate, blending between productive ability, perversion, and neurosis. A sub-species of sublimation is the suppression through *reaction-formation*, which, as we have found, begins even in the latency period of infancy, only to continue throughout life in favorable cases. What we call the *character* of a person is built up to a great extent from the material of sexual excitations; it is composed of impulses fixed since infancy and won through sublimation, and of such constructions as are destined to suppress effectually those perverse feelings which are recognized as useless. The general perverse sexual disposition of childhood can therefore be esteemed as a source of a number of our virtues, insofar as it incites their creation through the formation of reactions.[14]

Accidental Experiences.—All other influences lose in significance when compared with the sexual discharges, shifts of repressions, and sublimations; the inner determinations for the last two processes are totally unknown to us. He who includes repressions and sublimations among constitutional predispositions, and considers them as the living manifestations of the same, has surely the right to maintain that the final structure of the sexual life is above all the result of the congenital constitution. No intelligent person, however, will dispute that in such a coöperation of factors there is also room for the modifying influences of occasional factors derived from experience in childhood and later on.

It is not easy to estimate the effectiveness of the constitutional and of the occasional factors in their relation to each other. Theory is always inclined to overestimate the first while therapeutic practice renders prominent the significance of the latter. By no means should it be forgotten that between the two there exists a relation of coöperation and not of exclusion. The constitutional factor must wait for experiences which bring it to the surface, while the occasional needs the support of the constitutional factor in order to become effective. For the majority of cases one can imagine a so-called "etiological group" in which the declining intensities of one factor become balanced by the rise in the others, but there is no reason to deny the existence of extremes at the ends of the group.

It would be still more in harmony with psychoanalytic investigation if the experiences of early childhood would get a place of preference among the occasional factors. The one etiological group then becomes split up into two which may be designated as the dispositional and the definitive groups. Constitution and occasional infantile experiences are just as coöperative in the first as disposition and later traumatic experiences in the second group. All the factors which injure the sexual development show their effect in that they produce a *regression*, or a return to a former phase of development.

We may now continue with our task of enumerating the factors which have become known to us as influential for the sexual development, whether they be active forces or merely manifestations of the same.

Prematurity.—Such a factor is the spontaneous sexual *prematurity* which can be definitely demonstrated at least in the etiology of the neuroses, though in itself it is as little adequate for causation as the other factors. It manifests itself in a breaking through, shortening, or suspending of the infantile latency period and becomes a cause of disturbances inasmuch as it provokes sexual manifestations which, either on account of the unready state of the sexual inhibitions or because of the undeveloped state of the genital system, can only carry along the character of perversions. These tendencies to perversion may either remain as such, or after the repression sets in they may become motive powers for neurotic symptoms; at all events, the sexual prematurity renders difficult the desirable later control of the sexual impulse by the higher psychic influences, and enhances the compulsive-like character which even without this prematurity would be claimed by the psychic representatives of the impulse. Sexual prematurity often runs parallel with premature intellectual development; it is found as such in the infantile history of the most distinguished and most

111

productive individuals, and in such connection it does not seem to act as pathogenically as when appearing isolated.

Temporal Factors.—Just like prematurity, other factors, which under the designation of *temporal* can be added to prematurity, also demand consideration. It seems to be phylogenetically established in what sequence the individual impulsive feelings become active, and how long they can manifest themselves before they succumb to the influence of a newly appearing active impulse or to a typical repression. But both in this temporal succession as well as in the duration of the same, variations seem to occur, which must exercise a definite influence on the experience. It cannot be a matter of indifference whether a certain stream appears earlier or later than its counterstream, for the effect of a repression cannot be made retrogressive; a temporal deviation in the composition of the components regularly produces a change in the result. On the other hand impulsive feelings which appear with special intensity often come to a surprisingly rapid end, as in the case of the heterosexual attachment of the later manifest homosexuals. The strivings of childhood which manifest themselves most impetuously do not justify the fear that they will lastingly dominate the character of the grown-up; one has as much right to expect that they will disappear in order to make room for their counterparts. (Harsh masters do not rule long.) To what one may attribute such temporal confusions of the processes of development we are hardly able to suggest. A view is opened here to a deeper phalanx of biological, and perhaps also historical problems, which we have not yet approached within fighting distance.

Adhesion.—The significance of all premature sexual manifestations is enhanced by a psychic factor of unknown origin which at present can be put down only as a psychological preliminary. I believe that it is the *heightened adhesion* or *fixedness* of these impressions of the sexual life which in later neurotics, as well as in perverts, must be added for the completion of the other facts; for the same premature sexual manifestations in other persons cannot impress themselves deeply enough to repeat themselves compulsively and to succeed in prescribing the way for the sexual impulse throughout later life. Perhaps a part of the explanation for this adhesion lies in another psychic factor which we cannot miss in the causation of the neuroses, namely, in the preponderance which in the psychic life falls to the share of memory traces as compared with recent impressions. This factor is apparently dependent on the intellectual development and grows with the growth of personal culture. In contrast to this the savage has been characterized as "the unfortunate child of the moment."[15] Owing to the oppositional relation existing between culture and the free development of sexuality, the results of which may be traced far into the formation of our life, the problem how the sexual life of the child evolves is of very little importance for the later life in the lower stages of culture and civilization, and of very great importance in the higher.

Fixation.—The influence of the psychic factors just mentioned favored the development of the accidentally experienced impulses of the infantile sexuality. The latter (especially in the form of seductions through other children or through adults) produce the material which, with the help of the former, may become fixed as a permanent disturbance. A considerable number of the deviations from the normal sexual life observed later have been thus established in neurotics and perverts from the beginning through the impressions received during the alleged sexually free period of childhood. The causation is produced by the responsiveness of the constitution, the prematurity, the quality of heightened adhesion, and the accidental excitement of the sexual impulse through outside influence.

The unsatisfactory conclusions which have resulted from this investigation of the disturbances of the sexual life is due to the fact that we as yet know too little concerning the biological processes in which the nature of sexuality consists to form from our isolated examinations a satisfactory theory for the explanation of either the normal or the pathological.

1   The differences will be emphasized in the schematic representation given in the text. To what extent the infantile sexuality approaches the definitive sexual organization through its object selection has been discussed before (p. 60).

2   See my work, Wit and its Relation to the Unconscious, translated by A.A. Brill, Moffat Yard Pub. Co., New York: "The fore-pleasure gained by the technique of wit is utilized for the purpose of setting free a greater pleasure by the removal of inner inhibitions."

3   Cf. Zur Einführung des Narzismus, Jahrbuch der Psychoanalyse, VI, 1913.

4   It is necessary to make clear that the conceptions "masculine" and "feminine," whose content seems so unequivocal to the ordinary meaning, belong to the most confused terms in science and can be cut up into at least three paths. One uses masculine and feminine at times in the sense of activity and passivity, again, in the biological sense, and then also in the sociological sense. The first of these three meanings is the essential one and the only one utilizable in psychoanalysis. It agrees with the masculine designation of the libido in the text above, for the libido is always active even when it is directed to a passive aim. The second, the biological significance of masculine and feminine, is the one which permits the clearest determination. Masculine and feminine are here characterized by the presence of semen or ovum and through the functions emanating from them. The activity and its secondary manifestations, like stronger developed muscles, aggression, a greater intensity of libido, are as a rule soldered to the biological masculinity but not necessarily connected with it, for there are species of animals in whom these qualities are attributed to the female. The third, the sociological meaning, receives its content through the observation of the actual existing male and female individuals. The result of this in man is that there is no pure masculinity or feminity either in the biological or psychological sense. On the contrary every individual person shows a mixture of his own biological sex characteristics with the biological traits of the other sex and a union of activity and passivity; this is the case whether these psychological characteristic features depend on the biological or whether they are independent of it.

5   Psychoanalysis teaches that there are two paths of object-finding; the first is the one discussed in the text which is guided by the early infantile prototypes. The second is the narcissistic which seeks its own ego and finds it in the other. The latter is of particularly great significance for the pathological outcomes, but does not fit into the connection treated here.

6   Those to whom this conception appears "wicked" may read Havelock Ellis's treatise on the relations between mother and child which expresses almost the same ideas (The Sexual Impulse, p. 16).

7   For the explanation of the origin of the infantile fear I am indebted to a three-year-old boy whom I once heard calling from a dark room: "Aunt, talk to me, I am afraid because it is dark." "How will that help you," answered the aunt; "you cannot see anyhow." "That's nothing," answered the child; "if some one talks then it becomes light."—He was, as we see, not afraid of the darkness but he was afraid because he missed the person he loved, and he could promise to calm down as soon as he was assured of her presence.

8   Cf. here what was said on page 83 concerning the object selection of the child; the "tender stream."

9   The incest barrier probably belongs to the historical acquisitions of humanity and like other moral taboos it must be fixed in many individuals through organic heredity. (Cf. my work, Totem and Taboo, 1913.) Psychoanalytic studies show, however, how intensively the individual struggles with the incest temptations during his development and how frequently he puts them into phantasies and even into reality.

10   Compare the description concerning the inevitable relation in the Oedipus legend (The Interpretation of Dreams, p. 222, translated by A.A. Brill, The Macmillan Co., New York, and Allen & Unwin, London).

11   Innumerable peculiarities of the human love-life as well as the compulsiveness of being in love itself can surely only be understood through a reference to childhood or as an effective remnant of the same.

12   This was true not only of the "negative" tendencies to perversion appearing in the neurosis, but also of the so-called positive perversions. The latter are not only to be attributed to the fixation of the infantile tendencies, but also to regression to these tendencies owing to the misplacement of other paths of the sexual stream. Hence the positive perversions are also accessible to psychoanalytic therapy. (Cf. the works of Sadger, Ferenczi, and Brill.)

13   Here one often sees that at first a normal sexual stream begins at the age of puberty, but owing to its inner weakness it breaks down at the first outer hindrance and then changes from regression, to perverse fixation.

14   That keen observer of human nature, E. Zola, describes a girl in his book, La Joie de vivre, who in cheerful self renunciation offers all she has in possession or expectation, her fortune and her life's hopes to those she loves without thought of return. The childhood of this girl was dominated by an insatiable desire for love which whenever she was depreciated caused her to merge into a fit of cruelty.

15   It is possible that the heightened adhesion is only the result of a special intensive somatic sexual manifestation of former years.

DREAM PSYCHOLOGY

Psychoanalysis for Beginners

AUTHORIZED ENGLISH TRANSLATION BY
M.D. EDER

WITH AN INTRODUCTION BY
ANDRÉ TRIDON
Author of "Psychoanalysis, its History, Theory and Practice."
"Psychoanalysis and Behavior" and "Psychoanalysis, Sleep and Dreams"

INTRODUCTION

The medical profession is justly conservative. Human life should not be considered as the proper material for wild experiments.

Conservatism, however, is too often a welcome excuse for lazy minds, loath to adapt themselves to fast changing conditions.

Remember the scornful reception which first was accorded to Freud's discoveries in the domain of the unconscious.

When after years of patient observations, he finally decided to appear before medical bodies to tell them modestly of some facts which always recurred in his dream and his patients' dreams, he was first laughed at and then avoided as a crank.

The words "dream interpretation" were and still are indeed fraught with unpleasant, unscientific associations. They remind one of all sorts of childish, superstitious notions, which make up the thread and woof of dream books, read by none but the ignorant and the primitive.

The wealth of detail, the infinite care never to let anything pass unexplained, with which he presented to the public the result of his investigations, are impressing more and more serious-minded scientists, but the examination of his evidential data demands arduous work and presupposes an absolutely open mind.

This is why we still encounter men, totally unfamiliar with Freud's writings, men who were not even interested enough in the subject to attempt an interpretation of their dreams or their patients' dreams, deriding Freud's theories and combatting them with the help of statements which he never made.

Some of them, like Professor Boris Sidis, reach at times conclusions which are strangely similar to Freud's, but in their ignorance of psychoanalytic literature, they fail to credit Freud for observations antedating theirs.

Besides those who sneer at dream study, because they have never looked into the subject, there are those who do not dare to face the facts revealed by dream study. Dreams tell us many an unpleasant biological truth about ourselves and only very free minds can thrive on such a diet. Self-deception is a plant which withers fast in the pellucid atmosphere of dream investigation.

The weakling and the neurotic attached to his neurosis are not anxious to turn such a powerful searchlight upon the dark corners of their psychology.

Freud's theories are anything but theoretical.

He was moved by the fact that there always seemed to be a close connection between his patients' dreams and their mental abnormalities, to collect thousands of dreams and to compare them with the case histories in his possession.

He did not start out with a preconceived bias, hoping to find evidence which might support his views. He looked at facts a thousand times "until they began to tell him something."

His attitude toward dream study was, in other words, that of a statistician who does not know, and has no means of foreseeing, what conclusions will be forced on him by the information he is gathering, but who is fully prepared to accept those unavoidable conclusions.

This was indeed a novel way in psychology. Psychologists had always been wont to build, in what Bleuler calls "autistic ways," that is through methods in no wise supported by evidence, some attractive hypothesis, which sprung from their brain, like Minerva from Jove's brain, fully armed.

After which, they would stretch upon that unyielding frame the hide of a reality which they had previously killed.

It is only to minds suffering from the same distortions, to minds also autistically inclined, that those empty, artificial structures appear acceptable molds for philosophic thinking.

The pragmatic view that "truth is what works" had not been as yet expressed when Freud published his revolutionary views on the psychology of dreams.

Five facts of first magnitude were made obvious to the world by his interpretation of dreams.

First of all, Freud pointed out a constant connection between some part of every dream and some detail of the dreamer's life during the previous waking state. This positively establishes a relation between sleeping states and waking states and disposes of the widely prevalent view that dreams are purely nonsensical phenomena coming from nowhere and leading nowhere.

Secondly, Freud, after studying the dreamer's life and modes of thought, after noting down all his mannerisms and the apparently insignificant details of his conduct which reveal his secret thoughts, came to the conclusion that there was in every dream the attempted or successful gratification of some wish, conscious or unconscious.

Thirdly, he proved that many of our dream visions are symbolical, which causes us to consider them as absurd and unintelligible; the universality of those symbols, however, makes them very transparent to the trained observer.

Fourthly, Freud showed that sexual desires play an enormous part in our unconscious, a part which puritanical hypocrisy has always tried to minimize, if not to ignore entirely.

Finally, Freud established a direct connection between dreams and insanity, between the symbolic visions of our sleep and the symbolic actions of the mentally deranged.

There were, of course, many other observations which Freud made while dissecting the dreams of his patients, but not all of them present as much interest as the foregoing nor were they as revolutionary or likely to wield as much influence on modern psychiatry.

Other explorers have struck the path blazed by Freud and leading into man's unconscious. Jung of Zurich, Adler of Vienna and Kempf of Washington, D.C., have made to the study of the unconscious, contributions which have brought that study into fields which Freud himself never dreamt of invading.

One fact which cannot be too emphatically stated, however, is that but for Freud's wishfulfillment theory of dreams, neither Jung's "energic theory," nor Adler's theory of "organ inferiority and compensation," nor Kempf's "dynamic mechanism" might have been formulated.

Freud is the father of modern abnormal psychology and he established the psychoanalytical point of view. No one who is not well grounded in Freudian lore can hope to achieve any work of value in the field of psychoanalysis.

On the other hand, let no one repeat the absurd assertion that Freudism is a sort of religion bounded with dogmas and requiring an act of faith. Freudism as such was merely a stage in the development of psychoanalysis, a stage out of which all but a few bigoted camp followers, totally lacking in originality, have evolved. Thousands of stones have been added to the structure erected by the Viennese physician and many more will be added in the course of time.

But the new additions to that structure would collapse like a house of cards but for the original foundations which are as indestructible as Harvey's statement as to the circulation of the blood.

Regardless of whatever additions or changes have been made to the original structure, the analytic point of view remains unchanged.

That point of view is not only revolutionising all the methods of diagnosis and treatment of mental derangements, but compelling the intelligent, up-to-date physician to revise entirely his attitude to almost every kind of disease.

The insane are no longer absurd and pitiable people, to be herded in asylums till nature either cures them or relieves them, through death, of their misery. The insane who have not been made so by actual injury to their brain or nervous system, are the victims of unconscious forces which cause them to do abnormally things which they might be helped to do normally.

Insight into one's psychology is replacing victoriously sedatives and rest cures.

Physicians dealing with "purely" physical cases have begun to take into serious consideration the "mental" factors which have predisposed a patient to certain ailments.

Freud's views have also made a revision of all ethical and social values unavoidable and have thrown an unexpected flood of light upon literary and artistic accomplishment.

But the Freudian point of view, or more broadly speaking, the psychoanalytic point of view, shall ever remain a puzzle to those who, from laziness or indifference, refuse to survey with the great Viennese the field over which he carefully groped his way. We shall never be convinced until we repeat under his guidance all his laboratory experiments.

We must follow him through the thickets of the unconscious, through the land which had never been charted because academic philosophers, following the line of least effort, had decided *a priori* that it could not be charted.

Ancient geographers, when exhausting their store of information about distant lands, yielded to an unscientific craving for romance and, without any evidence to support their day dreams, filled the blank spaces left on their maps by unexplored tracts with amusing inserts such as "Here there are lions."

Thanks to Freud's interpretation of dreams the "royal road" into the unconscious is now open to all explorers. They shall not find lions, they shall find man himself, and the record of all his life and of his struggle with reality.

123

And it is only after seeing man as his unconscious, revealed by his dreams, presents him to us that we shall understand him fully. For as Freud said to Putnam: "We are what we are because we have been what we have been."

Not a few serious-minded students, however, have been discouraged from attempting a study of Freud's dream psychology.

The book in which he originally offered to the world his interpretation of dreams was as circumstantial as a legal record to be pondered over by scientists at their leisure, not to be assimilated in a few hours by the average alert reader. In those days, Freud could not leave out any detail likely to make his extremely novel thesis evidentially acceptable to those willing to sift data.

Freud himself, however, realized the magnitude of the task which the reading of his *magnum opus* imposed upon those who have not been prepared for it by long psychological and scientific training and he abstracted from that gigantic work the parts which constitute the essential of his discoveries.

The publishers of the present book deserve credit for presenting to the reading public the gist of Freud's psychology in the master's own words, and in a form which shall neither discourage beginners, nor appear too elementary to those who are more advanced in psychoanalytic study.

Dream psychology is the key to Freud's works and to all modern psychology. With a simple, compact manual such as *Dream Psychology* there shall be no longer any excuse for ignorance of the most revolutionary psychological system of modern times.

ANDRÉ TRIDON.

121 Madison Avenue, New York.
November, 1920.

I

DREAMS HAVE A MEANING

In what we may term "prescientific days" people were in no uncertainty about the interpretation of dreams. When they were recalled after awakening they were regarded as either the friendly or hostile manifestation of some higher powers, demoniacal and Divine. With the rise of scientific thought the whole of this expressive mythology was transferred to psychology; today there is but a small minority among educated persons who doubt that the dream is the dreamer's own psychical act.

But since the downfall of the mythological hypothesis an interpretation of the dream has been wanting. The conditions of its origin; its relationship to our psychical life when we are awake; its independence of disturbances which, during the state of sleep, seem to compel notice; its many peculiarities repugnant to our waking thought; the incongruence between its images and the feelings they engender; then the dream's evanescence, the way in which, on awakening, our thoughts thrust it aside as something bizarre, and our reminiscences mutilating or rejecting it—all these and many other problems have for many hundred years demanded answers which up till now could never have been satisfactory. Before all there is the question as to the meaning of the dream, a question which is in itself double-sided. There is, firstly, the psychical significance of the dream, its position with regard to the psychical processes, as to a possible biological function; secondly, has the dream a meaning—can sense be made of each single dream as of other mental syntheses?

Three tendencies can be observed in the estimation of dreams. Many philosophers have given currency to one of these tendencies, one which at the same time preserves something of the dream's former over-valuation. The foundation of dream life is for them a peculiar state of psychical activity, which they even celebrate as elevation to some higher state. Schubert, for instance, claims: "The dream is the liberation of the spirit from the pressure of external nature, a detachment of the soul from the fetters of matter." Not all go so far as this, but many maintain that dreams have their origin in real spiritual excitations, and are the outward manifestations of spiritual powers whose free movements have been hampered during the day ("Dream Phantasies," Scherner, Volkelt). A large number of observers acknowledge that dream life is capable of extraordinary achievements—at any rate, in certain fields ("Memory").

In striking contradiction with this the majority of medical writers hardly admit that the dream is a psychical phenomenon at all. According to them dreams are provoked and initiated exclusively by stimuli proceeding from the senses or the body, which either reach the sleeper from without or are accidental disturbances of his internal organs. The dream has no greater claim to meaning and importance than the sound called forth by the ten fingers of a person quite unacquainted with music running his fingers over the keys of an instrument. The dream is to be regarded, says Binz, "as a physical process always useless, frequently morbid." All the peculiarities of dream life are explicable as the incoherent effort, due to some physiological stimulus, of certain organs, or of the cortical elements of a brain otherwise asleep.

But slightly affected by scientific opinion and untroubled as to the origin of dreams, the popular view holds firmly to the belief that dreams really have got a meaning, in some way they do foretell the future, whilst the meaning can be unravelled in some way or other from its oft bizarre and enigmatical content. The reading of dreams consists in replacing the events of the dream, so far as remembered, by other events. This is done either scene by scene, *according to some rigid key*, or the dream as a whole is replaced by something else of which it was a *symbol*. Serious-minded persons laugh at these efforts—"Dreams are but sea-foam!"

One day I discovered to my amazement that the popular view grounded in superstition, and not the medical one, comes nearer to the truth about dreams. I arrived at new conclusions about dreams by the use of a new method of psychological investigation, one which had rendered me good service in the investigation of phobias, obsessions, illusions, and the like, and which, under the name "psycho-analysis," had found acceptance by a whole school of investigators. The manifold analogies of dream life with the most diverse conditions of psychical disease in the waking state have been rightly insisted upon by a number of medical observers. It seemed, therefore, *a priori*, hopeful to apply to the interpretation of dreams methods of investigation which had been tested in psychopathological processes. Obsessions and those peculiar sensations of haunting dread remain as strange to normal consciousness as do dreams to our waking consciousness; their origin is as unknown to consciousness as is that of dreams. It was practical ends that impelled us, in these diseases, to fathom their origin and formation. Experience had shown us that a cure and a consequent mastery of the obsessing ideas did result when once those thoughts, the connecting links between the morbid ideas and the rest of the psychical content, were revealed which were heretofore veiled from consciousness. The procedure I employed for the interpretation of dreams thus arose from psychotherapy.

This procedure is readily described, although its practice demands instruction and experience. Suppose the patient is suffering from intense morbid dread. He is requested to direct his attention to the idea in question, without, however, as he has so frequently done, meditating upon it. Every impression about it, without any exception, which occurs to him should be imparted to the doctor. The statement which will be perhaps then made, that he cannot concentrate his attention upon anything at all, is to be countered by assuring him most positively that such a blank state of mind is utterly impossible. As a matter of fact, a great number of impressions will soon occur, with which others will associate themselves. These will be invariably accompanied by the expression of the observer's opinion that they have no meaning or are unimportant. It will be at once noticed that it is this self-criticism which prevented the patient from imparting the ideas, which had indeed already excluded them from consciousness. If the patient can be induced to abandon this self-criticism and to pursue the trains of thought which are yielded by concentrating the attention, most significant matter will be obtained, matter which will be presently seen to be clearly linked to the morbid idea in question. Its connection with other ideas will be manifest, and later on will permit the replacement of the morbid idea by a fresh one, which is perfectly adapted to psychical continuity.

This is not the place to examine thoroughly the hypothesis upon which this experiment rests, or the deductions which follow from its invariable success. It must suffice to state that we obtain matter enough for the resolution of every morbid idea if we especially direct our attention to the *unbidden* associations *which disturb our thoughts*—those which are otherwise put aside by the critic as worthless refuse. If the procedure is exercised on oneself, the best plan of helping the experiment is to write down at once all one's first indistinct fancies.

I will now point out where this method leads when I apply it to the examination of dreams. Any dream could be made use of in this way. From certain motives I, however, choose a dream of my own, which appears confused and meaningless to my memory, and one which has the advantage of brevity. Probably my dream of last night satisfies the requirements. Its content, fixed immediately after awakening, runs as follows:

"Company; at table or table d'hôte . . . Spinach is served. Mrs. E.L., sitting next to me, gives me her undivided attention, and places her hand familiarly upon my knee. In defence I remove her hand. Then she says: 'But you have always had such beautiful eyes.' . . . I then distinctly see something like two eyes as a sketch or as the contour of a spectacle lens . . ."

This is the whole dream, or, at all events, all that I can remember. It appears to me not only obscure and meaningless, but more especially odd. Mrs. E.L. is a person with whom I am scarcely on visiting terms, nor to my knowledge have I ever desired any more cordial relationship. I have not seen her for a long time, and do not think there was any mention of her recently. No emotion whatever accompanied the dream process.

Reflecting upon this dream does not make it a bit clearer to my mind. I will now, however, present the ideas, without premeditation and without criticism, which introspection yielded. I soon notice that it is an advantage to break up the dream into its elements, and to search out the ideas which link themselves to each fragment.

Company; at table or table d'hôte. The recollection of the slight event with which the evening of yesterday ended is at once called up. I left a small party in the company of a friend, who offered to drive me home in his cab. "I prefer a taxi," he said; "that gives one such a pleasant occupation; there is always something to look at." When we were in the cab, and the cab-driver turned the disc so that the first sixty hellers were visible, I continued the jest. "We have hardly got in and we already owe sixty hellers. The taxi always reminds me of the table d'hôte. It makes me avaricious and selfish by continuously reminding me of my debt. It seems to me to mount up too quickly, and I am always afraid that I shall be at a disadvantage, just as I cannot resist at table d'hôte the comical fear that I am getting too little, that I must look after myself." In far-fetched connection with this I quote:

"To earth, this weary earth, ye bring us,
To guilt ye let us heedless go."

Another idea about the table d'hôte. A few weeks ago I was very cross with my dear wife at the dinner-table at a Tyrolese health resort, because she was not sufficiently reserved with some neighbors with whom I wished to have absolutely nothing to do. I begged her to occupy herself rather with me than with the strangers. That is just as if I had *been at a disadvantage at the table d'hôte*. The contrast between the behavior of my wife at the table and that of Mrs. E.L. in the dream now strikes me: *"Addresses herself entirely to me."*

Further, I now notice that the dream is the reproduction of a little scene which transpired between my wife and myself when I was secretly courting her. The caressing under cover of the tablecloth was an answer to a wooer's passionate letter. In the dream, however, my wife is replaced by the unfamiliar E.L.

Mrs. E.L. is the daughter of a man to whom I *owed money!* I cannot help noticing that here there is revealed an unsuspected connection between the dream content and my thoughts. If the chain of associations be followed up which proceeds from one element of the dream one is soon led back to another of its elements. The thoughts evoked by the dream stir up associations which were not noticeable in the dream itself.

Is it not customary, when some one expects others to look after his interests without any advantage to themselves, to ask the innocent question satirically: "Do you think this will be done *for the sake of your beautiful eyes?*" Hence Mrs. E.L.'s speech in the dream. "You have always had such beautiful eyes," means nothing but "people always do everything to you for love of you; you have had *everything for nothing.*" The contrary is, of course, the truth; I have always paid dearly for whatever kindness others have shown me. Still, the fact that *I had a ride for nothing* yesterday when my friend drove me home in his cab must have made an impression upon me.

In any case, the friend whose guests we were yesterday has often made me his debtor. Recently I allowed an opportunity of requiting him to go by. He has had only one present from me, an antique shawl, upon which eyes are painted all round, a so-called Occhiale, as a *charm* against the *Malocchio*. Moreover, he is an *eye specialist*. That same evening I had asked him after a patient whom I had sent to him for *glasses*.

As I remarked, nearly all parts of the dream have been brought into this new connection. I still might ask why in the dream it was *spinach* that was served up. Because spinach called up a little scene which recently occurred at our table. A child, whose *beautiful eyes* are really deserving of praise, refused to eat spinach. As a child I was just the same; for a long time I loathed *spinach*, until in later life my tastes altered, and it became one of my favorite dishes. The mention of this dish brings my own childhood and that of my child's near together. "You should be glad that you have some spinach," his mother had said to the little gourmet. "Some children would be very glad to get spinach." Thus I am reminded of the parents' duties towards their children. Goethe's words—

"To earth, this weary earth, ye bring us,
To guilt ye let us heedless go"—

take on another meaning in this connection.

Here I will stop in order that I may recapitulate the results of the analysis of the dream. By following the associations which were linked to the single elements of the dream torn from their context, I have been led to a series of thoughts and reminiscences where I am bound to recognize interesting expressions of my psychical life. The matter yielded by an analysis of the dream stands in intimate relationship with the dream content, but this relationship is so special that I should never have been able to have inferred the new discoveries directly from the dream itself. The dream was passionless, disconnected, and unintelligible. During the time that I am unfolding the thoughts at the back of the dream I feel intense and well-grounded emotions. The thoughts themselves fit beautifully together into chains logically bound together with certain central ideas which ever repeat themselves. Such ideas not represented in the dream itself are in this instance the antitheses *selfish, unselfish, to be indebted, to work for nothing*. I could draw closer the threads of the web which analysis has disclosed, and would then be able to show how they

131

all run together into a single knot; I am debarred from making this work public by considerations of a private, not of a scientific, nature. After having cleared up many things which I do not willingly acknowledge as mine, I should have much to reveal which had better remain my secret. Why, then, do not I choose another dream whose analysis would be more suitable for publication, so that I could awaken a fairer conviction of the sense and cohesion of the results disclosed by analysis? The answer is, because every dream which I investigate leads to the same difficulties and places me under the same need of discretion; nor should I forgo this difficulty any the more were I to analyze the dream of some one else. That could only be done when opportunity allowed all concealment to be dropped without injury to those who trusted me.

The conclusion which is now forced upon me is that the dream is a *sort of substitution* for those emotional and intellectual trains of thought which I attained after complete analysis. I do not yet know the process by which the dream arose from those thoughts, but I perceive that it is wrong to regard the dream as psychically unimportant, a purely physical process which has arisen from the activity of isolated cortical elements awakened out of sleep.

I must further remark that the dream is far shorter than the thoughts which I hold it replaces; whilst analysis discovered that the dream was provoked by an unimportant occurrence the evening before the dream.

Naturally, I would not draw such far-reaching conclusions if only one analysis were known to me. Experience has shown me that when the associations of any dream are honestly followed such a chain of thought is revealed, the constituent parts of the dream reappear correctly and sensibly linked together; the slight suspicion that this concatenation was merely an accident of a single first observation must, therefore, be absolutely relinquished. I regard it, therefore, as my right to establish this new view by a proper nomenclature. I contrast the dream which my memory evokes with the dream and other added matter revealed by analysis: the former I call the dream's *manifest content*; the latter, without at first further subdivision, its *latent content*. I arrive at two new problems hitherto unformulated: (1) What is the psychical process which has transformed the latent content of the dream into its manifest content? (2) What is the motive or the motives which have made such transformation exigent? The process by which the change from latent to manifest content is executed I name the *dream-work*. In contrast with this is the *work of analysis*, which produces the reverse transformation. The other problems of the dream—the inquiry as to its stimuli, as to the source of its materials, as to its possible purpose, the function of dreaming, the forgetting of dreams—these I will discuss in connection with the latent dream-content.

I shall take every care to avoid a confusion between the *manifest* and the *latent content*, for I ascribe all the contradictory as well as the incorrect accounts of dream-life to the ignorance of this latent content, now first laid bare through analysis.

The conversion of the latent dream thoughts into those manifest deserves our close study as the first known example of the transformation of psychical stuff from one mode of expression into another. From a mode of expression which, moreover, is readily intelligible into another which we can only penetrate by effort and with guidance, although this new mode must be equally reckoned as an effort of our own psychical activity. From the standpoint of the relationship of latent to manifest dream-content, dreams can be divided into three classes. We can, in the first place, distinguish those dreams which have a *meaning* and are, at the same time, *intelligible*, which allow us to penetrate into our psychical life without further ado. Such dreams are numerous; they are usually short, and, as a general rule, do not seem very noticeable, because everything remarkable or exciting surprise is absent. Their occurrence is, moreover, a strong argument against the doctrine which derives the dream from the isolated activity of certain cortical elements. All signs of a lowered or subdivided psychical activity are wanting. Yet we never raise any objection to characterizing them as dreams, nor do we confound them with the products of our waking life.

A second group is formed by those dreams which are indeed self-coherent and have a distinct meaning, but appear strange because we are unable to reconcile their meaning with our mental life. That is the case when we dream, for instance, that some dear relative has died of plague when we know of no ground for expecting, apprehending, or assuming anything of the sort; we can only ask ourself wonderingly: "What brought that into my head?" To the third group those dreams belong which are void of both meaning and intelligibility; they are *incoherent, complicated, and meaningless*. The overwhelming number of our dreams partake of this character, and this has given rise to the contemptuous attitude towards dreams and the medical theory of their limited psychical activity. It is especially in the longer and more complicated dream-plots that signs of incoherence are seldom missing.

The contrast between manifest and latent dream-content is clearly only of value for the dreams of the second and more especially for those of the third class. Here are problems which are only solved when the manifest dream is replaced by its latent content; it was an example of this kind, a complicated and unintelligible dream, that we subjected to analysis. Against our expectation we, however, struck upon reasons which prevented a complete cognizance of the latent dream thought. On the repetition of this same experience we were forced to the supposition that there is an *intimate bond, with laws of its own, between the unintelligible and complicated nature of the dream and the difficulties attending communication of the thoughts connected with the dream*. Before investigating the nature of this bond, it will be advantageous to turn our attention to the more readily intelligible dreams of the first class where, the manifest and latent content being identical, the dream work seems to be omitted.

The investigation of these dreams is also advisable from another standpoint. The dreams of *children* are of this nature; they have a meaning, and are not bizarre. This, by the way, is a further objection to reducing dreams to a dissociation of cerebral activity in sleep, for why should such a lowering of psychical functions belong to the nature of sleep in adults, but not in children? We are, however, fully justified in expecting that the explanation of psychical processes in children, essentially simplified as they may be, should serve as an indispensable preparation towards the psychology of the adult.

I shall therefore cite some examples of dreams which I have gathered from children. A girl of nineteen months was made to go without food for a day because she had been sick in the morning, and, according to nurse, had made herself ill through eating strawberries. During the night, after her day of fasting, she was heard calling out her name during sleep, and adding: *"Tawberry, eggs, pap."* She is dreaming that she is eating, and selects out of her menu exactly what she supposes she will not get much of just now.

The same kind of dream about a forbidden dish was that of a little boy of twenty-two months. The day before he was told to offer his uncle a present of a small basket of cherries, of which the child was, of course, only allowed one to taste. He woke up with the joyful news: "Hermann eaten up all the cherries."

A girl of three and a half years had made during the day a sea trip which was too short for her, and she cried when she had to get out of the boat. The next morning her story was that during the night she had been on the sea, thus continuing the interrupted trip.

A boy of five and a half years was not at all pleased with his party during a walk in the Dachstein region. Whenever a new peak came into sight he asked if that were the Dachstein, and, finally, refused to accompany the party to the waterfall. His behavior was ascribed to fatigue; but a better explanation was forthcoming when the next morning he told his dream: *he had ascended the Dachstein.* Obviously he expected the ascent of the Dachstein to be the object of the excursion, and was vexed by not getting a glimpse of the mountain. The dream gave him what the day had withheld. The dream of a girl of six was similar; her father had cut

135

short the walk before reaching the promised objective on account of the lateness of the hour. On the way back she noticed a signpost giving the name of another place for excursions; her father promised to take her there also some other day. She greeted her father next day with the news that she had dreamt that *her father had been with her to both places.*

What is common in all these dreams is obvious. They completely satisfy wishes excited during the day which remain unrealized. They are simply and undisguisedly realizations of wishes.

The following child-dream, not quite understandable at first sight, is nothing else than a wish realized. On account of poliomyelitis a girl, not quite four years of age, was brought from the country into town, and remained over night with a childless aunt in a big—for her, naturally, huge—bed. The next morning she stated that she had dreamt that *the bed was much too small for her, so that she could find no place in it.* To explain this dream as a wish is easy when we remember that to be "big" is a frequently expressed wish of all children. The bigness of the bed reminded Miss Little-Would-be-Big only too forcibly of her smallness. This nasty situation became righted in her dream, and she grew so big that the bed now became too small for her.

Even when children's dreams are complicated and polished, their comprehension as a realization of desire is fairly evident. A boy of eight dreamt that he was being driven with Achilles in a war-chariot, guided by Diomedes. The day before he was assiduously reading about great heroes. It is easy to show that he took these heroes as his models, and regretted that he was not living in those days.

From this short collection a further characteristic of the dreams of children is manifest—*their connection with the life of the day.* The desires which are realized in these dreams are left over from the day or, as a rule, the day previous, and the feeling has become intently emphasized and fixed during the day thoughts. Accidental and indifferent matters, or what must appear so to the child, find no acceptance in the contents of the dream.

136

Innumerable instances of such dreams of the infantile type can be found among adults also, but, as mentioned, these are mostly exactly like the manifest content. Thus, a random selection of persons will generally respond to thirst at night-time with a dream about drinking, thus striving to get rid of the sensation and to let sleep continue. Many persons frequently have these comforting *dreams* before waking, just when they are called. They then dream that they are already up, that they are washing, or already in school, at the office, etc., where they ought to be at a given time. The night before an intended journey one not infrequently dreams that one has already arrived at the destination; before going to a play or to a party the dream not infrequently anticipates, in impatience, as it were, the expected pleasure. At other times the dream expresses the realization of the desire somewhat indirectly; some connection, some sequel must be known—the first step towards recognizing the desire. Thus, when a husband related to me the dream of his young wife, that her monthly period had begun, I had to bethink myself that the young wife would have expected a pregnancy if the period had been absent. The dream is then a sign of pregnancy. Its meaning is that it shows the wish realized that pregnancy should not occur just yet. Under unusual and extreme circumstances, these dreams of the infantile type become very frequent. The leader of a polar expedition tells us, for instance, that during the wintering amid the ice the crew, with their monotonous diet and slight rations, dreamt regularly, like children, of fine meals, of mountains of tobacco, and of home.

It is not uncommon that out of some long, complicated and intricate dream one specially lucid part stands out containing unmistakably the realization of a desire, but bound up with much unintelligible matter. On more frequently analyzing the seemingly more transparent dreams of adults, it is astonishing to discover that these are rarely as simple as the dreams of children, and that they cover another meaning beyond that of the realization of a wish.

It would certainly be a simple and convenient solution of the riddle if the work of analysis made it at all possible for us to trace the meaningless and intricate dreams of adults back to the infantile type, to the realization of some intensely experienced desire of the day. But there is no warrant for such an expectation. Their dreams are generally full of the most indifferent and bizarre matter, and no trace of the realization of the wish is to be found in their content.

Before leaving these infantile dreams, which are obviously unrealized desires, we must not fail to mention another chief characteristic of dreams, one that has been long noticed, and one which stands out most clearly in this class. I can replace any of these dreams by a phrase expressing a desire. If the sea trip had only lasted longer; if I were only washed and dressed; if I had only been allowed to keep the cherries instead of giving them to my uncle. But the dream gives something more than the choice, for here the desire is already realized; its realization is real and actual. The dream presentations consist chiefly, if not wholly, of scenes and mainly of visual sense images. Hence a kind of transformation is not entirely absent in this class of dreams, and this may be fairly designated as the dream work. *An idea merely existing in the region of possibility is replaced by a vision of its accomplishment.*

II

THE DREAM MECHANISM

We are compelled to assume that such transformation of scene has also taken place in intricate dreams, though we do not know whether it has encountered any possible desire. The dream instanced at the commencement, which we analyzed somewhat thoroughly, did give us occasion in two places to suspect something of the kind. Analysis brought out that my wife was occupied with others at table, and that I did not like it; in the dream itself *exactly the opposite* occurs, for the person who replaces my wife gives me her undivided attention. But can one wish for anything pleasanter after a disagreeable incident than that the exact contrary should have occurred, just as the dream has it? The stinging thought in the analysis, that I have never had anything for nothing, is similarly connected with the woman's remark in the dream: "You have always had such beautiful eyes." Some portion of the opposition between the latent and manifest content of the dream must be therefore derived from the realization of a wish.

Another manifestation of the dream work which all incoherent dreams have in common is still more noticeable. Choose any instance, and compare the number of separate elements in it, or the extent of the dream, if written down, with the dream thoughts yielded by analysis, and of which but a trace can be refound in the dream itself. There can be no doubt that the dream working has resulted in an extraordinary compression or *condensation*. It is not at first easy to form an opinion as to the extent of the condensation; the more deeply you go into the analysis, the more deeply you are impressed by it. There will be found no factor in the dream whence the chains of associations do not lead in two or more directions, no scene which has not been pieced together out of two or more impressions and events. For instance, I once dreamt about a kind of swimming-bath where the bathers suddenly separated in all directions; at one place on the edge a person stood bending towards one of the bathers as if to drag him out. The scene was a composite one, made up out of an event that occurred at the time of puberty, and of two pictures, one of which I had seen just shortly before the dream. The two pictures were The Surprise in the Bath, from Schwind's Cycle of the Melusine (note the bathers suddenly separating), and The Flood, by an Italian master. The little incident was that I once witnessed a lady, who had tarried in the swimming-bath until the men's hour, being helped out of the water by the swimming-master. The scene in the dream which was selected for analysis led to a whole group of reminiscences, each one of which had contributed to the dream content. First of all came the little episode from the time of my courting, of which I have already spoken; the pressure of a hand under the table gave rise in the dream to the "under the table," which I had subsequently to find a place for in my recollection. There was, of course, at the time not a word about "undivided attention." Analysis taught me that this factor is the realization of a desire through its contradictory and related to the behavior of my wife at the table d'hôte. An exactly similar and much more important episode of our courtship, one which separated us for an entire day, lies hidden behind this recent recollection. The intimacy, the hand resting upon the knee, refers to a quite different connection and to quite other persons. This element in the dream becomes again the starting-point of two distinct series of reminiscences, and so on.

The stuff of the dream thoughts which has been accumulated for the formation of the dream scene must be naturally fit for this application. There must be one or more common factors. The dream work proceeds like Francis Galton with his family photographs. The different elements are put one on top of the other; what is common to the composite picture stands out clearly, the opposing details cancel each other. This process of reproduction partly explains the wavering statements, of a peculiar vagueness, in so many elements of the dream. For the interpretation of dreams this rule holds good: When analysis discloses *uncertainty*, as to *either—or* read *and*, *taking* each section of the apparent alternatives as a separate outlet for a series of impressions.

When there is nothing in common between the dream thoughts, the dream work takes the trouble to create a something, in order to make a common presentation feasible in the dream. The simplest way to approximate two dream thoughts, which have as yet nothing in common, consists in making such a change in the actual expression of one idea as will meet a slight responsive recasting in the form of the other idea. The process is analogous to that of rhyme, when consonance supplies the desired common factor. A good deal of the dream work consists in the creation of those frequently very witty, but often exaggerated, digressions. These vary from the common presentation in the dream content to dream thoughts which are as varied as are the causes in form and essence which give rise to them. In the analysis of our example of a dream, I find a like case of the transformation of a thought in order that it might agree with another essentially foreign one. In following out the analysis I struck upon the thought: *I should like to have something for nothing.* But this formula is not serviceable to the dream. Hence it is replaced by another one: "I should like to enjoy something free of cost."[1] The word "kost" (taste), with its double meaning, is appropriate to a table d'hôte; it, moreover, is in place through the special sense in the dream. At home if there is a dish which the children decline, their mother first tries gentle persuasion, with a "Just taste it." That the dream work should unhesitatingly use the double meaning of the word is certainly remarkable; ample experience has shown, however, that the occurrence is quite usual.

Through condensation of the dream certain constituent parts of its content are explicable which are peculiar to the dream life alone, and which are not found in the waking state. Such are the composite and mixed persons, the extraordinary mixed figures, creations comparable with the fantastic animal compositions of Orientals; a moment's thought and these are reduced to unity, whilst the fancies of the dream are ever formed anew in an inexhaustible profusion. Every one knows such images in his own dreams; manifold are their origins. I can build up a person by borrowing one feature from one person and one from another, or by giving to the form of one the name of another in my dream. I can also visualize one person, but place him in a position which has occurred to another. There is a meaning in all these cases when different persons are amalgamated into one substitute. Such cases denote an "and," a "just like," a comparison of the original person from a certain point of view, a comparison which can be also realized in the dream itself. As a rule, however, the identity of the blended persons is only discoverable by analysis, and is only indicated in the dream content by the formation of the "combined" person.

The same diversity in their ways of formation and the same rules for its solution hold good also for the innumerable medley of dream contents, examples of which I need scarcely adduce. Their strangeness quite disappears when we resolve not to place them on a level with the objects of perception as known to us when awake, but to remember that they represent the art of dream condensation by an exclusion of unnecessary detail. Prominence is given to the common character of the combination. Analysis must also generally supply the common features. The dream says simply: *All these things have an "x" in common.* The decomposition of these mixed images by analysis is often the quickest way to an interpretation of the dream. Thus I once dreamt that I was sitting with one of my former university tutors on a bench, which was undergoing a rapid continuous movement amidst other benches. This was a combination of lecture-room and moving staircase. I will not pursue the further result of the thought. Another time I was sitting in a carriage, and on my lap an object in shape like a top-hat, which, however, was made of transparent glass. The scene at once brought to my mind the proverb: "He who keeps his hat in his hand will travel safely through the land." By a slight turn the *glass hat* reminded me of *Auer's light*, and I knew that I was about to invent something which was to make me as rich and independent as his invention had made my countryman, Dr. Auer, of Welsbach; then I should be able to travel instead of remaining in Vienna. In the dream I was traveling with my invention, with the, it is true, rather awkward glass top-hat. The dream work is peculiarly adept at representing two contradictory conceptions by means of the same mixed image. Thus, for instance, a woman dreamt of herself carrying a tall flower-stalk, as in the picture of the Annunciation (Chastity-Mary is her own name), but the stalk was bedecked with thick white blossoms resembling camellias (contrast with chastity: La dame aux Camelias).

A great deal of what we have called "dream condensation" can be thus formulated. Each one of the elements of the dream content is *overdetermined* by the matter of the dream thoughts; it is not derived from one element of these thoughts, but from a whole series. These are not necessarily interconnected in any way, but may belong to the most diverse spheres of thought. The dream element truly represents all this disparate matter in the dream content. Analysis, moreover, discloses another side of the relationship between dream content and dream thoughts. Just as one element of the dream leads to associations with several dream thoughts, so, as a rule, the *one dream thought represents more than one dream element*. The threads of the association do not simply converge from the dream thoughts to the dream content, but on the way they overlap and interweave in every way.

Next to the transformation of one thought in the scene (its "dramatization"), condensation is the most important and most characteristic feature of the dream work. We have as yet no clue as to the motive calling for such compression of the content.

In the complicated and intricate dreams with which we are now concerned, condensation and dramatization do not wholly account for the difference between dream contents and dream thoughts. There is evidence of a third factor, which deserves careful consideration.

When I have arrived at an understanding of the dream thoughts by my analysis I notice, above all, that the matter of the manifest is very different from that of the latent dream content. That is, I admit, only an apparent difference which vanishes on closer investigation, for in the end I find the whole dream content carried out in the dream thoughts, nearly all the dream thoughts again represented in the dream content. Nevertheless, there does remain a certain amount of difference.

The essential content which stood out clearly and broadly in the dream must, after analysis, rest satisfied with a very subordinate rôle among the dream thoughts. These very dream thoughts which, going by my feelings, have a claim to the greatest importance are either not present at all in the dream content, or are represented by some remote allusion in some obscure region of the dream. I can thus describe these phenomena: *During the dream work the psychical intensity of those thoughts and conceptions to which it properly pertains flows to others which, in my judgment, have no claim to such emphasis.* There is no other process which contributes so much to concealment of the dream's meaning and to make the connection between the dream content and dream ideas irrecognizable. During this process, which I will call *the dream displacement*, I notice also the psychical intensity, significance, or emotional nature of the thoughts become transposed in sensory vividness. What was clearest in the dream seems to me, without further consideration, the most important; but often in some obscure element of the dream I can recognize the most direct offspring of the principal dream thought.

I could only designate this dream displacement as the *transvaluation of psychical values*. The phenomena will not have been considered in all its bearings unless I add that this displacement or transvaluation is shared by different dreams in extremely varying degrees. There are dreams which take place almost without any displacement. These have the same time, meaning, and intelligibility as we found in the dreams which recorded a desire. In other dreams not a bit of the dream idea has retained its own psychical value, or everything essential in these dream ideas has been replaced by unessentials, whilst every kind of transition between these conditions can be found. The more obscure and intricate a dream is, the greater is the part to be ascribed to the impetus of displacement in its formation.

The example that we chose for analysis shows, at least, this much of displacement—that its content has a different center of interest from that of the dream ideas. In the forefront of the dream content the main scene appears as if a woman wished to make advances to me; in the dream idea the chief interest rests on the desire to enjoy disinterested love which shall "cost nothing"; this idea lies at the back of the talk about the beautiful eyes and the far-fetched allusion to "spinach."

If we abolish the dream displacement, we attain through analysis quite certain conclusions regarding two problems of the dream which are most disputed—as to what provokes a dream at all, and as to the connection of the dream with our waking life. There are dreams which at once expose their links with the events of the day; in others no trace of such a connection can be found. By the aid of analysis it can be shown that every dream, without any exception, is linked up with our impression of the day, or perhaps it would be more correct to say of the day previous to the dream. The impressions which have incited the dream may be so important that we are not surprised at our being occupied with them whilst awake; in this case we are right in saying that the dream carries on the chief interest of our waking life. More usually, however, when the dream contains anything relating to the impressions of the day, it is so trivial, unimportant, and so deserving of oblivion, that we can only recall it with an effort. The dream content appears, then, even when coherent and intelligible, to be concerned with those indifferent trifles of thought undeserving of our waking interest. The depreciation of dreams is largely due to the predominance of the indifferent and the worthless in their content.

Analysis destroys the appearance upon which this derogatory judgment is based. When the dream content discloses nothing but some indifferent impression as instigating the dream, analysis ever indicates some significant event, which has been replaced by something indifferent with which it has entered into abundant associations. Where the dream is concerned with uninteresting and unimportant conceptions, analysis reveals the numerous associative paths which connect the trivial with the momentous in the psychical estimation of the individual. *It is only the action of displacement if what is indifferent obtains recognition in the dream content instead of those impressions which are really the stimulus, or instead of the things of real interest.* In answering the question as to what provokes the dream, as to the connection of the dream, in the daily troubles, we must say, in terms of the insight given us by replacing the manifest latent dream content: *The dream does never trouble itself about things which are not deserving of our concern during the day, and trivialities which do not trouble us during the day have no power to pursue us whilst asleep.*

What provoked the dream in the example which we have analyzed? The really unimportant event, that a friend invited me to a *free ride in his cab.* The table d'hôte scene in the dream contains an allusion to this indifferent motive, for in conversation I had brought the taxi parallel with the table d'hôte. But I can indicate the important event which has as its substitute the trivial one. A few days before I had disbursed a large sum of money for a member of my family who is very dear to me. Small wonder, says the dream thought, if this person is grateful to me for this—this love is not cost-free. But love that shall cost nothing is one of the prime thoughts of the dream. The fact that shortly before this I had had several *drives* with the relative in question puts the one drive with my friend in a position to recall the connection with the other person. The indifferent impression which, by such ramifications, provokes the dream is subservient to another condition which is not true of the real source

146

of the dream—the impression must be a recent one, everything arising from the day of the dream.

I cannot leave the question of dream displacement without the consideration of a remarkable process in the formation of dreams in which condensation and displacement work together towards one end. In condensation we have already considered the case where two conceptions in the dream having something in common, some point of contact, are replaced in the dream content by a mixed image, where the distinct germ corresponds to what is common, and the indistinct secondary modifications to what is distinctive. If displacement is added to condensation, there is no formation of a mixed image, but a *common mean* which bears the same relationship to the individual elements as does the resultant in the parallelogram of forces to its components. In one of my dreams, for instance, there is talk of an injection with *propyl*. On first analysis I discovered an indifferent but true incident where *amyl* played a part as the excitant of the dream. I cannot yet vindicate the exchange of amyl for propyl. To the round of ideas of the same dream, however, there belongs the recollection of my first visit to Munich, when the *Propyloea* struck me. The attendant circumstances of the analysis render it admissible that the influence of this second group of conceptions caused the displacement of amyl to propyl. *Propyl* is, so to say, the mean idea between *amyl* and *propyloea*; it got into the dream as a kind of *compromise* by simultaneous condensation and displacement.

The need of discovering some motive for this bewildering work of the dream is even more called for in the case of displacement than in condensation.

Although the work of displacement must be held mainly responsible if the dream thoughts are not refound or recognized in the dream content (unless the motive of the changes be guessed), it is another and milder kind of transformation which will be considered with the dream thoughts which leads to the discovery of a new but readily understood act of the dream work. The first dream thoughts which are unravelled

147

by analysis frequently strike one by their unusual wording. They do not appear to be expressed in the sober form which our thinking prefers; rather are they expressed symbolically by allegories and metaphors like the figurative language of the poets. It is not difficult to find the motives for this degree of constraint in the expression of dream ideas. The dream content consists chiefly of visual scenes; hence the dream ideas must, in the first place, be prepared to make use of these forms of presentation. Conceive that a political leader's or a barrister's address had to be transposed into pantomime, and it will be easy to understand the transformations to which the dream work is constrained by regard for this *dramatization of the dream content.*

Around the psychical stuff of dream thoughts there are ever found reminiscences of impressions, not infrequently of early childhood—scenes which, as a rule, have been visually grasped. Whenever possible, this portion of the dream ideas exercises a definite influence upon the modelling of the dream content; it works like a center of crystallization, by attracting and rearranging the stuff of the dream thoughts. The scene of the dream is not infrequently nothing but a modified repetition, complicated by interpolations of events that have left such an impression; the dream but very seldom reproduces accurate and unmixed reproductions of real scenes.

The dream content does not, however, consist exclusively of scenes, but it also includes scattered fragments of visual images, conversations, and even bits of unchanged thoughts. It will be perhaps to the point if we instance in the briefest way the means of dramatization which are at the disposal of the dream work for the repetition of the dream thoughts in the peculiar language of the dream.

The dream thoughts which we learn from the analysis exhibit themselves as a psychical complex of the most complicated superstructure. Their parts stand in the most diverse relationship to each other; they form backgrounds and foregrounds, stipulations, digressions, illustrations, demonstrations, and protestations. It may be said to be almost the rule that one train of thought is followed by its contradictory. No feature known to our reason whilst awake is absent. If a dream is to grow out of all this, the psychical matter is submitted to a pressure which condenses it extremely, to an inner shrinking and displacement, creating at the same time fresh surfaces, to a selective interweaving among the constituents best adapted for the construction of these scenes. Having regard to the origin of this stuff, the term *regression* can be fairly applied to this process. The logical chains which hitherto held the psychical stuff together become lost in this transformation to the dream content. The dream work takes on, as it were, only the essential content of the dream thoughts for elaboration. It is left to analysis to restore the connection which the dream work has destroyed.

The dream's means of expression must therefore be regarded as meager in comparison with those of our imagination, though the dream does not renounce all claims to the restitution of logical relation to the dream thoughts. It rather succeeds with tolerable frequency in replacing these by formal characters of its own.

By reason of the undoubted connection existing between all the parts of dream thoughts, the dream is able to embody this matter into a single scene. It upholds a *logical connection* as *approximation in time and space*, just as the painter, who groups all the poets for his picture of Parnassus who, though they have never been all together on a mountain peak, yet form ideally a community. The dream continues this method of presentation in individual dreams, and often when it displays two elements close together in the dream content it warrants some special inner connection between what they represent in the dream thoughts. It should be, moreover, observed that all the dreams of one night prove on analysis to originate from the same sphere of thought.

The causal connection between two ideas is either left without presentation, or replaced by two different long portions of dreams one after the other. This presentation is frequently a reversed one, the beginning of the dream being the deduction, and its end the hypothesis.

The direct *transformation* of one thing into another in the dream seems to serve the relationship of *cause* and *effect*.

The dream never utters the *alternative* *"either-or,"* but accepts both as having equal rights in the same connection. When "either-or" is used in the reproduction of dreams, it is, as I have already mentioned, to be replaced by *"and."*

Conceptions which stand in opposition to one another are preferably expressed in dreams by the same element.[2] There seems no "not" in dreams. Opposition between two ideas, the relation of conversion, is represented in dreams in a very remarkable way. It is expressed by the reversal of another part of the dream content just as if by way of appendix. We shall later on deal with another form of expressing disagreement. The common dream sensation of *movement checked* serves the purpose of representing disagreement of impulses—a *conflict of the will*.

Only one of the logical relationships—that of *similarity, identity, agreement*— is found highly developed in the mechanism of dream formation. Dream work makes use of these cases as a starting-point for condensation, drawing together everything which shows such agreement to a *fresh unity*.

These short, crude observations naturally do not suffice as an estimate of the abundance of the dream's formal means of presenting the logical relationships of the dream thoughts. In this respect, individual dreams are worked up more nicely or more carelessly, our text will have been followed more or less closely, auxiliaries of the dream work will have been taken more or less into consideration. In the latter case they appear obscure, intricate, incoherent. When the dream appears openly absurd, when it contains an obvious paradox in its content, it is so of purpose. Through its apparent disregard of all logical claims, it expresses a part of the intellectual content of the dream ideas. Absurdity in the dream denotes *disagreement, scorn, disdain* in the dream thoughts. As this explanation is in entire disagreement with the view that the dream owes its origin to dissociated, uncritical cerebral activity, I will emphasize my view by an example:

"*One of my acquaintances, Mr. M——, has been attacked by no less a person than Goethe in an essay with, we all maintain, unwarrantable violence. Mr. M——has naturally been ruined by this attack. He complains very bitterly of this at a dinner-party, but his respect for Goethe has not diminished through this personal experience. I now attempt to clear up the chronological relations which strike me as improbable. Goethe died in 1832. As his attack upon Mr. M——must, of course, have taken place before, Mr. M——must have been then a very young man. It seems to me plausible that he was eighteen. I am not certain, however, what year we are actually in, and the whole calculation falls into obscurity. The attack was, moreover, contained in Goethe's well-known essay on 'Nature.'*"

The absurdity of the dream becomes the more glaring when I state that Mr. M——is a young business man without any poetical or literary interests. My analysis of the dream will show what method there is in this madness. The dream has derived its material from three sources:

1. Mr. M——, to whom I was introduced at a dinner-party, begged me one day to examine his elder brother, who showed signs of mental trouble. In conversation with the patient, an unpleasant episode occurred. Without the slightest occasion he disclosed one of his brother's *youthful escapades*. I had asked the patient the *year of his birth* (*year of death* in dream), and led him to various calculations which might show up his want of memory.

2. A medical journal which displayed my name among others on the cover had published a *ruinous* review of a book by my friend F——of Berlin, from the pen of a very *juvenile* reviewer. I communicated with the editor, who, indeed, expressed his regret, but would not promise any redress. Thereupon I broke off my connection with the paper; in my letter of resignation I expressed the hope that our *personal relations would not suffer from this*. Here is the real source of the dream. The derogatory reception of my friend's work had made a deep impression upon me. In my judgment, it contained a fundamental biological discovery which only now, several years later, commences to find favor among the professors.

3. A little while before, a patient gave me the medical history of her brother, who, exclaiming *"Nature, Nature!"* had gone out of his mind. The doctors considered that the exclamation arose from a study of *Goethe's* beautiful essay, and indicated that the patient had been overworking. I expressed the opinion that it seemed more *plausible* to me that the exclamation "Nature!" was to be taken in that sexual meaning known also to the less educated in our country. It seemed to me that this view had something in it, because the unfortunate youth afterwards mutilated his genital organs. The patient was eighteen years old when the attack occurred.

The first person in the dream-thoughts behind the ego was my friend who had been so scandalously treated. *"I now attempted to clear up the chronological relation."* My friend's book deals with the chronological relations of life, and, amongst other things, correlates *Goethe's* duration of life with a number of days in many ways important to biology. The ego is, however, represented as a general paralytic *("I am not certain what year we are actually in")*. The dream exhibits my friend as behaving like a general paralytic, and thus riots in absurdity. But the dream thoughts run ironically. "Of course he is a madman, a fool, and you are the genius who understands all about it. But shouldn't it be the *other way round?"* This inversion obviously took place in the dream when Goethe attacked the young man, which is absurd, whilst any one, however young, can today easily attack the great Goethe.

I am prepared to maintain that no dream is inspired by other than egoistic emotions. The ego in the dream does not, indeed, represent only my friend, but stands for myself also. I identify myself with him because the fate of his discovery appears to me typical of the acceptance of *my own.* If I were to publish my own theory, which gives sexuality predominance in the ætiology of psychoneurotic disorders (see the allusion to the eighteen-year-old patient—*'Nature, Nature!'*), the same criticism would be leveled at me, and it would even now meet with the same contempt.

When I follow out the dream thoughts closely, I ever find only *scorn* and *contempt* as *correlated with the dream's absurdity*. It is well known that the discovery of a cracked sheep's skull on the Lido in Venice gave Goethe the hint for the so-called vertebral theory of the skull. My friend plumes himself on having as a student raised a hubbub for the resignation of an aged professor who had done good work (including some in this very subject of comparative anatomy), but who, on account of *decrepitude*, had become quite incapable of teaching. The agitation my friend inspired was so successful because in the German Universities an *age limit* is not demanded for academic work. *Age is no protection against folly.* In the hospital here I had for years the honor to serve under a chief who, long fossilized, was for decades notoriously *feebleminded*, and was yet permitted to continue in his responsible office. A trait, after the manner of the find in the Lido, forces itself upon me here. It was to this man that some youthful colleagues in the hospital adapted the then popular slang of that day: "No Goethe has written that," "No Schiller composed that," etc.

We have not exhausted our valuation of the dream work. In addition to condensation, displacement, and definite arrangement of the psychical matter, we must ascribe to it yet another activity—one which is, indeed, not shared by every dream. I shall not treat this position of the dream work exhaustively; I will only point out that the readiest way to arrive at a conception of it is to take for granted, probably unfairly, that it *only subsequently influences the dream content which has already been built up*. Its mode of action thus consists in so coördinating the parts of the dream that these coalesce to a coherent whole, to a dream composition. The dream gets a kind of façade which, it is true, does not conceal the whole of its content. There is a sort of preliminary explanation to be strengthened by interpolations and slight alterations. Such elaboration of the dream content must not be too pronounced; the misconception of the dream thoughts to which it gives rise is merely superficial, and our first piece of work in analyzing a dream is to get rid of these early attempts at interpretation.

The motives for this part of the dream work are easily gauged. This final elaboration of the dream is due to a *regard for intelligibility*—a fact at once betraying the origin of an action which behaves towards the actual dream content just as our normal psychical action behaves towards some proffered perception that is to our liking. The dream content is thus secured under the pretense of certain expectations, is perceptually classified by the supposition of its intelligibility, thereby risking its falsification, whilst, in fact, the most extraordinary misconceptions arise if the dream can be correlated with nothing familiar. Every one is aware that we are unable to look at any series of unfamiliar signs, or to listen to a discussion of unknown words, without at once making perpetual changes through *our regard for intelligibility*, through our falling back upon what is familiar.

We can call those dreams *properly made up* which are the result of an elaboration in every way analogous to the psychical action of our waking life. In other dreams there is no such action; not even an attempt is made to bring about order and meaning. We regard the dream as "quite mad," because on awaking it is with this last-named part of the dream work, the dream elaboration, that we identify ourselves. So far, however, as our analysis is concerned, the dream, which resembles a medley of disconnected fragments, is of as much value as the one with a smooth and beautifully polished surface. In the former case we are spared, to some extent, the trouble of breaking down the super-elaboration of the dream content.

All the same, it would be an error to see in the dream façade nothing but the misunderstood and somewhat arbitrary elaboration of the dream carried out at the instance of our psychical life. Wishes and phantasies are not infrequently employed in the erection of this façade, which were already fashioned in the dream thoughts; they are akin to those of our waking life—"day-dreams," as they are very properly called. These wishes and phantasies, which analysis discloses in our dreams at night, often present themselves as repetitions and refashionings of the scenes of infancy. Thus the dream façade may show us directly the true core of the dream, distorted through admixture with other matter.

154

Beyond these four activities there is nothing else to be discovered in the dream work. If we keep closely to the definition that dream work denotes the transference of dream thoughts to dream content, we are compelled to say that the dream work is not creative; it develops no fancies of its own, it judges nothing, decides nothing. It does nothing but prepare the matter for condensation and displacement, and refashions it for dramatization, to which must be added the inconstant last-named mechanism—that of explanatory elaboration. It is true that a good deal is found in the dream content which might be understood as the result of another and more intellectual performance; but analysis shows conclusively every time that these *intellectual operations were already present in the dream thoughts, and have only been taken over by the dream content.* A syllogism in the dream is nothing other than the repetition of a syllogism in the dream thoughts; it seems inoffensive if it has been transferred to the dream without alteration; it becomes absurd if in the dream work it has been transferred to other matter. A calculation in the dream content simply means that there was a calculation in the dream thoughts; whilst this is always correct, the calculation in the dream can furnish the silliest results by the condensation of its factors and the displacement of the same operations to other things. Even speeches which are found in the dream content are not new compositions; they prove to be pieced together out of speeches which have been made or heard or read; the words are faithfully copied, but the occasion of their utterance is quite overlooked, and their meaning is most violently changed.

It is, perhaps, not superfluous to support these assertions by examples:

1. *A seemingly inoffensive, well-made dream of a patient. She was going to market with her cook, who carried the basket. The butcher said to her when she asked him for something: "That is all gone," and wished to give her something else, remarking: "That's very good." She declines, and goes to the greengrocer, who wants to sell her a peculiar vegetable which is bound up in bundles and of a black color. She says: "I don't know that; I won't take it."*

The remark "That is all gone" arose from the treatment. A few days before I said myself to the patient that the earliest reminiscences of childhood *are all gone* as such, but are replaced by transferences and dreams. Thus I am the butcher.

The second remark, *"I don't know that"* arose in a very different connection. The day before she had herself called out in rebuke to the cook (who, moreover, also appears in the dream): *"Behave yourself properly*; I don't know *that"*—that is, "I don't know this kind of behavior; I won't have it." The more harmless portion of this speech was arrived at by a displacement of the dream content; in the dream thoughts only the other portion of the speech played a part, because the dream work changed an imaginary situation into utter irrecognizability and complete inoffensiveness (while in a certain sense I behave in an unseemly way to the lady). The situation resulting in this phantasy is, however, nothing but a new edition of one that actually took place.

2. A dream apparently meaningless relates to figures. *"She wants to pay something; her daughter takes three florins sixty-five kreuzers out of her purse; but she says: What are you doing? It only cost twenty-one kreuzers."*

The dreamer was a stranger who had placed her child at school in Vienna, and who was able to continue under my treatment so long as her daughter remained at Vienna. The day before the dream the directress of the school had recommended her to keep the child another year at school. In this case she would have been able to prolong her treatment by one year. The figures in the dream become important if it be remembered that time is money. One year equals 365 days, or, expressed in kreuzers, 365 kreuzers, which is three florins sixty-five kreuzers. The twenty-one kreuzers correspond with the three weeks which remained from the day of the dream to the end of the school term, and thus to the end of the treatment. It was obviously financial considerations which had moved the lady to refuse the proposal of the directress, and which were answerable for the triviality of the amount in the dream.

3. A lady, young, but already ten years married, heard that a friend of hers, Miss Elise L——, of about the same age, had become engaged. This gave rise to the following dream:

She was sitting with her husband in the theater; the one side of the stalls was quite empty. Her husband tells her, Elise L——and her fiancé had intended coming, but could only get some cheap seats, three for one florin fifty kreuzers, and these they would not take. In her opinion, that would not have mattered very much.

The origin of the figures from the matter of the dream thoughts and the changes the figures underwent are of interest. Whence came the one florin fifty kreuzers? From a trifling occurrence of the previous day. Her sister-in-law had received 150 florins as a present from her husband, and had quickly got rid of it by buying some ornament. Note that 150 florins is one hundred times one florin fifty kreuzers. For the *three* concerned with the tickets, the only link is that Elise L——is exactly three months younger than the dreamer. The scene in the dream is the repetition of a little adventure for which she has often been teased by her husband. She was once in a great hurry to get tickets in time for a piece, and when she came to the theater *one side of the stalls was almost empty*. It was therefore quite unnecessary for her to have been in *such a hurry*. Nor must we overlook the absurdity of the dream that two persons should take three tickets for the theater.

Now for the dream ideas. It was *stupid* to have married so early; I *need not* have been *in so great a hurry*. Elise L——'s example shows me that I should have been able to get a husband later; indeed, one a *hundred times better* if I had but waited. I could have bought *three* such men with the money (dowry).

---

1   "Ich möchte gerne etwas geniessen ohne 'Kosten' zu haben." A a pun upon the word "kosten," which has two meanings—"taste" and "cost." In "Die Traumdeutung," third edition, p. 71 footnote, Professor Freud remarks that "the finest example of dream interpretation left us by the ancients is based upon a pun" (from "The Interpretation of Dreams," by Artemidorus

Daldianus). "Moreover, dreams are so intimately bound up with language that Ferenczi truly points out that every tongue has its own language of dreams. A dream is as a rule untranslatable into other languages."—TRANSLATOR.

2   It is worthy of remark that eminent philologists maintain that the oldest languages used the same word for expressing quite general antitheses. In C. Abel's essay, "Ueber den Gegensinn der Urworter" (1884, the following examples of such words in England are given: "gleam—gloom"; "to lock—loch"; "down—The Downs"; "to step—to stop." In his essay on "The Origin of Language" ("Linguistic Essays," p. 240), Abel says: "When the Englishman says 'without,' is not his judgment based upon the comparative juxtaposition of two opposites, 'with' and 'out'; 'with' itself originally meant 'without,' as may still be seen in 'withdraw.' 'Bid' includes the opposite sense of giving and of proffering." Abel, "The English Verbs of Command," "Linguistic Essays," p. 104; see also Freud, "Ueber den Gegensinn der Urworte"; *Jahrbuch für Psychoanalytische und Psychopathologische Forschungen*, Band II., part i., p. 179).— TRANSLATOR.

III

WHY THE DREAM DISGUISES THE DESIRES

In the foregoing exposition we have now learnt something of the dream work; we must regard it as a quite special psychical process, which, so far as we are aware, resembles nothing else. To the dream work has been transferred that bewilderment which its product, the dream, has aroused in us. In truth, the dream work is only the first recognition of a group of psychical processes to which must be referred the origin of hysterical symptoms, the ideas of morbid dread, obsession, and illusion. Condensation, and especially displacement, are never-failing features in these other processes. The regard for appearance remains, on the other hand, peculiar to the dream work. If this explanation brings the dream into line with the formation of psychical disease, it becomes the more important to fathom the essential conditions of processes like dream building. It will be probably a surprise to hear that neither the state of sleep nor illness is among the indispensable conditions. A whole number of phenomena of the everyday life of healthy persons, forgetfulness, slips in speaking and in holding things, together with a certain class of mistakes, are due to a psychical mechanism analogous to that of the dream and the other members of this group.

Displacement is the core of the problem, and the most striking of all the dream performances. A thorough investigation of the subject shows that the essential condition of displacement is purely psychological; it is in the nature of a motive. We get on the track by thrashing out experiences which one cannot avoid in the analysis of dreams. I had to break off the relations of my dream thoughts in the analysis of my dream on p. 8 because I found some experiences which I do not wish strangers to know, and which I could not relate without serious damage to important considerations. I added, it would be no use were I to select another instead of that particular dream; in every dream where the content is obscure or intricate, I should hit upon dream thoughts which call for secrecy. If, however, I continue the analysis for myself, without regard to those others, for whom, indeed, so personal an event as my dream cannot matter, I arrive finally at ideas which surprise me, which I have not known to be mine, which not only appear *foreign* to me, but which are *unpleasant*, and which I would like to oppose vehemently, whilst the chain of ideas running through the analysis intrudes upon me inexorably. I can only take these circumstances into account by admitting that these thoughts are actually part of my psychical life, possessing a certain psychical intensity or energy. However, by virtue of a particular psychological condition, the *thoughts could not become conscious to me*. I call this particular condition *"Repression."* It is therefore impossible for me not to recognize some casual relationship between the obscurity of the dream content and this state of repression—this *incapacity of consciousness*. Whence I conclude that the cause of the obscurity is *the desire to conceal these thoughts*. Thus I arrive at the conception of the *dream distortion* as the deed of the dream work, and of *displacement* serving to disguise this object.

I will test this in my own dream, and ask myself, What is the thought which, quite innocuous in its distorted form, provokes my liveliest opposition in its real form? I remember that the free drive reminded me of the last expensive drive with a member of my family, the interpretation of the dream being: I should for once like to experience affection for which I should not have to pay, and that shortly before the dream I had to make a heavy disbursement for this very person. In this connection, I cannot get away from the thought *that I regret this disbursement.* It is only when I acknowledge this feeling that there is any sense in my wishing in the dream for an affection that should entail no outlay. And yet I can state on my honor that I did not hesitate for a moment when it became necessary to expend that sum. The regret, the counter-current, was unconscious to me. Why it was unconscious is quite another question which would lead us far away from the answer which, though within my knowledge, belongs elsewhere.

If I subject the dream of another person instead of one of my own to analysis, the result is the same; the motives for convincing others is, however, changed. In the dream of a healthy person the only way for me to enable him to accept this repressed idea is the coherence of the dream thoughts. He is at liberty to reject this explanation. But if we are dealing with a person suffering from any neurosis—say from hysteria—the recognition of these repressed ideas is compulsory by reason of their connection with the symptoms of his illness and of the improvement resulting from exchanging the symptoms for the repressed ideas. Take the patient from whom I got the last dream about the three tickets for one florin fifty kreuzers. Analysis shows that she does not think highly of her husband, that she regrets having married him, that she would be glad to change him for some one else. It is true that she maintains that she loves her husband, that her emotional life knows nothing about this depreciation (a hundred times better!), but all her symptoms lead to the same conclusion as this dream. When her repressed memories had rewakened a certain period when she was conscious that she did not love her husband, her symptoms disappeared, and therewith disappeared her resistance to the interpretation of the dream.

This conception of repression once fixed, together with the distortion of the dream in relation to repressed psychical matter, we are in a position to give a general exposition of the principal results which the analysis of dreams supplies. We learnt that the most intelligible and meaningful dreams are unrealized desires; the desires they pictured as realized are known to consciousness, have been held over from the daytime, and are of

161

absorbing interest. The analysis of obscure and intricate dreams discloses something very similar; the dream scene again pictures as realized some desire which regularly proceeds from the dream ideas, but the picture is unrecognizable, and is only cleared up in the analysis. The desire itself is either one repressed, foreign to consciousness, or it is closely bound up with repressed ideas. The formula for these dreams may be thus stated: *They are concealed realizations of repressed desires*. It is interesting to note that they are right who regard the dream as foretelling the future. Although the future which the dream shows us is not that which will occur, but that which we would like to occur. Folk psychology proceeds here according to its wont; it believes what it wishes to believe.

Dreams can be divided into three classes according to their relation towards the realization of desire. Firstly come those which exhibit a *non-repressed, non-concealed desire*; these are dreams of the infantile type, becoming ever rarer among adults. Secondly, dreams which express in *veiled* form some *repressed desire*; these constitute by far the larger number of our dreams, and they require analysis for their understanding. Thirdly, these dreams where repression exists, but *without* or with but slight concealment. These dreams are invariably accompanied by a feeling of dread which brings the dream to an end. This feeling of dread here replaces dream displacement; I regarded the dream work as having prevented this in the dream of the second class. It is not very difficult to prove that what is now present as intense dread in the dream was once desire, and is now secondary to the repression.

There are also definite dreams with a painful content, without the presence of any anxiety in the dream. These cannot be reckoned among dreams of dread; they have, however, always been used to prove the unimportance and the psychical futility of dreams. An analysis of such an example will show that it belongs to our second class of dreams—a *perfectly concealed* realization of repressed desires. Analysis will demonstrate at the same time how excellently adapted is the work of displacement to the concealment of desires.

A girl dreamt that she saw lying dead before her the only surviving child of her sister amid the same surroundings as a few years before she saw the first child lying dead. She was not sensible of any pain, but naturally combatted the view that the scene represented a desire of hers. Nor was that view necessary. Years ago it was at the funeral of the child that she had last seen and spoken to the man she loved. Were the second child to die, she would be sure to meet this man again in her sister's house. She is longing to meet him, but struggles against this feeling. The day of the dream she had taken a ticket for a lecture, which announced the presence of the man she always loved. The dream is simply a dream of impatience common to those which happen before a journey, theater, or simply anticipated pleasures. The longing is concealed by the shifting of the scene to the occasion when any joyous feeling were out of place, and yet where it did once exist. Note, further, that the emotional behavior in the dream is adapted, not to the displaced, but to the real but suppressed dream ideas. The scene anticipates the long-hoped-for meeting; there is here no call for painful emotions.

There has hitherto been no occasion for philosophers to bestir themselves with a psychology of repression. We must be allowed to construct some clear conception as to the origin of dreams as the first steps in this unknown territory. The scheme which we have formulated not only from a study of dreams is, it is true, already somewhat complicated, but we cannot find any simpler one that will suffice. We hold that our psychical apparatus contains two procedures for the construction of thoughts. The second one has the advantage that its products find an open path to consciousness, whilst the activity of the first procedure is unknown to itself, and can only arrive at consciousness through the second one. At the borderland of these two procedures, where the first passes over into the second, a censorship is established which only passes what pleases it, keeping back everything else. That which is rejected by the censorship is, according to our definition, in a state of repression. Under certain conditions, one of which is the sleeping state, the balance of power between the two procedures is so changed that what is repressed can no longer be kept back. In the sleeping state this may possibly occur through the negligence of the censor; what has been hitherto repressed will now succeed in finding its way to consciousness. But as the censorship is never absent, but merely off guard, certain alterations must be conceded so as to placate it. It is a compromise which becomes conscious in this case—a compromise between what one procedure has in view and the demands of the other. *Repression, laxity of the censor, compromise*—this is the foundation for the origin of many another psychological process, just as it is for the dream. In such compromises we can observe the processes of condensation, of displacement, the acceptance of superficial associations, which we have found in the dream work.

It is not for us to deny the demonic element which has played a part in constructing our explanation of dream work. The impression left is that the formation of obscure dreams proceeds as if a person had something to say which must be agreeable for another person upon whom he is dependent to hear. It is by the use of this image that we figure to ourselves the conception of the *dream distortion* and of the censorship, and ventured to crystallize our impression in a rather crude, but at least definite, psychological theory. Whatever explanation the future may offer of these first and second procedures, we shall expect a confirmation of our correlate that the second procedure commands the entrance to consciousness, and can exclude the first from consciousness.

Once the sleeping state overcome, the censorship resumes complete sway, and is now able to revoke that which was granted in a moment of weakness. That the *forgetting* of dreams explains this in part, at least, we are convinced by our experience, confirmed again and again. During the relation of a dream, or during analysis of one, it not infrequently happens that some fragment of the dream is suddenly forgotten. This fragment so forgotten invariably contains the best and readiest approach to an understanding of the dream. Probably that is why it sinks into oblivion—*i.e.*, into a renewed suppression.

Viewing the dream content as the representation of a realized desire, and referring its vagueness to the changes made by the censor in the repressed matter, it is no longer difficult to grasp the function of dreams. In fundamental contrast with those saws which assume that sleep is disturbed by dreams, we hold the *dream as the guardian of sleep*. So far as children's dreams are concerned, our view should find ready acceptance.

The sleeping state or the psychical change to sleep, whatsoever it be, is brought about by the child being sent to sleep or compelled thereto by fatigue, only assisted by the removal of all stimuli which might open other objects to the psychical apparatus. The means which serve to keep external stimuli distant are known; but what are the means we can employ to depress the internal psychical stimuli which frustrate sleep? Look at a mother getting her child to sleep. The child is full of beseeching; he wants another kiss; he wants to play yet awhile. His requirements are in part met, in part drastically put off till the following day. Clearly these desires and needs, which agitate him, are hindrances to sleep. Every one knows the charming story of the bad boy (Baldwin Groller's) who awoke at night bellowing out, *"I want the rhinoceros."* A really good boy, instead of bellowing, would have *dreamt* that he was playing with the rhinoceros. Because the dream which realizes his desire is believed during sleep, it removes the desire and makes sleep possible. It cannot be denied that this belief accords with the dream image, because it is arrayed in the psychical appearance of probability; the child is without the capacity which it will acquire later to distinguish hallucinations or phantasies from reality.

The adult has learnt this differentiation; he has also learnt the futility of desire, and by continuous practice manages to postpone his aspirations, until they can be granted in some roundabout method by a change in the external world. For this reason it is rare for him to have his wishes realized during sleep in the short psychical way. It is even possible that this never happens, and that everything which appears to us like a child's dream demands a much more elaborate explanation. Thus it is that for adults—for every sane person without exception—a differentiation of the psychical matter has been fashioned which the child knew not. A psychical procedure has been reached which, informed by the experience of life, exercises with jealous power a dominating and restraining influence upon psychical emotions; by its relation to consciousness, and by its spontaneous mobility, it is endowed with the greatest means of psychical power. A portion of the infantile emotions has been withheld from this procedure as useless to life, and all the thoughts which flow from these are found in the state of repression.

Whilst the procedure in which we recognize our normal ego reposes upon the desire for sleep, it appears compelled by the psycho-physiological conditions of sleep to abandon some of the energy with which it was wont during the day to keep down what was repressed. This neglect is really harmless; however much the emotions of the child's spirit may be stirred, they find the approach to consciousness rendered difficult, and that to movement blocked in consequence of the state of sleep. The danger of their disturbing sleep must, however, be avoided. Moreover, we must admit that even in deep sleep some amount of free attention is exerted as a protection against sense-stimuli which might, perchance, make an awakening seem wiser than the continuance of sleep. Otherwise we could not explain the fact of our being always awakened by stimuli of certain quality. As the old physiologist Burdach pointed out, the mother is awakened by the whimpering of her child, the miller by the cessation of his mill, most people by gently calling out their names. This attention, thus on the alert, makes use of the internal stimuli arising from repressed desires, and fuses them into the dream, which as a compromise satisfies both procedures at the same time. The dream creates a form of psychical release for the wish which is either suppressed or formed by the aid of repression, inasmuch as it presents it as realized. The other procedure is also satisfied, since the continuance of the sleep is assured. Our ego here gladly behaves like a child; it makes the dream pictures believable, saying, as it were, "Quite right, but let me sleep." The contempt which, once awakened, we bear the dream, and which rests upon the absurdity and apparent illogicality of the dream, is probably nothing but the reasoning of our sleeping ego on the feelings about what was repressed; with greater right it should rest upon the incompetency of this disturber of our sleep. In sleep we are now and then aware of this contempt; the dream content transcends the censorship rather too much, we think, "It's only a dream," and sleep on.

It is no objection to this view if there are borderlines for the dream where its function, to preserve sleep from interruption, can no longer be maintained—as in the dreams of impending dread. It is here changed for another function—to suspend the sleep at the proper time. It acts like a conscientious night-watchman, who first does his duty by quelling disturbances so as not to waken the citizen, but equally does his duty quite properly when he awakens the street should the causes of the trouble seem to him serious and himself unable to cope with them alone.

This function of dreams becomes especially well marked when there arises some incentive for the sense perception. That the senses aroused during sleep influence the dream is well known, and can be experimentally verified; it is one of the certain but much overestimated results of the medical investigation of dreams. Hitherto there has been an insoluble riddle connected with this discovery. The stimulus to the sense by which the investigator affects the sleeper is not properly recognized in the dream, but is intermingled with a number of indefinite interpretations, whose determination appears left to psychical free-will. There is, of course, no such psychical free-will. To an external sense-stimulus the sleeper can react in many ways. Either he awakens or he succeeds in sleeping on. In the latter case he can make use of the dream to dismiss the external stimulus, and this, again, in more ways than one. For instance, he can stay the stimulus by dreaming of a scene which is absolutely intolerable to him. This was the means used by one who was troubled by a painful perineal abscess. He dreamt that he was on horseback, and made use of the poultice, which was intended to alleviate his pain, as a saddle, and thus got away from the cause of the trouble. Or, as is more frequently the case, the external stimulus undergoes a new rendering, which leads him to connect it with a repressed desire seeking its realization, and robs him of its reality, and is treated as if it were a part of the psychical matter. Thus, some one dreamt that he had written a comedy which embodied a definite *motif*; it was being performed; the first act was over amid enthusiastic applause; there was great clapping. At this moment the dreamer must have succeeded in prolonging his sleep despite the disturbance, for when he woke he no longer heard the noise; he concluded rightly that some one must have been beating a carpet or bed. The dreams which come with a loud noise just before waking have all attempted to cover the stimulus to waking by some other explanation, and thus to prolong the sleep for a little while.

Whosoever has firmly accepted this *censorship* as the chief motive for the distortion of dreams will not be surprised to learn as the result of dream interpretation that most of the dreams of adults are traced by analysis to erotic desires. This assertion is not drawn from dreams obviously of a sexual nature, which are known to all dreamers from their own experience, and are the only ones usually described as "sexual dreams." These dreams are ever sufficiently mysterious by reason of the choice of persons who are made the objects of sex, the removal of all the barriers which cry halt to the dreamer's sexual needs in his waking state, the many strange reminders as to details of what are called perversions. But analysis discovers that, in many other dreams in whose manifest content nothing erotic can be found, the work of interpretation shows them up as, in reality, realization of sexual desires; whilst, on the other hand, that much of the thought-making when awake, the thoughts saved us as surplus from the day only, reaches presentation in dreams with the help of repressed erotic desires.

Towards the explanation of this statement, which is no theoretical postulate, it must be remembered that no other class of instincts has required so vast a suppression at the behest of civilization as the sexual, whilst their mastery by the highest psychical processes are in most persons

168

soonest of all relinquished. Since we have learnt to understand *infantile sexuality*, often so vague in its expression, so invariably overlooked and misunderstood, we are justified in saying that nearly every civilized person has retained at some point or other the infantile type of sex life; thus we understand that repressed infantile sex desires furnish the most frequent and most powerful impulses for the formation of dreams.[1]

If the dream, which is the expression of some erotic desire, succeeds in making its manifest content appear innocently asexual, it is only possible in one way. The matter of these sexual presentations cannot be exhibited as such, but must be replaced by allusions, suggestions, and similar indirect means; differing from other cases of indirect presentation, those used in dreams must be deprived of direct understanding. The means of presentation which answer these requirements are commonly termed "symbols." A special interest has been directed towards these, since it has been observed that the dreamers of the same language use the like symbols—indeed, that in certain cases community of symbol is greater than community of speech. Since the dreamers do not themselves know the meaning of the symbols they use, it remains a puzzle whence arises their relationship with what they replace and denote. The fact itself is undoubted, and becomes of importance for the technique of the interpretation of dreams, since by the aid of a knowledge of this symbolism it is possible to understand the meaning of the elements of a dream, or parts of a dream, occasionally even the whole dream itself, without having to question the dreamer as to his own ideas. We thus come near to the popular idea of an interpretation of dreams, and, on the other hand, possess again the technique of the ancients, among whom the interpretation of dreams was identical with their explanation through symbolism.

Though the study of dream symbolism is far removed from finality, we now possess a series of general statements and of particular observations which are quite certain. There are symbols which practically always have the same meaning: Emperor and Empress (King and Queen) always mean the parents; room, a woman[2], and so on. The sexes are represented by a great variety of symbols, many of which would be at first quite incomprehensible had not the clews to the meaning been often obtained through other channels.

There are symbols of universal circulation, found in all dreamers, of one range of speech and culture; there are others of the narrowest individual significance which an individual has built up out of his own material. In the first class those can be differentiated whose claim can be at once recognized by the replacement of sexual things in common speech (those, for instance, arising from agriculture, as reproduction, seed) from others whose sexual references appear to reach back to the earliest times and to the obscurest depths of our image-building. The power of building symbols in both these special forms of symbols has not died out. Recently discovered things, like the airship, are at once brought into universal use as sex symbols.

It would be quite an error to suppose that a profounder knowledge of dream symbolism (the "Language of Dreams") would make us independent of questioning the dreamer regarding his impressions about the dream, and would give us back the whole technique of ancient dream interpreters. Apart from individual symbols and the variations in the use of what is general, one never knows whether an element in the dream is to be understood symbolically or in its proper meaning; the whole content of the dream is certainly not to be interpreted symbolically. The knowledge of dream symbols will only help us in understanding portions of the dream content, and does not render the use of the technical rules previously given at all superfluous. But it must be of the greatest service in interpreting a dream just when the impressions of the dreamer are withheld or are insufficient.

Dream symbolism proves also indispensable for understanding the so-called "typical" dreams and the dreams that "repeat themselves." Dream symbolism leads us far beyond the dream; it does not belong only to dreams, but is likewise dominant in legend, myth, and saga, in wit and in folklore. It compels us to pursue the inner meaning of the dream in these productions. But we must acknowledge that symbolism is not a result of the dream work, but is a peculiarity probably of our unconscious thinking, which furnishes to the dream work the matter for condensation, displacement, and dramatization.

1   Freud, "Three Contributions to Sexual Theory," translated by A.A. Brill *(Journal of Nervous and Mental Disease* Publishing Company, New York).
2   The words from "and" to "channels" in the next sentence is a short summary of the passage in the original. As this book will be read by other than professional people the passage has not been translated, in deference to English opinion.—TRANSLATOR.

IV

DREAM ANALYSIS

Perhaps we shall now begin to suspect that dream interpretation is capable of giving us hints about the structure of our psychic apparatus which we have thus far expected in vain from philosophy. We shall not, however, follow this track, but return to our original problem as soon as we have cleared up the subject of dream-disfigurement. The question has arisen how dreams with disagreeable content can be analyzed as the fulfillment of wishes. We see now that this is possible in case dream-disfigurement has taken place, in case the disagreeable content serves only as a disguise for what is wished. Keeping in mind our assumptions in regard to the two psychic instances, we may now proceed to say: disagreeable dreams, as a matter of fact, contain something which is disagreeable to the second instance, but which at the same time fulfills a wish of the first instance. They are wish dreams in the sense that every dream originates in the first instance, while the second instance acts towards the dream only in repelling, not in a creative manner. If we limit ourselves to a consideration of what the second instance contributes to the dream, we can never understand the dream. If we do so, all the riddles which the authors have found in the dream remain unsolved.

That the dream actually has a secret meaning, which turns out to be the fulfillment of a wish, must be proved afresh for every case by means of an analysis. I therefore select several dreams which have painful contents and attempt an analysis of them. They are partly dreams of hysterical subjects, which require long preliminary statements, and now and then also an examination of the psychic processes which occur in hysteria. I cannot, however, avoid this added difficulty in the exposition.

When I give a psychoneurotic patient analytical treatment, dreams are always, as I have said, the subject of our discussion. It must, therefore, give him all the psychological explanations through whose aid I myself have come to an understanding of his symptoms, and here I undergo an unsparing criticism, which is perhaps not less keen than that I must expect from my colleagues. Contradiction of the thesis that all dreams are the fulfillments of wishes is raised by my patients with perfect regularity. Here are several examples of the dream material which is offered me to refute this position.

"You always tell me that the dream is a wish fulfilled," begins a clever lady patient. "Now I shall tell you a dream in which the content is quite the opposite, in which a wish of mine is *not* fulfilled. How do you reconcile that with your theory? The dream is as follows:—

"I want to give a supper, but having nothing at hand except some smoked salmon, I think of going marketing, but I remember that it is Sunday afternoon, when all the shops are closed. I next try to telephone to some caterers, but the telephone is out of order . . . Thus I must resign my wish to give a supper."

I answer, of course, that only the analysis can decide the meaning of this dream, although I admit that at first sight it seems sensible and coherent, and looks like the opposite of a wish-fulfillment. "But what occurrence has given rise to this dream?" I ask. "You know that the stimulus for a dream always lies among the experiences of the preceding day."

Analysis.—The husband of the patient, an upright and conscientious wholesale butcher, had told her the day before that he is growing too fat, and that he must, therefore, begin treatment for obesity. He was going to get up early, take exercise, keep to a strict diet, and above all accept no more invitations to suppers. She proceeds laughingly to relate how her husband at an inn table had made the acquaintance of an artist, who insisted upon painting his portrait because he, the painter, had never found such an expressive head. But her husband had answered in his rough way, that he was very thankful for the honor, but that he was quite convinced that a portion of the backside of a pretty young girl would please the artist better than his whole face[1]. She said that she was at the time very much in love with her husband, and teased him a good deal. She had also asked him not to send her any caviare. What does that mean?

As a matter of fact, she had wanted for a long time to eat a caviare sandwich every forenoon, but had grudged herself the expense. Of course, she would at once get the caviare from her husband, as soon as she asked him for it. But she had begged him, on the contrary, not to send her the caviare, in order that she might tease him about it longer.

This explanation seems far-fetched to me. Unadmitted motives are in the habit of hiding behind such unsatisfactory explanations. We are reminded of subjects hypnotized by Bernheim, who carried out a posthypnotic order, and who, upon being asked for their motives, instead of answering: "I do not know why I did that," had to invent a reason that was obviously inadequate. Something similar is probably the case with the caviare of my patient. I see that she is compelled to create an unfulfilled wish in life. Her dream also shows the reproduction of the wish as accomplished. But why does she need an unfulfilled wish?

The ideas so far produced are insufficient for the interpretation of the dream. I beg for more. After a short pause, which corresponds to the overcoming of a resistance, she reports further that the day before she had made a visit to a friend, of whom she is really jealous, because her husband is always praising this woman so much. Fortunately, this friend is very lean and thin, and her husband likes well-rounded figures. Now of what did this lean friend speak? Naturally of her wish to become somewhat stouter. She also asked my patient: "When are you going to invite us again? You always have such a good table."

Now the meaning of the dream is clear. I may say to the patient: "It is just as though you had thought at the time of the request: 'Of course, I'll invite you, so you can eat yourself fat at my house and become still more pleasing to my husband. I would rather give no more suppers.' The dream then tells you that you cannot give a supper, thereby fulfilling your wish not to contribute anything to the rounding out of your friend's figure. The resolution of your husband to refuse invitations to supper for the sake of getting thin teaches you that one grows fat on the things served in company." Now only some conversation is necessary to confirm the solution. The smoked salmon in the dream has not yet been traced. "How did the salmon mentioned in the dream occur to you?" "Smoked salmon is the favorite dish of this friend," she answered. I happen to know the lady, and may corroborate this by saying that she grudges herself the salmon just as much as my patient grudges herself the caviare.

The dream admits of still another and more exact interpretation, which is necessitated only by a subordinate circumstance. The two interpretations do not contradict one another, but rather cover each other and furnish a neat example of the usual ambiguity of dreams as well as of all other psychopathological formations. We have seen that at the same time that she dreams of the denial of the wish, the patient is in reality occupied in securing an unfulfilled wish (the caviare sandwiches). Her friend, too, had expressed a wish, namely, to get fatter, and it would not surprise us if our lady had dreamt that the wish of the friend was not being fulfilled. For it is her own wish that a wish of her friend's—for increase in weight—should not be fulfilled. Instead of this, however, she dreams that one of her own wishes is not fulfilled. The dream becomes capable of a new interpretation, if in the dream she does not intend herself, but her friend, if she has put herself in the place of her friend, or, as we may say, has identified herself with her friend.

I think she has actually done this, and as a sign of this identification she has created an unfulfilled wish in reality. But what is the meaning of this hysterical identification? To clear this up a thorough exposition is necessary. Identification is a highly important factor in the mechanism of hysterical symptoms; by this means patients are enabled in their symptoms to represent not merely their own experiences, but the experiences of a great number of other persons, and can suffer, as it were, for a whole mass of people, and fill all the parts of a drama by means of their own personalities alone. It will here be objected that this is well-known hysterical imitation, the ability of hysteric subjects to copy all the symptoms which impress them when they occur in others, as though their pity were stimulated to the point of reproduction. But this only indicates the way in which the psychic process is discharged in hysterical imitation; the way in which a psychic act proceeds and the act itself are two different things. The latter is slightly more complicated than one is apt to imagine the imitation of hysterical subjects to be: it corresponds to an unconscious concluded process, as an example will show. The physician who has a female patient with a particular kind of twitching, lodged in the company of other patients in the same room of the hospital, is not surprised when some morning he learns that this peculiar hysterical attack has found imitations. He simply says to himself: The others have seen her and have done likewise: that is psychic infection. Yes, but psychic infection proceeds in somewhat the following manner: As a rule, patients know more about one another than the physician knows about each of them, and they are concerned about each other when the visit of the doctor is over. Some of them have an attack today: soon it is known among the rest that a letter from home, a return of lovesickness or the like, is the cause of it. Their sympathy is aroused, and the following syllogism, which does not reach consciousness, is completed in them: "If it is possible to have this kind of an attack from such causes, I too may have this kind of an attack, for I have the same reasons." If this were a cycle capable of becoming conscious, it would perhaps express itself in *fear* of getting the same attack; but it takes place in another psychic sphere, and, therefore, ends in the realization of the dreaded symptom. Identification is therefore not a simple imitation, but a sympathy based upon the same etiological claim; it expresses an "as though," and refers to some common quality which has remained in the unconscious.

176

Identification is most often used in hysteria to express sexual community. An hysterical woman identifies herself most readily—although not exclusively—with persons with whom she has had sexual relations, or who have sexual intercourse with the same persons as herself. Language takes such a conception into consideration: two lovers are "one." In the hysterical phantasy, as well as in the dream, it is sufficient for the identification if one thinks of sexual relations, whether or not they become real. The patient, then, only follows the rules of the hysterical thought processes when she gives expression to her jealousy of her friend (which, moreover, she herself admits to be unjustified, in that she puts herself in her place and identifies herself with her by creating a symptom—the denied wish). I might further clarify the process specifically as follows: She puts herself in the place of her friend in the dream, because her friend has taken her own place relation to her husband, and because she would like to take her friend's place in the esteem of her husband[2].

The contradiction to my theory of dreams in the case of another female patient, the most witty among all my dreamers, was solved in a simpler manner, although according to the scheme that the non-fulfillment of one wish signifies the fulfillment of another. I had one day explained to her that the dream is a wish of fulfillment. The next day she brought me a dream to the effect that she was traveling with her mother-in-law to their common summer resort. Now I knew that she had struggled violently against spending the summer in the neighborhood of her mother-in-law. I also knew that she had luckily avoided her mother-in-law by renting an estate in a far-distant country resort. Now the dream reversed this wished-for solution; was not this in the flattest contradiction to my theory of wish-fulfillment in the dream? Certainly, it was only necessary to draw the inferences from this dream in order to get at its interpretation. According to this dream, I was in the wrong. *It was thus her wish that I should be in the wrong, and this wish the dream showed her as fulfilled.* But the wish that I should be in the wrong, which was fulfilled in the theme of the country home, referred to a more serious matter. At that time I had made up my mind, from the material furnished by her analysis, that something of significance for her illness must have occurred at a certain time in her life. She had denied it because it was not present in her memory. We soon came to see that I was in the right. Her wish that I should be in the wrong, which is transformed into the dream, thus corresponded to the justifiable wish that those things, which at the time had only been suspected, had never occurred at all.

Without an analysis, and merely by means of an assumption, I took the liberty of interpreting a little occurrence in the case of a friend, who had been my colleague through the eight classes of the Gymnasium. He once heard a lecture of mine delivered to a small assemblage, on the novel subject of the dream as the fulfillment of a wish. He went home, dreamt *that he had lost all his suits*—he was a lawyer—and then complained to me about it. I took refuge in the evasion: "One can't win all one's suits," but I thought to myself: "If for eight years I sat as Primus on the first bench, while he moved around somewhere in the middle of the class, may he not naturally have had a wish from his boyhood days that I, too, might for once completely disgrace myself?"

In the same way another dream of a more gloomy character was offered me by a female patient as a contradiction to my theory of the wish-dream. The patient, a young girl, began as follows: "You remember that my sister has now only one boy, Charles: she lost the elder one, Otto, while I was still at her house. Otto was my favorite; it was I who really brought him up. I like the other little fellow, too, but of course not nearly as much as the dead one. Now I dreamt last night that *I saw Charles lying dead before me. He was lying in his little coffin, his hands folded: there were candles all about, and, in short, it was just like the time of little Otto's death, which shocked me so profoundly.* Now tell me, what does this mean? You know me: am I really bad enough to wish my sister to lose the only child she has left? Or does the dream mean that I wish Charles to be dead rather than Otto, whom I like so much better?"

I assured her that this interpretation was impossible. After some reflection I was able to give her the interpretation of the dream, which I subsequently made her confirm.

Having become an orphan at an early age, the girl had been brought up in the house of a much older sister, and had met among the friends and visitors who came to the house, a man who made a lasting impression upon her heart. It looked for a time as though these barely expressed relations were to end in marriage, but this happy culmination was frustrated by the sister, whose motives have never found a complete explanation. After the break, the man who was loved by our patient avoided the house: she herself became independent some time after little Otto's death, to whom her affection had now turned. But she did not succeed in freeing herself from the inclination for her sister's friend in which she had become involved. Her pride commanded her to avoid him; but it was impossible for her to transfer her love to the other suitors who presented themselves in order. Whenever the man whom she loved, who was a member of the literary profession, announced a lecture anywhere, she was sure to be found in the audience; she also seized every other opportunity to see him from a distance unobserved by him. I remembered that on the day before she had told me that the Professor was going to a certain concert, and that she was also going there, in order to enjoy the sight of him. This was on the day of the dream; and the concert was to take place on the day on which she told me the dream. I could now easily see the correct interpretation, and I asked her whether she could think of any event which had happened after the death of little Otto. She answered immediately: "Certainly; at that time the Professor returned after a long absence, and I saw him once more beside the coffin of little Otto." It was exactly as I had expected. I interpreted the dream in the following manner: "If now the other boy were to die, the same thing would be repeated. You would spend the day with your sister, the Professor would surely come in order to offer condolence, and you would see him again under the same circumstances as at that time. The dream signifies nothing

179

but this wish of yours to see him again, against which you are fighting inwardly. I know that you are carrying the ticket for today's concert in your bag. Your dream is a dream of impatience; it has anticipated the meeting which is to take place today by several hours."

In order to disguise her wish she had obviously selected a situation in which wishes of that sort are commonly suppressed—a situation which is so filled with sorrow that love is not thought of. And yet, it is very easily probable that even in the actual situation at the bier of the second, more dearly loved boy, which the dream copied faithfully, she had not been able to suppress her feelings of affection for the visitor whom she had missed for so long a time.

A different explanation was found in the case of a similar dream of another female patient, who was distinguished in her earlier years by her quick wit and her cheerful demeanors and who still showed these qualities at least in the notion, which occurred to her in the course of treatment. In connection with a longer dream, it seemed to this lady that she saw her fifteen-year-old daughter lying dead before her in a box. She was strongly inclined to convert this dream-image into an objection to the theory of wish-fulfillment, but herself suspected that the detail of the box must lead to a different conception of the dream.[3] In the course of the analysis it occurred to her that on the evening before, the conversation of the company had turned upon the English word "box," and upon the numerous translations of it into German, such as box, theater box, chest, box on the ear, &c. From other components of the same dream it is now possible to add that the lady had guessed the relationship between the English word "box" and the German *Büchse*, and had then been haunted by the memory that *Büchse* (as well as "box") is used in vulgar speech to designate the female genital organ. It was therefore possible, making a certain allowance for her notions on the subject of topographical anatomy, to assume that the child in the box signified a child in the womb of the mother. At this stage of the explanation she no longer denied that the picture of the dream really corresponded to one of her wishes. Like so many other young women, she was by no means happy when she became pregnant, and admitted to me more than once the wish that her child might die before its birth; in a fit of anger following a violent scene with her husband she had even struck her abdomen with her fists in order to hit the child within. The dead child was, therefore, really the fulfillment of a wish, but a wish which had been put aside for fifteen years, and it is not surprising that the fulfillment of the wish was no longer recognized after so long an interval. For there had been many changes meanwhile.

The group of dreams to which the two last mentioned belong, having as content the death of beloved relatives, will be considered again under the head of "Typical Dreams." I shall there be able to show by new examples that in spite of their undesirable content, all these dreams must be interpreted as wish-fulfillments. For the following dream, which again was told me in order to deter me from a hasty generalization of the theory of wishing in dreams, I am indebted, not to a patient, but to an intelligent jurist of my acquaintance. *"I dream,"* my informant tells me, *"that I am walking in front of my house with a lady on my arm. Here a closed wagon is waiting, a gentleman steps up to me, gives his authority as an agent of the police, and demands that I should follow him. I only ask for time in which to arrange my affairs.* Can you possibly suppose this is a wish of mine to be arrested?" "Of course not," I must admit. "Do you happen to know upon what charge you were arrested?" "Yes; I believe for infanticide." "Infanticide? But you know that only a mother can commit this crime upon her newly born child?" "That is true."[4] "And under what circumstances did you dream; what happened on the evening before?" "I would rather not tell you that; it is a delicate matter." "But I must have it, otherwise we must forgo the interpretation of the dream." "Well, then, I will tell you. I spent the night, not at home, but at the house of a lady who means very much to me. When we awoke in the morning, something again passed between us. Then I went to sleep again, and dreamt what I have told you." "The woman is married?" "Yes." "And you do not wish her to conceive a child?" "No; that might betray us." "Then you do not practice normal coitus?"

181

"I take the precaution to withdraw before ejaculation." "Am I permitted to assume that you did this trick several times during the night, and that in the morning you were not quite sure whether you had succeeded?" "That might be the case." "Then your dream is the fulfillment of a wish. By means of it you secure the assurance that you have not begotten a child, or, what amounts to the same thing, that you have killed a child. I can easily demonstrate the connecting links. Do you remember, a few days ago we were talking about the distress of matrimony (Ehenot), and about the inconsistency of permitting the practice of coitus as long as no impregnation takes place, while every delinquency after the ovum and the semen meet and a foetus is formed is punished as a crime? In connection with this, we also recalled the mediæval controversy about the moment of time at which the soul is really lodged in the foetus, since the concept of murder becomes admissible only from that point on. Doubtless you also know the gruesome poem by Lenau, which puts infanticide and the prevention of children on the same plane." "Strangely enough, I had happened to think of Lenau during the afternoon." "Another echo of your dream. And now I shall demonstrate to you another subordinate wish-fulfillment in your dream. You walk in front of your house with the lady on your arm. So you take her home, instead of spending the night at her house, as you do in actuality. The fact that the wish-fulfillment, which is the essence of the dream, disguises itself in such an unpleasant form, has perhaps more than one reason. From my essay on the etiology of anxiety neuroses, you will see that I note interrupted coitus as one of the factors which cause the development of neurotic fear. It would be consistent with this that if after repeated cohabitation of the kind mentioned you should be left in an uncomfortable mood, which now becomes an element in the composition of your dream. You also make use of this unpleasant state of mind to conceal the wish-fulfillment. Furthermore, the mention of infanticide has not yet been explained. Why does this crime, which is peculiar to females, occur to you?" "I shall confess to you that I was involved in such an affair years ago. Through my fault a girl tried to protect herself from the consequences of a *liaison* with me by securing an abortion. I had nothing to do with carrying out the plan, but I was naturally for a long time worried lest the affair might be discovered." "I understand; this recollection furnished a second reason why the supposition that you had done your trick badly must have been painful to you."

A young physician, who had heard this dream of my colleague when it was told, must have felt implicated by it, for he hastened to imitate it in a dream of his own, applying its mode of thinking to another subject. The day before he had handed in a declaration of his income, which was perfectly honest, because he had little to declare. He dreamt that an acquaintance of his came from a meeting of the tax commission and informed him that all the other declarations of income had passed uncontested, but that his own had awakened general suspicion, and that he would be punished with a heavy fine. The dream is a poorly-concealed fulfillment of the wish to be known as a physician with a large income. It likewise recalls the story of the young girl who was advised against accepting her suitor because he was a man of quick temper who would surely treat her to blows after they were married.

The answer of the girl was: "I wish he *would* strike me!" Her wish to be married is so strong that she takes into the bargain the discomfort which is said to be connected with matrimony, and which is predicted for her, and even raises it to a wish.

If I group the very frequently occurring dreams of this sort, which seem flatly to contradict my theory, in that they contain the denial of a wish or some occurrence decidedly unwished for, under the head of "counter wish-dreams," I observe that they may all be referred to two principles, of which one has not yet been mentioned, although it plays a large part in the dreams of human beings. One of the motives inspiring these dreams is the wish that I should appear in the wrong. These dreams regularly occur in the course of my treatment if the patient shows a resistance against me, and I can count with a large degree of certainty upon causing such a dream after I have once explained to the patient my theory that the dream is a wish-fulfillment.[5] I may even expect this to be the case in a dream merely in order to fulfill the wish that I may appear in the wrong. The last dream which I shall tell from those occurring in the course of treatment again shows this very thing. A young girl who has struggled hard to continue my treatment, against the will of her relatives and the authorities whom she had consulted, dreams as follows: *She is forbidden at home to come to me any more. She then reminds me of the promise I made her to treat her for nothing if necessary, and I say to her: "I can show no consideration in money matters."*

It is not at all easy in this case to demonstrate the fulfillment of a wish, but in all cases of this kind there is a second problem, the solution of which helps also to solve the first. Where does she get the words which she puts into my mouth? Of course I have never told her anything like that, but one of her brothers, the very one who has the greatest influence over her, has been kind enough to make this remark about me. It is then the purpose of the dream that this brother should remain in the right; and she does not try to justify this brother merely in the dream; it is her purpose in life and the motive for her being ill.

The other motive for counter wish-dreams is so clear that there is danger of overlooking it, as for some time happened in my own case. In the sexual make-up of many people there is a masochistic component, which has arisen through the conversion of the aggressive, sadistic component into its opposite. Such people are called "ideal" masochists, if they seek pleasure not in the bodily pain which may be inflicted upon them, but in humiliation and in chastisement of the soul. It is obvious that such persons can have counter wish-dreams and disagreeable dreams, which, however, for them are nothing but wish-fulfillment, affording satisfaction for their masochistic inclinations. Here is such a dream. A young man, who has in earlier years tormented his elder brother, towards whom he was homosexually inclined, but who had undergone a complete change of character, has the following dream, which consists of three parts:

(1) *He is "insulted" by his brother.* (2) *Two adults are caressing each other with homosexual intentions.* (3) *His brother has sold the enterprise whose management the young man reserved for his own future.* He awakens from the last-mentioned dream with the most unpleasant feelings, and yet it is a masochistic wish-dream, which might be translated: It would serve me quite right if my brother were to make that sale against my interest, as a punishment for all the torments which he has suffered at my hands.

I hope that the above discussion and examples will suffice—until further objection can be raised—to make it seem credible that even dreams with a painful content are to be analyzed as the fulfillments of wishes. Nor will it seem a matter of chance that in the course of interpretation one always happens upon subjects of which one does not like to speak or think. The disagreeable sensation which such dreams arouse is simply identical with the antipathy which endeavors—usually with success—to restrain us from the treatment or discussion of such subjects, and which must be overcome by all of us, if, in spite of its unpleasantness, we find it necessary to take the matter in hand. But this disagreeable sensation, which occurs also in dreams, does not preclude the existence of a wish; every one has wishes which he would not like to tell to others, which he does not want to admit even to himself. We are, on other grounds, justified in connecting the disagreeable character of all these dreams with the fact of dream disfigurement, and in concluding that these dreams are distorted, and that the wish-fulfillment in them is disguised until recognition is impossible for no other reason than that a repugnance, a will to suppress, exists in relation to the subject-matter of the dream or in relation to the wish which the dream creates. Dream disfigurement, then, turns out in reality to be an act of the censor. We shall take into consideration everything which the analysis of disagreeable dreams has brought to light if we reword our formula as follows: *The dream is the (disguised) fulfillment of a (suppressed, repressed) wish.*

Now there still remain as a particular species of dreams with painful content, dreams of anxiety, the inclusion of which under dreams of

185

wishing will find least acceptance with the uninitiated. But I can settle the problem of anxiety dreams in very short order; for what they may reveal is not a new aspect of the dream problem; it is a question in their case of understanding neurotic anxiety in general. The fear which we experience in the dream is only seemingly explained by the dream content. If we subject the content of the dream to analysis, we become aware that the dream fear is no more justified by the dream content than the fear in a phobia is justified by the idea upon which the phobia depends. For example, it is true that it is possible to fall out of a window, and that some care must be exercised when one is near a window, but it is inexplicable why the anxiety in the corresponding phobia is so great, and why it follows its victims to an extent so much greater than is warranted by its origin. The same explanation, then, which applies to the phobia applies also to the dream of anxiety. In both cases the anxiety is only superficially attached to the idea which accompanies it and comes from another source.

On account of the intimate relation of dream fear to neurotic fear, discussion of the former obliges me to refer to the latter. In a little essay on "The Anxiety Neurosis,"[6] I maintained that neurotic fear has its origin in the sexual life, and corresponds to a libido which has been turned away from its object and has not succeeded in being applied. From this formula, which has since proved its validity more and more clearly, we may deduce the conclusion that the content of anxiety dreams is of a sexual nature, the libido belonging to which content has been transformed into fear.

1   To sit for the painter. Goethe: "And if he has no backside, how can the nobleman sit?"

2   I myself regret the introduction of such passages from the psychopathology of hysteria, which, because of their fragmentary representation and of being torn from all connection with the subject, cannot have a very enlightening influence. If these passages are capable of throwing light upon the intimate

relations between the dream and the psychoneuroses, they have served the purpose for which I have taken them up.

3   Something like the smoked salmon in the dream of the deferred supper.

4   It often happens that a dream is told incompletely, and that a recollection of the omitted portions appear only in the course of the analysis. These portions subsequently fitted in, regularly furnish the key to the interpretation. *Cf.* below, about forgetting in dreams.

5   Similar "counter wish-dreams" have been repeatedly reported to me within the last few years by my pupils who thus reacted to their first encounter with the "wish theory of the dream."

6   See *Selected Papers on Hysteria and other Psychoneuroses*, p. 133, translated by A.A. Brill, *Journal of Nervous and Mental Diseases*, Monograph Series.

V

SEX IN DREAMS

The more one is occupied with the solution of dreams, the more willing one must become to acknowledge that the majority of the dreams of adults treat of sexual material and give expression to erotic wishes. Only one who really analyzes dreams, that is to say, who pushes forward from their manifest content to the latent dream thoughts, can form an opinion on this subject—never the person who is satisfied with registering the manifest content (as, for example, Näcke in his works on sexual dreams). Let us recognize at once that this fact is not to be wondered at, but that it is in complete harmony with the fundamental assumptions of dream explanation. No other impulse has had to undergo so much suppression from the time of childhood as the sex impulse in its numerous components, from no other impulse have survived so many and such intense unconscious wishes, which now act in the sleeping state in such a manner as to produce dreams. In dream interpretation, this significance of sexual complexes must never be forgotten, nor must they, of course, be exaggerated to the point of being considered exclusive.

Of many dreams it can be ascertained by a careful interpretation that they are even to be taken bisexually, inasmuch as they result in an irrefutable secondary interpretation in which they realize homosexual feelings—that is, feelings that are common to the normal sexual activity of the dreaming person. But that all dreams are to be interpreted bisexually, seems to me to be a generalization as indemonstrable as it is improbable, which I should not like to support. Above all I should not know how to dispose of the apparent fact that there are many dreams satisfying other than—in the widest sense—erotic needs, as dreams of hunger, thirst, convenience, &c. Likewise the similar assertions "that behind every dream one finds the death sentence" (Stekel), and that every dream shows "a continuation from the feminine to the masculine line" (Adler), seem to me to proceed far beyond what is admissible in the interpretation of dreams.

We have already asserted elsewhere that dreams which are conspicuously innocent invariably embody coarse erotic wishes, and we might confirm this by means of numerous fresh examples. But many dreams which appear indifferent, and which would never be suspected of any particular significance, can be traced back, after analysis, to unmistakably sexual wish-feelings, which are often of an unexpected nature. For example, who would suspect a sexual wish in the following dream until the interpretation had been worked out? The dreamer relates: *Between two stately palaces stands a little house, receding somewhat, whose doors are closed. My wife leads me a little way along the street up to the little house, and pushes in the door, and then I slip quickly and easily into the interior of a courtyard that slants obliquely upwards.*

Any one who has had experience in the translating of dreams will, of course, immediately perceive that penetrating into narrow spaces, and opening locked doors, belong to the commonest sexual symbolism, and will easily find in this dream a representation of attempted coition from behind (between the two stately buttocks of the female body). The narrow slanting passage is of course the vagina; the assistance attributed to the wife of the dreamer requires the interpretation that in reality it is only consideration for the wife which is responsible for the detention from such an attempt. Moreover, inquiry shows that on the previous day a young girl had entered the household of the dreamer who had pleased him, and who had given him the impression that she would not be altogether opposed to an approach of this sort. The little house between the two palaces is taken from a reminiscence of the Hradschin in Prague, and thus points again to the girl who is a native of that city.

189

If with my patients I emphasize the frequency of the Oedipus dream—of having sexual intercourse with one's mother—I get the answer: "I cannot remember such a dream." Immediately afterwards, however, there arises the recollection of another disguised and indifferent dream, which has been dreamed repeatedly by the patient, and the analysis shows it to be a dream of this same content—that is, another Oedipus dream. I can assure the reader that veiled dreams of sexual intercourse with the mother are a great deal more frequent than open ones to the same effect.

There are dreams about landscapes and localities in which emphasis is always laid upon the assurance: "I have been there before." In this case the locality is always the genital organ of the mother; it can indeed be asserted with such certainty of no other locality that one "has been there before."

A large number of dreams, often full of fear, which are concerned with passing through narrow spaces or with staying, in the water, are based upon fancies about the embryonic life, about the sojourn in the mother's womb, and about the act of birth. The following is the dream of a young man who in his fancy has already while in embryo taken advantage of his opportunity to spy upon an act of coition between his parents.

"He is in a deep shaft, in which there is a window, as in the Semmering Tunnel. At first he sees an empty landscape through this window, and then he composes a picture into it, which is immediately at hand and which fills out the empty space. The picture represents a field which is being thoroughly harrowed by an implement, and the delightful air, the accompanying idea of hard work, and the bluish-black clods of earth make a pleasant impression. He then goes on and sees a primary school opened . . . and he is surprised that so much attention is devoted in it to the sexual feelings of the child, which makes him think of me."

Here is a pretty water-dream of a female patient, which was turned to extraordinary account in the course of treatment.

At her summer resort at the . . . Lake, she hurls herself into the dark water at a place where the pale moon is reflected in the water.

Dreams of this sort are parturition dreams; their interpretation is accomplished by reversing the fact reported in the manifest dream content; thus, instead of "throwing one's self into the water," read "coming out of the water," that is, "being born." The place from which one is born is recognized if one thinks of the bad sense of the French "la lune." The pale moon thus becomes the white "bottom" (Popo), which the child soon recognizes as the place from which it came. Now what can be the meaning of the patient's wishing to be born at her summer resort? I asked the dreamer this, and she answered without hesitation: "Hasn't the treatment made me as though I were born again?" Thus the dream becomes an invitation to continue the cure at this summer resort, that is, to visit her there; perhaps it also contains a very bashful allusion to the wish to become a mother herself.[1]

Another dream of parturition, with its interpretation, I take from the work of E. Jones. *"She stood at the seashore watching a small boy, who seemed to be hers, wading into the water. This he did till the water covered him, and she could only see his head bobbing up and down near the surface. The scene then changed to the crowded hall of a hotel. Her husband left her, and she 'entered into conversation with' a stranger."* The second half of the dream was discovered in the analysis to represent a flight from her husband, and the entering into intimate relations with a third person, behind whom was plainly indicated Mr. X.'s brother mentioned in a former dream. The first part of the dream was a fairly evident birth phantasy. In dreams as in mythology, the delivery of a child *from* the uterine waters is commonly presented by distortion as the entry of the child *into* water; among many others, the births of Adonis, Osiris, Moses, and Bacchus are well-known illustrations of this. The bobbing up and down of the head in the water at once recalled to the patient the sensation of quickening she had experienced in her only pregnancy. Thinking of the boy going into the water induced a reverie in which she saw herself taking him out of the water, carrying him into the nursery, washing him and dressing him, and installing him in her household.

The second half of the dream, therefore, represents thoughts concerning the elopement, which belonged to the first half of the underlying latent content; the first half of the dream corresponded with the second half of the latent content, the birth phantasy. Besides this inversion in order, further inversions took place in each half of the dream. In the first half the child *entered* the water, and then his head bobbed; in the underlying dream thoughts first the quickening occurred, and then the child left the water (a double inversion). In the second half her husband left her; in the dream thoughts she left her husband.

Another parturition dream is related by Abraham of a young woman looking forward to her first confinement. From a place in the floor of the house a subterranean canal leads directly into the water (parturition path, amniotic liquor). She lifts up a trap in the floor, and there immediately appears a creature dressed in a brownish fur, which almost resembles a seal. This creature changes into the younger brother of the dreamer, to whom she has always stood in maternal relationship.

Dreams of "saving" are connected with parturition dreams. To save, especially to save from the water, is equivalent to giving birth when dreamed by a woman; this sense is, however, modified when the dreamer is a man.

Robbers, burglars at night, and ghosts, of which we are afraid before going to bed, and which occasionally even disturb our sleep, originate in one and the same childish reminiscence. They are the nightly visitors who have awakened the child to set it on the chamber so that it may not wet the bed, or have lifted the cover in order to see clearly how the child is holding its hands while sleeping. I have been able to induce an exact recollection of the nocturnal visitor in the analysis of some of these anxiety dreams. The robbers were always the father, the ghosts more probably corresponded to feminine persons with white night-gowns.

When one has become familiar with the abundant use of symbolism for the representation of sexual material in dreams, one naturally raises the question whether there are not many of these symbols which

192

appear once and for all with a firmly established significance like the signs in stenography; and one is tempted to compile a new dream-book according to the cipher method. In this connection it may be remarked that this symbolism does not belong peculiarly to the dream, but rather to unconscious thinking, particularly that of the masses, and it is to be found in greater perfection in the folklore, in the myths, legends, and manners of speech, in the proverbial sayings, and in the current witticisms of a nation than in its dreams.

The dream takes advantage of this symbolism in order to give a disguised representation to its latent thoughts. Among the symbols which are used in this manner there are of course many which regularly, or almost regularly, mean the same thing. Only it is necessary to keep in mind the curious plasticity of psychic material. Now and then a symbol in the dream content may have to be interpreted not symbolically, but according to its real meaning; at another time the dreamer, owing to a peculiar set of recollections, may create for himself the right to use anything whatever as a sexual symbol, though it is not ordinarily used in that way. Nor are the most frequently used sexual symbols unambiguous every time.

After these limitations and reservations I may call attention to the following: Emperor and Empress (King and Queen) in most cases really represent the parents of the dreamer; the dreamer himself or herself is the prince or princess. All elongated objects, sticks, tree-trunks, and umbrellas (on account of the stretching-up which might be compared to an erection! all elongated and sharp weapons, knives, daggers, and pikes, are intended to represent the male member. A frequent, not very intelligible, symbol for the same is a nail-file (on account of the rubbing and scraping?). Little cases, boxes, caskets, closets, and stoves correspond to the female part. The symbolism of lock and key has been very gracefully employed by Uhland in his song about the "Grafen Eberstein," to make a common smutty joke. The dream of walking through a row of rooms is a brothel or harem dream. Staircases, ladders, and flights of stairs, or climbing on these, either upwards or downwards, are symbolic representations of the sexual act. Smooth walls over which one is climbing, façades of houses upon which one is letting oneself down, frequently under great anxiety, correspond to the erect human body, and probably repeat in the dream reminiscences of the upward climbing of little children on their parents or foster parents. "Smooth" walls are men. Often in a dream of anxiety one is holding on firmly to some projection from a house. Tables, set tables, and boards are women, perhaps on account of the opposition which does away with the bodily contours. Since "bed and board" *(mensa et thorus)* constitute marriage, the former are often put for the latter in the dream, and as far as practicable the sexual presentation complex is transposed to the eating complex. Of articles of dress the woman's hat may frequently be definitely interpreted as the male genital. In dreams of men one often finds the cravat as a symbol for the penis; this indeed is not only because cravats hang down long, and are characteristic of the man, but also because one can select them at pleasure, a freedom which is prohibited by nature in the original of the symbol. Persons who make use of this symbol in the dream are very extravagant with cravats, and possess regular collections of them. All complicated machines and apparatus in dream are very probably genitals, in the description of which dream symbolism shows itself to be as tireless as the activity of wit. Likewise many landscapes in dreams, especially with bridges or with wooded mountains, can be readily recognized as descriptions of the genitals. Finally where one finds incomprehensible neologisms one may think of combinations made up of components having a sexual significance. Children also in the dream often signify the genitals, as men and women are in the habit of fondly referring to their genital organ as their "little one." As a very recent symbol of the male genital may be mentioned the flying machine, utilization of which is justified by its relation to flying as well as occasionally by its form. To play with a little child or to beat a little one is often the dream's representation of onanism. A number of other symbols, in part not sufficiently verified are given by

Stekel, who illustrates them with examples. Right and left, according to him, are to be conceived in the dream in an ethical sense. "The right way always signifies the road to righteousness, the left the one to crime. Thus the left may signify homosexuality, incest, and perversion, while the right signifies marriage, relations with a prostitute, &c. The meaning is always determined by the individual moral view-point of the dreamer." Relatives in the dream generally play the rôle of genitals. Not to be able to catch up with a wagon is interpreted by Stekel as regret not to be able to come up to a difference in age. Baggage with which one travels is the burden of sin by which one is oppressed. Also numbers, which frequently occur in the dream, are assigned by Stekel a fixed symbolical meaning, but these interpretations seem neither sufficiently verified nor of general validity, although the interpretation in individual cases can generally be recognized as probable. In a recently published book by W. Stekel, *Die Sprache des Traumes*, which I was unable to utilize, there is a list of the most common sexual symbols, the object of which is to prove that all sexual symbols can be bisexually used. He states: "Is there a symbol which (if in any way permitted by the phantasy) may not be used simultaneously in the masculine and the feminine sense!" To be sure the clause in parentheses takes away much of the absoluteness of this assertion, for this is not at all permitted by the phantasy. I do not, however, think it superfluous to state that in my experience Stekel's general statement has to give way to the recognition of a greater manifoldness. Besides those symbols, which are just as frequent for the male as for the female genitals, there are others which preponderately, or almost exclusively, designate one of the sexes, and there are still others of which only the male or only the female signification is known. To use long, firm objects and weapons as symbols of the female genitals, or hollow objects (chests, pouches, &c.), as symbols of the male genitals, is indeed not allowed by the fancy.

It is true that the tendency of the dream and the unconscious fancy to utilize the sexual symbol bisexually betrays an archaic trend, for in childhood a difference in the genitals is unknown, and the same genitals are attributed to both sexes.

These very incomplete suggestions may suffice to stimulate others to make a more careful collection.

I shall now add a few examples of the application of such symbolisms in dreams, which will serve to show how impossible it becomes to interpret a dream without taking into account the symbolism of dreams, and how imperatively it obtrudes itself in many cases.

1. The hat as a symbol of the man (of the male genital): (a fragment from the dream of a young woman who suffered from agoraphobia on account of a fear of temptation).

"I am walking in the street in summer, I wear a straw hat of peculiar shape, the middle piece of which is bent upwards and the side pieces of which hang downwards (the description became here obstructed), and in such a fashion that one is lower than the other. I am cheerful and in a confidential mood, and as I pass a troop of young officers I think to myself: None of you can have any designs upon me."

As she could produce no associations to the hat, I said to her: "The hat is really a male genital, with its raised middle piece and the two downward hanging side pieces." I intentionally refrained from interpreting those details concerning the unequal downward hanging of the two side pieces, although just such individualities in the determinations lead the way to the interpretation. I continued by saying that if she only had a man with such a virile genital she would not have to fear the officers—that is, she would have nothing to wish from them, for she is mainly kept from going without protection and company by her fancies of temptation. This last explanation of her fear I had already been able to give her repeatedly on the basis of other material.

It is quite remarkable how the dreamer behaved after this interpretation. She withdrew her description of the hat, and claimed not to have said that the two side pieces were hanging downwards. I was, however, too sure of what I had heard to allow myself to be misled, and I persisted in it. She was quiet for a while, and then found the courage to ask why it was that one of her husband's testicles was lower than the other, and whether it was the same in all men. With this the peculiar detail of the hat was explained, and the whole interpretation was accepted by her. The hat symbol was familiar to me long before the patient related this dream. From other but less transparent cases I believe that the hat may also be taken as a female genital.

2. The little one as the genital—to be run over as a symbol of sexual intercourse (another dream of the same agoraphobic patient).

"Her mother sends away her little daughter so that she must go alone. She rides with her mother to the railroad and sees her little one walking directly upon the tracks, so that she cannot avoid being run over. She hears the bones crackle. (From this she experiences a feeling of discomfort but no real horror.) She then looks out through the car window to see whether the parts cannot be seen behind. She then reproaches her mother for allowing the little one to go out alone." Analysis. It is not an easy matter to give here a complete interpretation of the dream. It forms part of a cycle of dreams, and can be fully understood only in connection with the others. For it is not easy to get the necessary material sufficiently isolated to prove the symbolism. The patient at first finds that the railroad journey is to be interpreted historically as an allusion to a departure from a sanatorium for nervous diseases, with the superintendent of which she naturally was in love. Her mother took her away from this place, and the physician came to the railroad station and handed her a bouquet of flowers on leaving; she felt uncomfortable because her mother witnessed this homage. Here the mother, therefore, appears as a disturber of her love affairs, which is the rôle actually played by this strict woman during her daughter's girlhood. The next thought referred to the sentence: "She then looks to see whether the parts can be seen behind." In the dream façade one would naturally be compelled to think of the parts of the little daughter run over and ground up. The thought, however, turns in quite a different direction. She recalls that she once saw her father in the bath-room naked from behind; she then begins to talk about the sex differentiation, and asserts that in the man the genitals can be seen from behind, but in the woman they cannot. In this connection she now herself offers the interpretation that the little one is the genital, her little one (she has a four-year-old daughter) her own genital. She reproaches her mother for wanting her to live as though she had no genital, and recognizes this reproach in the introductory sentence of the dream; the mother sends away her little one so that she must go alone. In her phantasy going alone on the street signifies to have no man and no sexual relations (coire = to go together), and this she does not like. According to all her statements she really suffered as a girl on account of the jealousy of her mother, because she showed a preference for her father.

The "little one" has been noted as a symbol for the male or the female genitals by Stekel, who can refer in this connection to a very widespread usage of language.

The deeper interpretation of this dream depends upon another dream of the same night in which the dreamer identifies herself with her brother. She was a "tomboy," and was always being told that she should have been born a boy. This identification with the brother shows with special clearness that "the little one" signifies the genital. The mother threatened him (her) with castration, which could only be understood as a punishment for playing with the parts, and the identification, therefore, shows that she herself had masturbated as a child, though this fact she now retained only in memory concerning her brother. An early knowledge of the male genital which she later lost she must have acquired at that time according to the assertions of this second dream. Moreover the second dream points to the infantile sexual theory that girls originate from boys through castration. After I had told her of this childish belief, she at once confirmed it with an anecdote in which the boy asks the girl: "Was it cut off?" to which the girl replied, "No, it's always been so."

198

The sending away of the little one, of the genital, in the first dream therefore also refers to the threatened castration. Finally she blames her mother for not having been born a boy.

That "being run over" symbolizes sexual intercourse would not be evident from this dream if we were not sure of it from many other sources.

3. Representation of the genital by structures, stairways, and shafts. (Dream of a young man inhibited by a father complex.)

"He is taking a walk with his father in a place which is surely the Prater, for the *Rotunda* may be seen in front of which there is a small front structure to which is attached a captive balloon; the balloon, however, seems quite collapsed. His father asks him what this is all for; he is surprised at it, but he explains it to his father. They come into a court in which lies a large sheet of tin. His father wants to pull off a big piece of this, but first looks around to see if any one is watching. He tells his father that all he needs to do is to speak to the watchman, and then he can take without any further difficulty as much as he wants to. From this court a stairway leads down into a shaft, the walls of which are softly upholstered something like a leather pocketbook. At the end of this shaft there is a longer platform, and then a new shaft begins . . ."

Analysis. This dream belongs to a type of patient which is not favorable from a therapeutic point of view. They follow in the analysis without offering any resistances whatever up to a certain point, but from that point on they remain almost inaccessible. This dream he almost analyzed himself. "The Rotunda," he said, "is my genital, the captive balloon in front is my penis, about the weakness of which I have worried." We must, however, interpret in greater detail; the Rotunda is the buttock which is regularly associated by the child with the genital, the smaller front structure is the scrotum. In the dream his father asks him what this is all for—that is, he asks him about the purpose and arrangement of the genitals. It is quite evident that this state of affairs should be turned

199

around, and that he should be the questioner. As such a questioning on the side of the father has never taken place in reality, we must conceive the dream thought as a wish, or take it conditionally, as follows: "If I had only asked my father for sexual enlightenment." The continuation of this thought we shall soon find in another place.

The court in which the tin sheet is spread out is not to be conceived symbolically in the first instance, but originates from his father's place of business. For discretionary reasons I have inserted the tin for another material in which the father deals, without, however, changing anything in the verbal expression of the dream. The dreamer had entered his father's business, and had taken a terrible dislike to the questionable practices upon which profit mainly depends. Hence the continuation of the above dream thought ("if I had only asked him") would be: "He would have deceived me just as he does his customers." For the pulling off, which serves to represent commercial dishonesty, the dreamer himself gives a second explanation—namely, onanism. This is not only entirely familiar to us, but agrees very well with the fact that the secrecy of onanism is expressed by its opposite ("Why one can do it quite openly"). It, moreover, agrees entirely with our expectations that the onanistic activity is again put off on the father, just as was the questioning in the first scene of the dream. The shaft he at once interprets as the vagina by referring to the soft upholstering of the walls. That the act of coition in the vagina is described as a going down instead of in the usual way as a going up, I have also found true in other instances[2].

The details that at the end of the first shaft there is a longer platform and then a new shaft, he himself explains biographically. He had for some time consorted with women sexually, but had then given it up because of inhibitions and now hopes to be able to take it up again with the aid of the treatment. The dream, however, becomes indistinct toward the end, and to the experienced interpreter it becomes evident that in the second scene of the dream the influence of another subject has begun to assert itself; in this his father's business and his dishonest practices signify the first vagina represented as a shaft so that one might think of a reference to the mother.

4. The male genital symbolized by persons and the female by a landscape.

(Dream of a woman of the lower class, whose husband is a policeman, reported by B. Dattner.)

... Then some one broke into the house and anxiously called for a policeman. But he went with two tramps by mutual consent into a church,[3] to which led a great many stairs;[4] behind the church there was a mountain,[5] on top of which a dense forest.[6] The policeman was furnished with a helmet, a gorget, and a cloak.[7] The two vagrants, who went along with the policeman quite peaceably, had tied to their loins sack-like aprons.[8] A road led from the church to the mountain. This road was overgrown on each side with grass and brushwood, which became thicker and thicker as it reached the height of the mountain, where it spread out into quite a forest.

5. A stairway dream.

(Reported and interpreted by Otto Rank.)

For the following transparent pollution dream, I am indebted to the same colleague who furnished us with the dental-irritation dream.

"I am running down the stairway in the stair-house after a little girl, whom I wish to punish because she has done something to me. At the bottom of the stairs some one held the child for me. (A grown-up woman?) I grasp it, but do not know whether I have hit it, for I suddenly find myself in the middle of the stairway where I practice coitus with the child (in the air as it were). It is really no coitus, I only rub my genital on her external genital, and in doing this I see it very distinctly, as distinctly as I see her head which is lying sideways. During the sexual act I see hanging to the left and above me (also as if in the air) two small pictures, landscapes, representing a house on a green. On the smaller one my surname stood in the place where the painter's signature should be; it seemed to be intended for my birthday present. A small sign hung in front of the pictures to the effect that cheaper pictures could also be obtained. I then see myself very indistinctly lying in bed, just as I had seen myself at the foot of the stairs, and I am awakened by a feeling of dampness which came from the pollution."

Interpretation. The dreamer had been in a book-store on the evening of the day of the dream, where, while he was waiting, he examined some pictures which were exhibited, which represented motives similar to the dream pictures. He stepped nearer to a small picture which particularly took his fancy in order to see the name of the artist, which, however, was quite unknown to him.

Later in the same evening, in company, he heard about a Bohemian servant-girl who boasted that her illegitimate child "was made on the stairs." The dreamer inquired about the details of this unusual occurrence, and learned that the servant-girl went with her lover to the home of her parents, where there was no opportunity for sexual relations, and that the excited man performed the act on the stairs. In witty allusion to the mischievous expression used about wine-adulterers, the dreamer remarked, "The child really grew on the cellar steps."

These experiences of the day, which are quite prominent in the dream content, were readily reproduced by the dreamer. But he just as readily reproduced an old fragment of infantile recollection which was also utilized by the dream. The stair-house was the house in which he had spent the greatest part of his childhood, and in which he had first become acquainted with sexual problems. In this house he used, among other things, to slide down the banister astride which caused him to become sexually excited. In the dream he also comes down the stairs very rapidly—so rapidly that, according to his own distinct assertions, he hardly touched the individual stairs, but rather "flew" or "slid down," as we used to say. Upon reference to this infantile experience, the beginning of the dream seems to represent the factor of sexual excitement. In the same house and in the adjacent residence the dreamer used to play pugnacious games with the neighboring children, in which he satisfied himself just as he did in the dream.

If one recalls from Freud's investigation of sexual symbolism[9] that in the dream stairs or climbing stairs almost regularly symbolizes coitus, the dream becomes clear. Its motive power as well as its effect, as is shown by the pollution, is of a purely libidinous nature. Sexual excitement became aroused during the sleeping state (in the dream this is represented by the rapid running or sliding down the stairs) and the sadistic thread in this is, on the basis of the pugnacious playing, indicated in the pursuing and overcoming of the child. The libidinous excitement becomes enhanced and urges to sexual action (represented in the dream by the grasping of the child and the conveyance of it to the middle of the stairway). Up to this point the dream would be one of pure, sexual symbolism, and obscure for the unpracticed dream interpreter. But this symbolic gratification, which would have insured undisturbed sleep, was not sufficient for the powerful libidinous excitement. The excitement leads to an orgasm, and thus the whole stairway symbolism is unmasked as a substitute for coitus. Freud lays stress on the rhythmical character of both actions as one of the reasons for the sexual utilization of the stairway symbolism, and this dream especially seems to corroborate this, for, according to the express assertion of the dreamer, the rhythm of a sexual act was the most pronounced feature in the whole dream.

Still another remark concerning the two pictures, which, aside from their real significance, also have the value of "Weibsbilder" (literally *woman-pictures*, but idiomatically *women*). This is at once shown by the fact that the dream deals with a big and a little picture, just as the dream content presents a big (grown up) and a little girl. That cheap pictures could also be obtained points to the prostitution complex, just as the dreamer's surname on the little picture and the thought that it was intended for his birthday, point to the parent complex (to be born on the stairway—to be conceived in coitus).

The indistinct final scene, in which the dreamer sees himself on the staircase landing lying in bed and feeling wet, seems to go back into childhood even beyond the infantile onanism, and manifestly has its prototype in similarly pleasurable scenes of bed-wetting.

6. A modified stair-dream.

To one of my very nervous patients, who was an abstainer, whose fancy was fixed on his mother, and who repeatedly dreamed of climbing stairs accompanied by his mother, I once remarked that moderate masturbation would be less harmful to him than enforced abstinence. This influence provoked the following dream:

"His piano teacher reproaches him for neglecting his piano-playing, and for not practicing the *Etudes* of Moscheles and Clementi's *Gradus ad Parnassum.*" In relation to this he remarked that the *Gradus* is only a stairway, and that the piano itself is only a stairway as it has a scale.

It is correct to say that there is no series of associations which cannot be adapted to the representation of sexual facts. I conclude with the dream of a chemist, a young man, who has been trying to give up his habit of masturbation by replacing it with intercourse with women.

Preliminary statement.—On the day before the dream he had given a student instruction concerning Grignard's reaction, in which magnesium is to be dissolved in absolutely pure ether under the catalytic influence of iodine. Two days before, there had been an explosion in the course of the same reaction, in which the investigator had burned his hand.

Dream I. *He is to make phenylmagnesium-bromid; he sees the apparatus with particular clearness, but he has substituted himself for the magnesium. He is now in a curious swaying attitude. He keeps repeating to himself, "This is the right thing, it is working, my feet are beginning to dissolve and my knees are getting soft." Then he reaches down and feels for his feet, and meanwhile (he does not know how) he takes his legs out of the crucible, and then again he says to himself, "That cannot be . . . Yes, it must be so, it has been done correctly." Then he partially awakens, and repeats the dream to himself, because he wants to tell it to me. He is distinctly afraid of the analysis of the dream. He is much excited during this semi-sleeping state, and repeats continually, "Phenyl, phenyl."*

II. *He is in . . . ing with his whole family; at half-past eleven. He is to be at the Schottenthor for a rendezvous with a certain lady, but he does not wake up until half-past eleven. He says to himself, "It is too late now; when you get there it will be half-past twelve." The next instant he sees the whole family gathered about the table—his mother and the servant girl with the soup-tureen with particular clearness. Then he says to himself, "Well, if we are eating already, I certainly can't get away."*

Analysis: He feels sure that even the first dream contains a reference to the lady whom he is to meet at the rendezvous (the dream was dreamed during the night before the expected meeting). The student to whom he gave the instruction is a particularly unpleasant fellow; he had said to the chemist: "That isn't right," because the magnesium was still unaffected, and the latter answered as though he did not care anything about it: "It certainly isn't right." He himself must be this student; he is as indifferent towards his analysis as the student is towards his synthesis; the *He* in the dream, however, who accomplishes the operation, is myself. How unpleasant he must seem to me with his indifference towards the success achieved!

Moreover, he is the material with which the analysis (synthesis) is made. For it is a question of the success of the treatment. The legs in the dream recall an impression of the previous evening. He met a lady at a dancing lesson whom he wished to conquer; he pressed her to him so closely that she once cried out. After he had stopped pressing against her legs, he felt her firm responding pressure against his lower thighs as far as just above his knees, at the place mentioned in the dream. In this situation, then, the woman is the magnesium in the retort, which is at last working. He is feminine towards me, as he is masculine towards the woman. If it will work with the woman, the treatment will also work. Feeling and becoming aware of himself in the region of his knees refers to masturbation, and corresponds to his fatigue of the previous day . . . The rendezvous had actually been set for half-past eleven. His wish to oversleep and to remain with his usual sexual objects (that is, with masturbation) corresponds with his resistance.

1   It is only of late that I have learned to value the significance of fancies and unconscious thoughts about life in the womb. They contain the explanation of the curious fear felt by so many people of being buried alive, as well as the profoundest unconscious reason for the belief in a life after death which represents nothing but a projection into the future of this mysterious life before birth. *The act of birth, moreover, is the first experience with fear, and is thus the source and model of the emotion of fear.*
2   Cf. *Zentralblatt für psychoanalyse*, I.
3   Or chapel—vagina.
4   Symbol of coitus.
5   Mons veneris.
6   Crines pubis.
7   Demons in cloaks and capucines are, according to the explanation of a man versed in the subject, of a phallic nature.
8   The two halves of the scrotum.
9   See *Zentralblatt für Psychoanalyse*, vol. i., p. 2.

VI

THE WISH IN DREAMS

That the dream should be nothing but a wish-fulfillment surely seemed strange to us all—and that not alone because of the contradictions offered by the anxiety dream.

After learning from the first analytical explanations that the dream conceals sense and psychic validity, we could hardly expect so simple a determination of this sense. According to the correct but concise definition of Aristotle, the dream is a continuation of thinking in sleep (in so far as one sleeps). Considering that during the day our thoughts produce such a diversity of psychic acts—judgments, conclusions, contradictions, expectations, intentions, &c.—why should our sleeping thoughts be forced to confine themselves to the production of wishes? Are there not, on the contrary, many dreams that present a different psychic act in dream form, *e.g.*, a solicitude, and is not the very transparent father's dream mentioned above of just such a nature? From the gleam of light falling into his eyes while asleep the father draws the solicitous conclusion that a candle has been upset and may have set fire to the corpse; he transforms this conclusion into a dream by investing it with a senseful situation enacted in the present tense. What part is played in this dream by the wish-fulfillment, and which are we to suspect—the predominance of the thought continued from, the waking state or of the thought incited by the new sensory impression?

All these considerations are just, and force us to enter more deeply into the part played by the wish-fulfillment in the dream, and into the significance of the waking thoughts continued in sleep.

It is in fact the wish-fulfillment that has already induced us to separate dreams into two groups. We have found some dreams that were plainly wish-fulfillments; and others in which wish-fulfillment could not be recognized, and was frequently concealed by every available means. In this latter class of dreams we recognized the influence of the dream censor. The undisguised wish dreams were chiefly found in children, yet fleeting open-hearted wish dreams *seemed* (I purposely emphasize this word) to occur also in adults.

We may now ask whence the wish fulfilled in the dream originates. But to what opposition or to what diversity do we refer this "whence"? I think it is to the opposition between conscious daily life and a psychic activity remaining unconscious which can only make itself noticeable during the night. I thus find a threefold possibility for the origin of a wish. Firstly, it may have been incited during the day, and owing to external circumstances failed to find gratification, there is thus left for the night an acknowledged but unfulfilled wish. Secondly, it may come to the surface during the day but be rejected, leaving an unfulfilled but suppressed wish. Or, thirdly, it may have no relation to daily life, and belong to those wishes that originate during the night from the suppression. If we now follow our scheme of the psychic apparatus, we can localize a wish of the first order in the system Forec. We may assume that a wish of the second order has been forced back from the Forec. system into the Unc. system, where alone, if anywhere, it can maintain itself; while a wish-feeling of the third order we consider altogether incapable of leaving the Unc. system. This brings up the question whether wishes arising from these different sources possess the same value for the dream, and whether they have the same power to incite a dream.

On reviewing the dreams which we have at our disposal for answering this question, we are at once moved to add as a fourth source of the dream-wish the actual wish incitements arising during the night, such as thirst and sexual desire. It then becomes evident that the source of the dream-wish does not affect its capacity to incite a dream. That a wish suppressed during the day asserts itself in the dream can be shown by a great many examples. I shall mention a very simple example of this class. A somewhat sarcastic young lady, whose younger friend has become engaged to be married, is asked throughout the day by her acquaintances whether she knows and what she thinks of the fiancé. She answers with unqualified praise, thereby silencing her own judgment, as she would prefer to tell the truth, namely, that he is an ordinary person. The following night she dreams that the same question is put to her, and that she replies with the formula: "In case of subsequent orders it will suffice to mention the number." Finally, we have learned from numerous analyses that the wish in all dreams that have been subject to distortion has been derived from the unconscious, and has been unable to come to perception in the waking state. Thus it would appear that all wishes are of the same value and force for the dream formation.

I am at present unable to prove that the state of affairs is really different, but I am strongly inclined to assume a more stringent determination of the dream-wish. Children's dreams leave no doubt that an unfulfilled wish of the day may be the instigator of the dream. But we must not forget that it is, after all, the wish of a child, that it is a wish-feeling of infantile strength only. I have a strong doubt whether an unfulfilled wish from the day would suffice to create a dream in an adult. It would rather seem that as we learn to control our impulses by intellectual activity, we more and more reject as vain the formation or retention of such intense wishes as are natural to childhood. In this, indeed, there may be individual variations; some retain the infantile type of psychic processes longer than others. The differences are here the same as those found in the gradual decline of the originally distinct visual imagination.

In general, however, I am of the opinion that unfulfilled wishes of the day are insufficient to produce a dream in adults. I readily admit that the wish instigators originating in conscious like contribute towards the incitement of dreams, but that is probably all. The dream would not originate if the foreconscious wish were not reinforced from another source.

That source is the unconscious. I believe that *the conscious wish is a dream inciter only if it succeeds in arousing a similar unconscious wish which reinforces it.* Following the suggestions obtained through the psychoanalysis of the neuroses, I believe that these unconscious wishes are always active and ready for expression whenever they find an opportunity to unite themselves with an emotion from conscious life, and that they transfer their greater intensity to the lesser intensity of the latter.[1] It may therefore seem that the conscious wish alone has been realized in a dream; but a slight peculiarity in the formation of this dream will put us on the track of the powerful helper from the unconscious. These ever active and, as it were, immortal wishes from the unconscious recall the legendary Titans who from time immemorial have borne the ponderous mountains which were once rolled upon them by the victorious gods, and which even now quiver from time to time from the convulsions of their mighty limbs; I say that these wishes found in the repression are of themselves of an infantile origin, as we have learned from the psychological investigation of the neuroses. I should like, therefore, to withdraw the opinion previously expressed that it is unimportant whence the dream-wish originates, and replace it by another, as follows: *The wish manifested in the dream must be an infantile one.* In the adult it originates in the Unc., while in the child, where no separation and censor as yet exist between Forec. and Unc., or where these are only in the process of formation, it is an unfulfilled and unrepressed wish from the waking state. I am aware that this conception cannot be generally demonstrated, but I maintain nevertheless that it can be frequently demonstrated, even when it was not suspected, and that it cannot be generally refuted.

The wish-feelings which remain from the conscious waking state are, therefore, relegated to the background in the dream formation. In the dream content I shall attribute to them only the part attributed to the material of actual sensations during sleep. If I now take into account those other psychic instigations remaining from the waking state which are not wishes, I shall only adhere to the line mapped out for me by this train of thought. We may succeed in provisionally terminating the sum of energy of our waking thoughts by deciding to go to sleep. He is a good sleeper who can do this; Napoleon I. is reputed to have been a model of this sort. But we do not always succeed in accomplishing it, or in accomplishing it perfectly. Unsolved problems, harassing cares, overwhelming impressions continue the thinking activity even during sleep, maintaining psychic processes in the system which we have termed the foreconscious. These mental processes continuing into sleep may be divided into the following groups: 1, That which has not been terminated during the day owing to casual prevention; 2, that which has been left unfinished by temporary paralysis of our mental power, *i.e.* the unsolved; 3, that which has been rejected and suppressed during the day. This unites with a powerful group (4) formed by that which has been excited in our Unc. during the day by the work of the foreconscious. Finally, we may add group (5) consisting of the indifferent and hence unsettled impressions of the day.

We should not underrate the psychic intensities introduced into sleep by these remnants of waking life, especially those emanating from the group of the unsolved. These excitations surely continue to strive for expression during the night, and we may assume with equal certainty that the sleeping state renders impossible the usual continuation of the excitement in the foreconscious and the termination of the excitement by its becoming conscious. As far as we can normally become conscious of our mental processes, even during the night, in so far we are not asleep. I shall not venture to state what change is produced in the Forec. system by the sleeping state, but there is no doubt that the psychological character of sleep is essentially due to the change of energy in this very system, which also dominates the approach to motility, which is paralyzed

211

during sleep. In contradistinction to this, there seems to be nothing in the psychology of the dream to warrant the assumption that sleep produces any but secondary changes in the conditions of the Unc. system. Hence, for the nocturnal excitation in the Force, there remains no other path than that followed by the wish excitements from the Unc. This excitation must seek reinforcement from the Unc., and follow the detours of the unconscious excitations. But what is the relation of the foreconscious day remnants to the dream? There is no doubt that they penetrate abundantly into the dream, that they utilize the dream content to obtrude themselves upon consciousness even during the night; indeed, they occasionally even dominate the dream content, and impel it to continue the work of the day; it is also certain that the day remnants may just as well have any other character as that of wishes; but it is highly instructive and even decisive for the theory of wish-fulfillment to see what conditions they must comply with in order to be received into the dream.

Let us pick out one of the dreams cited above as examples, *e.g.*, the dream in which my friend Otto seems to show the symptoms of Basedow's disease. My friend Otto's appearance occasioned me some concern during the day, and this worry, like everything else referring to this person, affected me. I may also assume that these feelings followed me into sleep. I was probably bent on finding out what was the matter with him. In the night my worry found expression in the dream which I have reported, the content of which was not only senseless, but failed to show any wish-fulfillment. But I began to investigate for the source of this incongruous expression of the solicitude felt during the day, and analysis revealed the connection. I identified my friend Otto with a certain Baron L. and myself with a Professor R. There was only one explanation for my being impelled to select just this substitution for the day thought. I must have always been prepared in the Unc. to identify myself with Professor R., as it meant the realization of one of the immortal infantile wishes, viz. that of becoming great. Repulsive ideas respecting my friend, that would certainly have been repudiated in a waking state, took advantage of the opportunity to creep into the dream, but the worry of the day likewise found some form of expression through a substitution in the dream content. The day thought, which was no wish in itself but rather a worry, had in some way to find a connection with the infantile now unconscious and suppressed wish, which then allowed it, though already properly prepared, to "originate" for consciousness. The more dominating this worry, the stronger must be the connection to be established; between the contents of the wish and that of the worry there need be no connection, nor was there one in any of our examples.

We can now sharply define the significance of the unconscious wish for the dream. It may be admitted that there is a whole class of dreams in which the incitement originates preponderatingly or even exclusively from the remnants of daily life; and I believe that even my cherished desire to become at some future time a "professor extraordinarius" would have allowed me to slumber undisturbed that night had not my worry about my friend's health been still active. But this worry alone would not have produced a dream; the motive power needed by the dream had to be contributed by a wish, and it was the affair of the worriment to procure for itself such wish as a motive power of the dream. To speak figuratively, it is quite possible that a day thought plays the part of the contractor (*entrepreneur*) in the dream. But it is known that no matter what idea the contractor may have in mind, and how desirous he may be of putting it into operation, he can do nothing without capital; he must depend upon a capitalist to defray the necessary expenses, and this capitalist, who supplies the psychic expenditure for the dream is invariably and indisputably *a wish from the unconscious*, no matter what the nature of the waking thought may be.

In other cases the capitalist himself is the contractor for the dream; this, indeed, seems to be the more usual case. An unconscious wish is produced by the day's work, which in turn creates the dream. The dream processes, moreover, run parallel with all the other possibilities of the economic relationship used here as an illustration. Thus, the entrepreneur may contribute some capital himself, or several entrepreneurs may seek the aid of the same capitalist, or several capitalists may jointly supply the capital required by the entrepreneur. Thus there are dreams produced by more than one dream-wish, and many similar variations which may readily be passed over and are of no further interest to us. What we have left unfinished in this discussion of the dream-wish we shall be able to develop later.

The "tertium comparationis" in the comparisons just employed— *i.e.* the sum placed at our free disposal in proper allotment—admits of still finer application for the illustration of the dream structure. We can recognize in most dreams a center especially supplied with perceptible intensity. This is regularly the direct representation of the wish-fulfillment; for, if we undo the displacements of the dream-work by a process of retrogression, we find that the psychic intensity of the elements in the dream thoughts is replaced by the perceptible intensity of the elements in the dream content. The elements adjoining the wish-fulfillment have frequently nothing to do with its sense, but prove to be descendants of painful thoughts which oppose the wish. But, owing to their frequently artificial connection with the central element, they have acquired sufficient intensity to enable them to come to expression. Thus, the force of expression of the wish-fulfillment is diffused over a certain sphere of association, within which it raises to expression all elements, including those that are in themselves impotent. In dreams having several strong wishes we can readily separate from one another the spheres of the individual wish-fulfillments; the gaps in the dream likewise can often be explained as boundary zones.

Although the foregoing remarks have considerably limited the significance of the day remnants for the dream, it will nevertheless be worth our while to give them some attention. For they must be a necessary ingredient in the formation of the dream, inasmuch as experience reveals the surprising fact that every dream shows in its content a connection with some impression of a recent day, often of the most indifferent kind. So far we have failed to see any necessity for this addition to the dream mixture. This necessity appears only when we follow closely the part played by the unconscious wish, and then seek information in the psychology of the neuroses. We thus learn that the unconscious idea, as such, is altogether incapable of entering into the foreconscious, and that it can exert an influence there only by uniting with a harmless idea already belonging to the foreconscious, to which it transfers its intensity and under which it allows itself to be concealed. This is the fact of transference which furnishes an explanation for so many surprising occurrences in the psychic life of neurotics.

The idea from the foreconscious which thus obtains an unmerited abundance of intensity may be left unchanged by the transference, or it may have forced upon it a modification from the content of the transferring idea. I trust the reader will pardon my fondness for comparisons from daily life, but I feel tempted to say that the relations existing for the repressed idea are similar to the situations existing in Austria for the American dentist, who is forbidden to practise unless he gets permission from a regular physician to use his name on the public signboard and thus cover the legal requirements. Moreover, just as it is naturally not the busiest physicians who form such alliances with dental practitioners, so in the psychic life only such foreconscious or conscious ideas are chosen to cover a repressed idea as have not themselves attracted much of the attention which is operative in the foreconscious. The unconscious entangles with its connections preferentially either those impressions and ideas of the foreconscious which have been left unnoticed as indifferent, or those that have soon been deprived of this attention through rejection. It is a familiar fact from the association studies confirmed by every experience, that ideas which have formed intimate connections in one direction assume an almost negative attitude to whole groups of new connections. I once tried from this principle to develop a theory for hysterical paralysis.

If we assume that the same need for the transference of the repressed ideas which we have learned to know from the analysis of the neuroses makes its influence felt in the dream as well, we can at once explain two riddles of the dream, viz. that every dream analysis shows an interweaving of a recent impression, and that this recent element is frequently of the most indifferent character. We may add what we have already learned elsewhere, that these recent and indifferent elements come so frequently into the dream content as a substitute for the most deep-lying of the dream thoughts, for the further reason that they have least to fear from the resisting censor. But while this freedom from censorship explains only the preference for trivial elements, the constant presence of recent elements points to the fact that there is a need for transference. Both groups of impressions satisfy the demand of the repression for material still free from associations, the indifferent ones because they have offered no inducement for extensive associations, and the recent ones because they have had insufficient time to form such associations.

We thus see that the day remnants, among which we may now include the indifferent impressions when they participate in the dream formation, not only borrow from the Unc. the motive power at the disposal of the repressed wish, but also offer to the unconscious something indispensable, namely, the attachment necessary to the transference. If we here attempted to penetrate more deeply into the psychic processes, we should first have to throw more light on the play of emotions between the foreconscious and the unconscious, to which, indeed, we are urged by the study of the psychoneuroses, whereas the dream itself offers no assistance in this respect.

Just one further remark about the day remnants. There is no doubt that they are the actual disturbers of sleep, and not the dream, which, on the contrary, strives to guard sleep. But we shall return to this point later.

We have so far discussed the dream-wish, we have traced it to the sphere of the Unc., and analyzed its relations to the day remnants, which in turn may be either wishes, psychic emotions of any other kind, or simply recent impressions. We have thus made room for any claims that may be made for the importance of conscious thought activity in dream formations in all its variations. Relying upon our thought series, it would not be at all impossible for us to explain even those extreme cases in which the dream as a continuer of the day work brings to a happy conclusion and unsolved problem possess an example, the analysis of which might reveal the infantile or repressed wish source furnishing such alliance and successful strengthening of the efforts of the foreconscious activity. But we have not come one step nearer a solution of the riddle: Why can the unconscious furnish the motive power for the wish-fulfillment only during sleep? The answer to this question must throw light on the psychic nature of wishes; and it will be given with the aid of the diagram of the psychic apparatus.

We do not doubt that even this apparatus attained its present perfection through a long course of development. Let us attempt to restore it as it existed in an early phase of its activity. From assumptions, to be confirmed elsewhere, we know that at first the apparatus strove to keep as free from excitement as possible, and in its first formation, therefore, the scheme took the form of a reflex apparatus, which enabled it promptly to discharge through the motor tracts any sensible stimulus reaching it from without. But this simple function was disturbed by the wants of life, which likewise furnish the impulse for the further development of the apparatus. The wants of life first manifested themselves to it in the form of the great physical needs. The excitement aroused by the inner want seeks an outlet in motility, which may be designated as "inner changes" or as an "expression of the emotions." The hungry child cries or fidgets helplessly, but its situation remains unchanged; for the excitation proceeding from an inner want requires, not a momentary outbreak, but a force working continuously. A change can occur only if in some way a feeling of gratification is experienced—which in the case of the child must be through outside help—in order to remove the inner excitement.

An essential constituent of this experience is the appearance of a certain perception (of food in our example), the memory picture of which thereafter remains associated with the memory trace of the excitation of want.

Thanks to the established connection, there results at the next appearance of this want a psychic feeling which revives the memory picture of the former perception, and thus recalls the former perception itself, *i.e.* it actually re-establishes the situation of the first gratification. We call such a feeling a wish; the reappearance of the perception constitutes the wish-fulfillment, and the full revival of the perception by the want excitement constitutes the shortest road to the wish-fulfillment. We may assume a primitive condition of the psychic apparatus in which this road is really followed, *i.e.* where the wishing merges into an hallucination, This first psychic activity therefore aims at an identity of perception, *i.e.* it aims at a repetition of that perception which is connected with the fulfillment of the want.

This primitive mental activity must have been modified by bitter practical experience into a more expedient secondary activity. The establishment of the identity perception on the short regressive road within the apparatus does not in another respect carry with it the result which inevitably follows the revival of the same perception from without. The gratification does not take place, and the want continues. In order to equalize the internal with the external sum of energy, the former must be continually maintained, just as actually happens in the hallucinatory psychoses and in the deliriums of hunger which exhaust their psychic capacity in clinging to the object desired. In order to make more appropriate use of the psychic force, it becomes necessary to inhibit the full regression so as to prevent it from extending beyond the image of memory, whence it can select other paths leading ultimately to the establishment of the desired identity from the outer world. This inhibition and consequent deviation from the excitation becomes the task of a second system which dominates the voluntary motility, *i.e.* through whose activity the expenditure of motility is now devoted to previously recalled purposes. But this entire complicated mental activity which works its way from the memory picture to the establishment of the perception identity from the outer world merely represents a detour which has been forced upon the wish-fulfillment by experience.[2] Thinking is indeed nothing but the equivalent of the hallucinatory wish; and if the dream be called a wish-fulfillment this becomes self-evident, as nothing but a wish can impel our psychic apparatus to activity. The dream, which in fulfilling its wishes follows the short regressive path, thereby preserves for us only an example of the primary form of the psychic apparatus which has been abandoned as inexpedient. What once ruled in the waking state when the psychic life was still young and unfit seems to have been banished into the sleeping state, just as we see again in the nursery the bow and arrow, the discarded primitive weapons of grown-up humanity. *The dream is a fragment of the abandoned psychic life of the child.* In the psychoses these modes of operation of the psychic apparatus, which are normally suppressed in the waking state, reassert themselves, and then betray their inability to satisfy our wants in the outer world.

The unconscious wish-feelings evidently strive to assert themselves during the day also, and the fact of transference and the psychoses teach us that they endeavor to penetrate to consciousness and dominate motility by the road leading through the system of the foreconscious. It is, therefore, the censor lying between the Unc. and the Forec., the assumption of which is forced upon us by the dream, that we have to recognize and honor as the guardian of our psychic health. But is it not carelessness on the part of this guardian to diminish its vigilance during the night and to allow the suppressed emotions of the Unc. to come to expression, thus again making possible the hallucinatory regression? I think not, for when the critical guardian goes to rest—and we have proof that his slumber is not profound—he takes care to close the gate to motility. No matter what feelings from the otherwise inhibited Unc. may roam about on the scene, they need not be interfered with; they remain harmless because they are unable to put in motion the motor apparatus which alone can exert a modifying influence upon the outer world. Sleep guarantees the security of the fortress which is under guard. Conditions are less harmless when a displacement of forces is produced, not through a nocturnal diminution in the operation of the critical censor, but through pathological enfeeblement of the latter or through pathological reinforcement of the unconscious excitations, and this while the foreconscious is charged with energy and the avenues to motility are open. The guardian is then overpowered, the unconscious excitations subdue the Forec.; through it they dominate our speech and actions, or they enforce the hallucinatory regression, thus governing an apparatus not designed for them by virtue of the attraction exerted by the perceptions on the distribution of our psychic energy. We call this condition a psychosis.

We are now in the best position to complete our psychological construction, which has been interrupted by the introduction of the two systems, Unc. and Forec. We have still, however, ample reason for giving further consideration to the wish as the sole psychic motive power in the dream. We have explained that the reason why the dream is in every case a wish realization is because it is a product of the Unc., which knows no other aim in its activity but the fulfillment of wishes, and which has no other forces at its disposal but wish-feelings. If we avail ourselves for a moment longer of the right to elaborate from the dream interpretation such far-reaching psychological speculations, we are in duty bound to demonstrate that we are thereby bringing the dream into a relationship which may also comprise other psychic structures. If there exists a system of the Unc.—or something sufficiently analogous to it for the purpose of our discussion—the dream cannot be its sole manifestation; every dream may be a wish-fulfillment, but there must be other forms of abnormal wish-fulfillment beside this of dreams. Indeed, the theory of all psychoneurotic symptoms culminates in the proposition *that they too must be taken as wish-fulfillments of the unconscious.* Our explanation makes the dream only the first member of a group most important for the psychiatrist, an understanding of which means the solution of the purely psychological part of the psychiatric problem. But other members of this group of wish-fulfillments, *e.g.*, the hysterical symptoms, evince one essential quality which I have so far failed to find in the dream. Thus, from the investigations frequently referred to in this treatise, I know that the formation of an hysterical symptom necessitates the combination of both streams of our psychic life. The symptom is not merely the expression of a realized unconscious wish, but it must be joined by another wish from the foreconscious which is fulfilled by the same symptom; so that the symptom is at least doubly determined, once by each one of the conflicting systems. Just as in the dream, there is no limit to further over-determination. The determination not derived from the Unc. is, as far as I can see, invariably a stream of thought in reaction against the unconscious wish, *e.g.*, a self-punishment. Hence I may say, in general, that *an hysterical symptom originates only where two contrasting wish-fulfillments, having their source in different psychic systems, are able to combine in one expression.* (Compare my latest formulation of the origin of the hysterical symptoms in a treatise published by the *Zeitschrift für Sexualwissenschaft*, by Hirschfeld and others, 1908). Examples on this point would prove of little value, as nothing but a complete unveiling of the complication in question would carry conviction. I therefore content myself with the mere assertion, and will cite an example, not for conviction but for explication. The hysterical vomiting of a female patient proved, on the one hand, to be the realization of an unconscious fancy from the time of puberty, that she might be continuously pregnant and have a multitude of children, and this was subsequently united with the wish that she might have them from as many men as possible. Against this immoderate wish there arose a powerful defensive impulse. But as the vomiting might spoil the patient's figure and beauty, so that she would not find favor in the eyes of mankind, the symptom was therefore in keeping with her punitive trend of thought, and, being thus admissible from both sides, it was allowed to become a reality. This is the same manner of

221

consenting to a wish-fulfillment which the queen of the Parthians chose for the triumvir Crassus. Believing that he had undertaken the campaign out of greed for gold, she caused molten gold to be poured into the throat of the corpse. "Now hast thou what thou hast longed for." As yet we know of the dream only that it expresses a wish-fulfillment of the unconscious; and apparently the dominating foreconscious permits this only after it has subjected the wish to some distortions. We are really in no position to demonstrate regularly a stream of thought antagonistic to the dream-wish which is realized in the dream as in its counterpart. Only now and then have we found in the dream traces of reaction formations, as, for instance, the tenderness toward friend R. in the "uncle dream." But the contribution from the foreconscious, which is missing here, may be found in another place. While the dominating system has withdrawn on the wish to sleep, the dream may bring to expression with manifold distortions a wish from the Unc., and realize this wish by producing the necessary changes of energy in the psychic apparatus, and may finally retain it through the entire duration of sleep.[3]

This persistent wish to sleep on the part of the foreconscious in general facilitates the formation of the dream. Let us refer to the dream of the father who, by the gleam of light from the death chamber, was brought to the conclusion that the body has been set on fire. We have shown that one of the psychic forces decisive in causing the father to form this conclusion, instead of being awakened by the gleam of light, was the wish to prolong the life of the child seen in the dream by one moment. Other wishes proceeding from the repression probably escape us, because we are unable to analyze this dream. But as a second motive power of the dream we may mention the father's desire to sleep, for, like the life of the child, the sleep of the father is prolonged for a moment by the dream. The underlying motive is: "Let the dream go on, otherwise I must wake up." As in this dream so also in all other dreams, the wish to sleep lends its support to the unconscious wish. We reported dreams which were apparently dreams of convenience. But, properly speaking, all dreams may claim this designation. The efficacy of the wish to continue to sleep is the most easily recognized in the waking dreams, which so transform the objective sensory stimulus as to render it compatible with the continuance of sleep; they interweave this stimulus with the dream in order to rob it of any claims it might make as a warning to the outer world. But this wish to continue to sleep must also participate in the formation of all other dreams which may disturb the sleeping state from within only. "Now, then, sleep on; why, it's but a dream"; this is in many cases the suggestion of the Forec. to consciousness when the dream goes too far; and this also describes in a general way the attitude of our dominating psychic activity toward dreaming, though the thought remains tacit. I must draw the conclusion that *throughout our entire sleeping state we are just as certain that we are dreaming as we are certain that we are sleeping.* We are compelled to disregard the objection urged against this conclusion that our consciousness is never directed to a knowledge of the former, and that it is directed to a knowledge of the latter only on special occasions when the censor is unexpectedly surprised. Against this objection we may say that there are persons who are entirely conscious of their sleeping and dreaming, and who are apparently endowed with the conscious faculty of guiding their dream life. Such a dreamer, when dissatisfied with the course taken by the dream, breaks it off without awakening, and begins it anew in order to continue it with a different turn, like the popular author who, on request, gives a happier ending to his play. Or, at another time, if placed by the dream in a sexually exciting situation, he thinks in his sleep: "I do not care to continue this dream and exhaust myself by a pollution; I prefer to defer it in favor of a real situation."

1   They share this character of indestructibility with all psychic acts that are really unconscious—that is, with psychic acts belonging to the system of the unconscious only. These paths are constantly open and never fall into disuse; they conduct the discharge of the exciting process as often as it becomes

endowed with unconscious excitement To speak metaphorically they suffer the same form of annihilation as the shades of the lower region in the *Odyssey*, who awoke to new life the moment they drank blood. The processes depending on the foreconscious system are destructible in a different way. The psychotherapy of the neuroses is based on this difference.

2   Le Lorrain justly extols the wish-fulfilment of the dream: "Sans fatigue sérieuse, sans être obligé de recourir à cette lutte opinâtre et longue qui use et corrode les jouissances poursuivies."

3   This idea has been borrowed from *The Theory of Sleep* by Liébault, who revived hypnotic investigation in our days. *(Du Sommeil provoqué*, etc.; Paris, 1889.)

VII

THE FUNCTION OF THE DREAM

Since we know that the foreconscious is suspended during the night by the wish to sleep, we can proceed to an intelligent investigation of the dream process. But let us first sum up the knowledge of this process already gained. We have shown that the waking activity leaves day remnants from which the sum of energy cannot be entirely removed; or the waking activity revives during the day one of the unconscious wishes; or both conditions occur simultaneously; we have already discovered the many variations that may take place. The unconscious wish has already made its way to the day remnants, either during the day or at any rate with the beginning of sleep, and has effected a transference to it. This produces a wish transferred to the recent material, or the suppressed recent wish comes to life again through a reinforcement from the unconscious. This wish now endeavors to make its way to consciousness on the normal path of the mental processes through the foreconscious, to which indeed it belongs through one of its constituent elements. It is confronted, however, by the censor, which is still active, and to the influence of which it now succumbs. It now takes on the distortion for which the way has already been paved by its transference to the recent material. Thus far it is in the way of becoming something resembling an obsession, delusion, or the like, *i.e.* a thought reinforced by a transference and distorted in expression by the censor. But its further progress is now checked through the dormant state of the foreconscious; this system has apparently protected itself against invasion by diminishing its excitements. The dream process, therefore, takes the regressive course, which has just been opened by the peculiarity of the sleeping state, and thereby follows the attraction exerted on it by the memory groups, which themselves exist in part only as visual energy not yet translated into terms of the later systems. On its way to regression the dream takes on the form of dramatization. The subject of compression will be discussed later. The dream process has now terminated the second part of its repeatedly impeded course. The first part expended itself progressively from the unconscious scenes or phantasies to the foreconscious, while the second part gravitates from the advent of the censor back to the perceptions. But when the dream process becomes a content of perception it has, so to speak, eluded the obstacle set up in the Forec. by the censor and by the sleeping state. It succeeds in drawing attention to itself and in being noticed by consciousness. For consciousness, which means to us a sensory organ for the reception of psychic qualities, may receive stimuli from two sources—first, from the periphery of the entire apparatus, viz. from the perception system, and, secondly, from the pleasure and pain stimuli, which constitute the sole psychic quality produced in the transformation of energy within the apparatus. All other processes in the system, even those in the foreconscious, are devoid of any psychic quality, and are therefore not objects of consciousness inasmuch as they do not furnish pleasure or pain for perception. We shall have to assume that those liberations of pleasure and pain automatically regulate the outlet of the occupation processes. But in order to make possible more delicate functions, it was later found necessary to render the course of the presentations more independent of the manifestations of pain. To accomplish this the Forec. system needed some qualities of its own which could attract consciousness, and most probably received them through the connection of the foreconscious processes with the memory system of the signs of speech, which is not devoid of qualities. Through the qualities of this system, consciousness, which had hitherto been a sensory organ only for the perceptions, now becomes also a sensory organ for a part of our mental processes. Thus we have now, as it were, two sensory surfaces, one directed to perceptions and the other to the foreconscious mental processes.

I must assume that the sensory surface of consciousness devoted to the Forec. is rendered less excitable by sleep than that directed to the P-systems. The giving up of interest for the nocturnal mental processes is indeed purposeful. Nothing is to disturb the mind; the Forec. wants to sleep. But once the dream becomes a perception, it is then capable of exciting consciousness through the qualities thus gained. The sensory stimulus accomplishes what it was really destined for, namely, it directs a part of the energy at the disposal of the Forec. in the form of attention upon the stimulant. We must, therefore, admit that the dream invariably awakens us, that is, it puts into activity a part of the dormant force of the Forec. This force imparts to the dream that influence which we have designated as secondary elaboration for the sake of connection and comprehensibility. This means that the dream is treated by it like any other content of perception; it is subjected to the same ideas of expectation, as far at least as the material admits. As far as the direction is concerned in this third part of the dream, it may be said that here again the movement is progressive.

To avoid misunderstanding, it will not be amiss to say a few words about the temporal peculiarities of these dream processes. In a very interesting discussion, apparently suggested by Maury's puzzling guillotine dream, Goblet tries to demonstrate that the dream requires no other time than the transition period between sleeping and awakening. The awakening requires time, as the dream takes place during that period. One is inclined to believe that the final picture of the dream is so strong that it forces the dreamer to awaken; but, as a matter of fact, this picture is strong only because the dreamer is already very near awakening when it appears. "Un rêve c'est un réveil qui commence."

227

It has already been emphasized by Dugas that Goblet was forced to repudiate many facts in order to generalize his theory. There are, moreover, dreams from which we do not awaken, *e.g.*, some dreams in which we dream that we dream. From our knowledge of the dream-work, we can by no means admit that it extends only over the period of awakening. On the contrary, we must consider it probable that the first part of the dream-work begins during the day when we are still under the domination of the foreconscious. The second phase of the dream-work, viz. the modification through the censor, the attraction by the unconscious scenes, and the penetration to perception must continue throughout the night. And we are probably always right when we assert that we feel as though we had been dreaming the whole night, although we cannot say what. I do not, however, think it necessary to assume that, up to the time of becoming conscious, the dream processes really follow the temporal sequence which we have described, viz. that there is first the transferred dream-wish, then the distortion of the censor, and consequently the change of direction to regression, and so on. We were forced to form such a succession for the sake of *description*; in reality, however, it is much rather a matter of simultaneously trying this path and that, and of emotions fluctuating to and fro, until finally, owing to the most expedient distribution, one particular grouping is secured which remains. From certain personal experiences, I am myself inclined to believe that the dream-work often requires more than one day and one night to produce its result; if this be true, the extraordinary art manifested in the construction of the dream loses all its marvels. In my opinion, even the regard for comprehensibility as an occurrence of perception may take effect before the dream attracts consciousness to itself. To be sure, from now on the process is accelerated, as the dream is henceforth subjected to the same treatment as any other perception. It is like fireworks, which require hours of preparation and only a moment for ignition.

Through the dream-work the dream process now gains either sufficient intensity to attract consciousness to itself and arouse the foreconscious, which is quite independent of the time or profundity of sleep, or, its intensity being insufficient it must wait until it meets the attention which is set in motion immediately before awakening. Most dreams seem to operate with relatively slight psychic intensities, for they wait for the awakening. This, however, explains the fact that we regularly perceive something dreamt on being suddenly aroused from a sound sleep. Here, as well as in spontaneous awakening, the first glance strikes the perception content created by the dream-work, while the next strikes the one produced from without.

But of greater theoretical interest are those dreams which are capable of waking us in the midst of sleep. We must bear in mind the expediency elsewhere universally demonstrated, and ask ourselves why the dream or the unconscious wish has the power to disturb sleep, *i.e.* the fulfillment of the foreconscious wish. This is probably due to certain relations of energy into which we have no insight. If we possessed such insight we should probably find that the freedom given to the dream and the expenditure of a certain amount of detached attention represent for the dream an economy in energy, keeping in view the fact that the unconscious must be held in check at night just as during the day. We know from experience that the dream, even if it interrupts sleep, repeatedly during the same night, still remains compatible with sleep. We wake up for an instant, and immediately resume our sleep. It is like driving off a fly during sleep, we awake *ad hoc*, and when we resume our sleep we have removed the disturbance. As demonstrated by familiar examples from the sleep of wet nurses, &c., the fulfillment of the wish to sleep is quite compatible with the retention of a certain amount of attention in a given direction.

But we must here take cognizance of an objection that is based on a better knowledge of the unconscious processes. Although we have ourselves described the unconscious wishes as always active, we have, nevertheless, asserted that they are not sufficiently strong during the day to make themselves perceptible. But when we sleep, and the unconscious wish has shown its power to form a dream, and with it to awaken the

229

foreconscious, why, then, does this power become exhausted after the dream has been taken cognizance of? Would it not seem more probable that the dream should continually renew itself, like the troublesome fly which, when driven away, takes pleasure in returning again and again? What justifies our assertion that the dream removes the disturbance of sleep?

That the unconscious wishes always remain active is quite true. They represent paths which are passable whenever a sum of excitement makes use of them. Moreover, a remarkable peculiarity of the unconscious processes is the fact that they remain indestructible. Nothing can be brought to an end in the unconscious; nothing can cease or be forgotten. This impression is most strongly gained in the study of the neuroses, especially of hysteria. The unconscious stream of thought which leads to the discharge through an attack becomes passable again as soon as there is an accumulation of a sufficient amount of excitement. The mortification brought on thirty years ago, after having gained access to the unconscious affective source, operates during all these thirty years like a recent one. Whenever its memory is touched, it is revived and shows itself to be supplied with the excitement which is discharged in a motor attack. It is just here that the office of psychotherapy begins, its task being to bring about adjustment and forgetfulness for the unconscious processes. Indeed, the fading of memories and the flagging of affects, which we are apt to take as self-evident and to explain as a primary influence of time on the psychic memories, are in reality secondary changes brought about by painstaking work. It is the foreconscious that accomplishes this work; and the only course to be pursued by psychotherapy is the subjugate the Unc, to the domination of the Forec.

There are, therefore, two exits for the individual unconscious emotional process. It is either left to itself, in which case it ultimately breaks through somewhere and secures for once a discharge for its excitation into motility; or it succumbs to the influence of the foreconscious, and its excitation becomes confined through this influence instead of being discharged. It is the latter process that occurs in the dream. Owing to the fact that it is directed by the conscious excitement, the energy from the Forec., which confronts the dream when grown to perception, restricts the unconscious excitement of the dream and renders it harmless as a disturbing factor. When the dreamer wakes up for a moment, he has actually chased away the fly that has threatened to disturb his sleep. We can now understand that it is really more expedient and economical to give full sway to the unconscious wish, and clear its way to regression so that it may form a dream, and then restrict and adjust this dream by means of a small expenditure of foreconscious labor, than to curb the unconscious throughout the entire period of sleep. We should, indeed, expect that the dream, even if it was not originally an expedient process, would have acquired some function in the play of forces of the psychic life. We now see what this function is. The dream has taken it upon itself to bring the liberated excitement of the Unc. back under the domination of the foreconscious; it thus affords relief for the excitement of the Unc. and acts as a safety-valve for the latter, and at the same time it insures the sleep of the foreconscious at a slight expenditure of the waking state. Like the other psychic formations of its group, the dream offers itself as a compromise serving simultaneously both systems by fulfilling both wishes in so far as they are compatible with each other. A glance at Robert's "elimination theory," will show that we must agree with this author in his main point, viz. in the determination of the function of the dream, though we differ from him in our hypotheses and in our treatment of the dream process.

The above qualification—in so far as the two wishes are compatible with each other—contains a suggestion that there may be cases in which the function of the dream suffers shipwreck. The dream process is in the first instance admitted as a wish-fulfillment of the unconscious, but if this tentative wish-fulfillment disturbs the foreconscious to such an extent that the latter can no longer maintain its rest, the dream then breaks the compromise and fails to perform the second part of its task. It is then at once broken off, and replaced by complete wakefulness. Here, too, it is not really the fault of the dream, if, while ordinarily the guardian of sleep, it is here compelled to appear as the disturber of sleep, nor should this cause us to entertain any doubts as to its efficacy. This is not the only case in the organism in which an otherwise efficacious arrangement became inefficacious and disturbing as soon as some element is changed in the conditions of its origin; the disturbance then serves at least the new purpose of announcing the change, and calling into play against it the means of adjustment of the organism. In this connection, I naturally bear in mind the case of the anxiety dream, and in order not to have the appearance of trying to exclude this testimony against the theory of wish-fulfillment wherever I encounter it, I will attempt an explanation of the anxiety dream, at least offering some suggestions.

That a psychic process developing anxiety may still be a wish-fulfillment has long ceased to impress us as a contradiction. We may explain this occurrence by the fact that the wish belongs to one system (the Unc.), while by the other system (the Forec.), this wish has been rejected and suppressed. The subjection of the Unc. by the Forec. is not complete even in perfect psychic health; the amount of this suppression shows the degree of our psychic normality. Neurotic symptoms show that there is a conflict between the two systems; the symptoms are the results of a compromise of this conflict, and they temporarily put an end to it. On the one hand, they afford the Unc. an outlet for the discharge of its excitement, and serve it as a sally port, while, on the other hand, they give the Forec. the capability of dominating the Unc. to some extent. It is highly instructive to consider, *e.g.*, the significance of any hysterical phobia or of an agoraphobia. Suppose a neurotic incapable of crossing the street alone, which we would justly call a "symptom." We attempt to remove this symptom by urging him to the action which he deems himself incapable of. The result will be an attack of anxiety, just as an attack of anxiety in the street has often been the cause of establishing an agoraphobia. We thus learn that the symptom has been constituted in order to guard against the outbreak of the anxiety. The phobia is thrown before the anxiety like a fortress on the frontier.

Unless we enter into the part played by the affects in these processes, which can be done here only imperfectly, we cannot continue our discussion. Let us therefore advance the proposition that the reason why the suppression of the unconscious becomes absolutely necessary is because, if the discharge of presentation should be left to itself, it would develop an affect in the Unc. which originally bore the character of pleasure, but which, since the appearance of the repression, bears the character of pain. The aim, as well as the result, of the suppression is to stop the development of this pain. The suppression extends over the unconscious ideation, because the liberation of pain might emanate from the ideation. The foundation is here laid for a very definite assumption concerning the nature of the affective development. It is regarded as a motor or secondary activity, the key to the innervation of which is located in the presentations of the Unc. Through the domination of the Forec. these presentations become, as it were, throttled and inhibited at the exit of the emotion-developing impulses. The danger, which is due to the fact that the Forec. ceases to occupy the energy, therefore consists in the fact that the unconscious excitations liberate such an affect as—in consequence of the repression that has previously taken place—can only be perceived as pain or anxiety.

This danger is released through the full sway of the dream process. The determinations for its realization consist in the fact that repressions have taken place, and that the suppressed emotional wishes shall become sufficiently strong. They thus stand entirely without the psychological realm of the dream structure. Were it not for the fact that our subject is connected through just one factor, namely, the freeing of the Unc. during sleep, with the subject of the development of anxiety, I could dispense with discussion of the anxiety dream, and thus avoid all obscurities connected with it.

As I have often repeated, the theory of the anxiety belongs to the psychology of the neuroses. I would say that the anxiety in the dream is an anxiety problem and not a dream problem. We have nothing further to do with it after having once demonstrated its point of contact with the subject of the dream process. There is only one thing left for me to do. As I have asserted that the neurotic anxiety originates from sexual sources, I can subject anxiety dreams to analysis in order to demonstrate the sexual material in their dream thoughts.

For good reasons I refrain from citing here any of the numerous examples placed at my disposal by neurotic patients, but prefer to give anxiety dreams from young persons.

Personally, I have had no real anxiety dream for decades, but I recall one from my seventh or eighth year which I subjected to interpretation about thirty years later. The dream was very vivid, and showed me *my beloved mother, with peculiarly calm sleeping countenance, carried into the room and laid on the bed by two (or three) persons with birds' beaks*. I awoke crying and screaming, and disturbed my parents. The very tall figures—draped in a peculiar manner—with beaks, I had taken from the illustrations of Philippson's bible; I believe they represented deities with heads of sparrowhawks from an Egyptian tomb relief. The analysis also introduced the reminiscence of a naughty janitor's boy, who used to play with us children on the meadow in front of the house; I would add that his name was Philip. I feel that I first heard from this boy the vulgar word signifying sexual intercourse, which is replaced among the educated by the Latin "coitus," but to which the dream distinctly alludes by the selection of the birds' heads. I must have suspected the sexual significance of the word from the facial expression of my worldly-wise teacher. My mother's features in the dream were copied from the countenance of my grandfather, whom I had seen a few days before his death snoring in the state of coma. The interpretation of the secondary elaboration in the dream must therefore have been that my mother was dying; the tomb relief, too, agrees with this. In this anxiety I awoke, and could not calm myself until I had awakened

234

my parents. I remember that I suddenly became calm on coming face to face with my mother, as if I needed the assurance that my mother was not dead. But this secondary interpretation of the dream had been effected only under the influence of the developed anxiety. I was not frightened because I dreamed that my mother was dying, but I interpreted the dream in this manner in the foreconscious elaboration because I was already under the domination of the anxiety. The latter, however, could be traced by means of the repression to an obscure obviously sexual desire, which had found its satisfying expression in the visual content of the dream.

A man twenty-seven years old who had been severely ill for a year had had many terrifying dreams between the ages of eleven and thirteen. He thought that a man with an ax was running after him; he wished to run, but felt paralyzed and could not move from the spot. This may be taken as a good example of a very common, and apparently sexually indifferent, anxiety dream. In the analysis the dreamer first thought of a story told him by his uncle, which chronologically was later than the dream, viz. that he was attacked at night by a suspicious-looking individual. This occurrence led him to believe that he himself might have already heard of a similar episode at the time of the dream. In connection with the ax he recalled that during that period of his life he once hurt his hand with an ax while chopping wood. This immediately led to his relations with his younger brother, whom he used to maltreat and knock down. In particular, he recalled an occasion when he struck his brother on the head with his boot until he bled, whereupon his mother remarked: "I fear he will kill him some day." While he was seemingly thinking of the subject of violence, a reminiscence from his ninth year suddenly occurred to him. His parents came home late and went to bed while he was feigning sleep. He soon heard panting and other noises that appeared strange to him, and he could also make out the position of his parents in bed. His further associations showed that he had established an analogy between this relation between his parents and his own relation toward his younger brother. He subsumed what occurred between his parents under the conception "violence and wrestling," and thus reached a sadistic conception of the coitus act, as often happens among children. The fact that he often noticed blood on his mother's bed corroborated his conception.

That the sexual intercourse of adults appears strange to children who observe it, and arouses fear in them, I dare say is a fact of daily experience. I have explained this fear by the fact that sexual excitement is not mastered by their understanding, and is probably also inacceptable to them because their parents are involved in it. For the same son this excitement is converted into fear. At a still earlier period of life sexual emotion directed toward the parent of opposite sex does not meet with repression but finds free expression, as we have seen before.

For the night terrors with hallucinations (*pavor nocturnus*) frequently found in children, I would unhesitatingly give the same explanation. Here, too, we are certainly dealing with the incomprehensible and rejected sexual feelings, which, if noted, would probably show a temporal periodicity, for an enhancement of the sexual *libido* may just as well be produced accidentally through emotional impressions as through the spontaneous and gradual processes of development.

I lack the necessary material to sustain these explanations from observation. On the other hand, the pediatrists seem to lack the point of view which alone makes comprehensible the whole series of phenomena, on the somatic as well as on the psychic side. To illustrate by a comical example how one wearing the blinders of medical mythology may miss the understanding of such cases I will relate a case which I found in a thesis on *pavor nocturnus* by *Debacker*, 1881. A thirteen-year-old boy of delicate health began to become anxious and dreamy; his sleep became restless, and about once a week it was interrupted by an acute attack of anxiety with hallucinations. The memory of these dreams was invariably very distinct. Thus, he related that the *devil* shouted at him: "Now we have you, now we have you," and this was followed by an odor of sulphur; the fire burned his skin. This dream aroused him, terror-stricken. He was unable to scream at first; then his voice returned, and he was heard to say distinctly: "No, no, not me; why, I have done nothing," or, "Please don't, I shall never do it again." Occasionally, also, he said: "Albert has not done that." Later he avoided undressing, because, as he said, the fire attacked him only when he was undressed. From amid these evil dreams, which menaced his health, he was sent into the country, where he recovered within a year and a half, but at the age of fifteen he once confessed: "Je n'osais pas l'avouer, mais j'éprouvais continuellement des picotements et des surexcitations aux *parties*; à la fin, cela m'énervait tant que plusieurs fois, j'ai pensé me jeter par la fenêtre au dortoir."

It is certainly not difficult to suspect: 1, that the boy had practiced masturbation in former years, that he probably denied it, and was threatened with severe punishment for his wrongdoing (his confession: Je ne le ferai plus; his denial: Albert n'a jamais fait ça). 2, That under the pressure of puberty the temptation to self-abuse through the tickling of the genitals was reawakened. 3, That now, however, a struggle of repression arose in him, suppressing the *libido* and changing it into fear, which subsequently took the form of the punishments with which he was then threatened.

Let us, however, quote the conclusions drawn by our author. This observation shows: 1, That the influence of puberty may produce in a boy of delicate health a condition of extreme weakness, and that it may lead to a *very marked cerebral anæmia*.

2. This cerebral anæmia produces a transformation of character, demonomaniacal hallucinations, and very violent nocturnal, perhaps also diurnal, states of anxiety.

3. Demonomania and the self-reproaches of the day can be traced to the influences of religious education which the subject underwent as a child.

4. All manifestations disappeared as a result of a lengthy sojourn in the country, bodily exercise, and the return of physical strength after the termination of the period of puberty.

5. A predisposing influence for the origin of the cerebral condition of the boy may be attributed to heredity and to the father's chronic syphilitic state.

The concluding remarks of the author read: "Nous avons fait entrer cette observation dans le cadre des délires apyrétiques d'inanition, car c'est à l'ischémie cérébrale que nous rattachons cet état particulier."

VIII

THE PRIMARY AND SECONDARY
PROCESS—REGRESSION

In venturing to attempt to penetrate more deeply into the psychology of the dream processes, I have undertaken a difficult task, to which, indeed, my power of description is hardly equal. To reproduce in description by a succession of words the simultaneousness of so complex a chain of events, and in doing so to appear unbiassed throughout the exposition, goes fairly beyond my powers. I have now to atone for the fact that I have been unable in my description of the dream psychology to follow the historic development of my views. The view-points for my conception of the dream were reached through earlier investigations in the psychology of the neuroses, to which I am not supposed to refer here, but to which I am repeatedly forced to refer, whereas I should prefer to proceed in the opposite direction, and, starting from the dream, to establish a connection with the psychology of the neuroses. I am well aware of all the inconveniences arising for the reader from this difficulty, but I know of no way to avoid them.

As I am dissatisfied with this state of affairs, I am glad to dwell upon another view-point which seems to raise the value of my efforts. As has been shown in the introduction to the first chapter, I found myself confronted with a theme which had been marked by the sharpest contradictions on the part of the authorities. After our elaboration of the dream problems we found room for most of these contradictions. We have been forced, however, to take decided exception to two of the views pronounced, viz. that the dream is a senseless and that it is a somatic process; apart from these cases we have had to accept all the contradictory views in one place or another of the complicated argument, and we have been able to demonstrate that they had discovered something that was correct. That the dream continues the impulses and interests of the waking state has been quite generally confirmed through the discovery of the latent thoughts of the dream. These thoughts concern themselves only with things that seem important and of momentous interest to us. The dream never occupies itself with trifles. But we have also concurred with the contrary view, viz., that the dream gathers up the indifferent remnants from the day, and that not until it has in some measure withdrawn itself from the waking activity can an important event of the day be taken up by the dream. We found this holding true for the dream content, which gives the dream thought its changed expression by means of disfigurement. We have said that from the nature of the association mechanism the dream process more easily takes possession of recent or indifferent material which has not yet been seized by the waking mental activity; and by reason of the censor it transfers the psychic intensity from the important but also disagreeable to the indifferent material. The hypermnesia of the dream and the resort to infantile material have become main supports in our theory. In our theory of the dream we have attributed to the wish originating from the infantile the part of an indispensable motor for the formation of the dream. We naturally could not think of doubting the experimentally demonstrated significance of the objective sensory stimuli during sleep; but we have brought this material into the same relation to the dream-wish as the thought remnants from the waking activity. There was no need of disputing the fact that the dream interprets the objective sensory stimuli after the manner of an illusion; but we have supplied the motive for this interpretation which has been left undecided by the authorities. The interpretation follows in such a manner that the perceived object is rendered harmless as a sleep disturber and becomes available for the wish-fulfillment. Though we do not admit as special sources of the dream the subjective state of excitement of the sensory organs during sleep, which seems to have been demonstrated by Trumbull Ladd, we are nevertheless able to explain this excitement through the regressive revival of active memories behind the dream. A modest part in our conception has also been assigned to the inner organic sensations which are wont to be taken as the cardinal point in the explanation of the dream. These—the sensation of falling, flying, or inhibition—stand as an ever ready material to be used by the dream-work to express the dream thought as often as need arises.

That the dream process is a rapid and momentary one seems to be true for the perception through consciousness of the already prepared dream content; the preceding parts of the dream process probably take a slow, fluctuating course. We have solved the riddle of the superabundant dream content compressed within the briefest moment by explaining that this is due to the appropriation of almost fully formed structures from the psychic life. That the dream is disfigured and distorted by memory we found to be correct, but not troublesome, as this is only the last manifest operation in the work of disfigurement which has been active from the beginning of the dream-work. In the bitter and seemingly irreconcilable controversy as to whether the psychic life sleeps at night or can make the same use of all its capabilities as during the day, we have been able to agree with both sides, though not fully with either. We have found proof that the dream thoughts represent a most complicated intellectual activity, employing almost every means furnished by the psychic apparatus; still it cannot be denied that these dream thoughts have originated during the day, and it is indispensable to assume that there is a sleeping state of the psychic life. Thus, even the theory of partial sleep has come into play; but the characteristics of the sleeping state have been found not in the dilapidation of the psychic connections but in the cessation of the psychic system dominating the day, arising from its desire to sleep. The withdrawal from the outer world retains its significance also for our

241

conception; though not the only factor, it nevertheless helps the regression to make possible the representation of the dream. That we should reject the voluntary guidance of the presentation course is uncontestable; but the psychic life does not thereby become aimless, for we have seen that after the abandonment of the desired end-presentation undesired ones gain the mastery. The loose associative connection in the dream we have not only recognized, but we have placed under its control a far greater territory than could have been supposed; we have, however, found it merely the feigned substitute for another correct and senseful one. To be sure we, too, have called the dream absurd; but we have been able to learn from examples how wise the dream really is when it simulates absurdity. We do not deny any of the functions that have been attributed to the dream. That the dream relieves the mind like a valve, and that, according to Robert's assertion, all kinds of harmful material are rendered harmless through representation in the dream, not only exactly coincides with our theory of the twofold wish-fulfillment in the dream, but, in his own wording, becomes even more comprehensible for us than for Robert himself. The free indulgence of the psychic in the play of its faculties finds expression with us in the non-interference with the dream on the part of the foreconscious activity. The "return to the embryonal state of psychic life in the dream" and the observation of Havelock Ellis, "an archaic world of vast emotions and imperfect thoughts," appear to us as happy anticipations of our deductions to the effect that *primitive* modes of work suppressed during the day participate in the formation of the dream; and with us, as with Delage, the *suppressed* material becomes the mainspring of the dreaming.

We have fully recognized the rôle which Scherner ascribes to the dream phantasy, and even his interpretation; but we have been obliged, so to speak, to conduct them to another department in the problem. It is not the dream that produces the phantasy but the unconscious phantasy that takes the greatest part in the formation of the dream thoughts. We are indebted to Scherner for his clew to the source of the dream thoughts, but almost everything that he ascribes to the dream-work is attributable to the activity of the unconscious, which is at work during the day, and which supplies incitements not only for dreams but for neurotic symptoms as well. We have had to separate the dream-work from this activity as being something entirely different and far more restricted. Finally, we have by no means abandoned the relation of the dream to mental disturbances, but, on the contrary, we have given it a more solid foundation on new ground.

Thus held together by the new material of our theory as by a superior unity, we find the most varied and most contradictory conclusions of the authorities fitting into our structure; some of them are differently disposed, only a few of them are entirely rejected. But our own structure is still unfinished. For, disregarding the many obscurities which we have necessarily encountered in our advance into the darkness of psychology, we are now apparently embarrassed by a new contradiction. On the one hand, we have allowed the dream thoughts to proceed from perfectly normal mental operations, while, on the other hand, we have found among the dream thoughts a number of entirely abnormal mental processes which extend likewise to the dream contents. These, consequently, we have repeated in the interpretation of the dream. All that we have termed the "dream-work" seems so remote from the psychic processes recognized by us as correct, that the severest judgments of the authors as to the low psychic activity of dreaming seem to us well founded.

Perhaps only through still further advance can enlightenment and improvement be brought about. I shall pick out one of the constellations leading to the formation of dreams.

We have learned that the dream replaces a number of thoughts derived from daily life which are perfectly formed logically. We cannot therefore doubt that these thoughts originate from our normal mental life. All the qualities which we esteem in our mental operations, and which distinguish these as complicated activities of a high order, we find repeated in the dream thoughts. There is, however, no need of assuming that this mental work is performed during sleep, as this would materially impair the conception of the psychic state of sleep we have hitherto adhered to. These thoughts may just as well have originated from the day, and, unnoticed by our consciousness from their inception, they may have continued to develop until they stood complete at the onset of sleep. If we are to conclude anything from this state of affairs, it will at most prove *that the most complex mental operations are possible without the coöperation of consciousness,* which we have already learned independently from every psychoanalysis of persons suffering from hysteria or obsessions. These dream thoughts are in themselves surely not incapable of consciousness; if they have not become conscious to us during the day, this may have various reasons. The state of becoming conscious depends on the exercise of a certain psychic function, viz. attention, which seems to be extended only in a definite quantity, and which may have been withdrawn from the stream of thought in Question by other aims. Another way in which such mental streams are kept from consciousness is the following:— Our conscious reflection teaches us that when exercising attention we pursue a definite course. But if that course leads us to an idea which does not hold its own with the critic, we discontinue and cease to apply our attention. Now, apparently, the stream of thought thus started and abandoned may spin on without regaining attention unless it reaches a spot of especially marked intensity which forces the return of attention. An initial rejection, perhaps consciously brought about by the judgment on the ground of incorrectness or unfitness for the actual purpose of the mental act, may therefore account for the fact that a mental process continues until the onset of sleep unnoticed by consciousness.

Let us recapitulate by saying that we call such a stream of thought a foreconscious one, that we believe it to be perfectly correct, and that it may just as well be a more neglected one or an interrupted and suppressed one. Let us also state frankly in what manner we conceive this presentation course. We believe that a certain sum of excitement, which we call occupation energy, is displaced from an end-presentation along the association paths selected by that end-presentation. A "neglected" stream of thought has received no such occupation, and from a "suppressed" or "rejected" one this occupation has been withdrawn; both have thus been left to their own emotions. The end-stream of thought stocked with energy is under certain conditions able to draw to itself the attention of consciousness, through which means it then receives a "surplus of energy." We shall be obliged somewhat later to elucidate our assumption concerning the nature and activity of consciousness.

A train of thought thus incited in the Forec. may either disappear spontaneously or continue. The former issue we conceive as follows: It diffuses its energy through all the association paths emanating from it, and throws the entire chain of ideas into a state of excitement which, after lasting for a while, subsides through the transformation of the excitement requiring an outlet into dormant energy.[1] If this first issue is brought about the process has no further significance for the dream formation. But other end-presentations are lurking in our foreconscious that originate from the sources of our unconscious and from the ever active wishes. These may take possession of the excitations in the circle of thought thus left to itself, establish a connection between it and the unconscious wish, and transfer to it the energy inherent in the unconscious wish. Henceforth the neglected or suppressed train of thought is in a position to maintain itself, although this reinforcement does not help it to gain access to consciousness. We may say that the hitherto foreconscious train of thought has been drawn into the unconscious.

Other constellations for the dream formation would result if the foreconscious train of thought had from the beginning been connected with the unconscious wish, and for that reason met with rejection by the dominating end-occupation; or if an unconscious wish were made active for other—possibly somatic—reasons and of its own accord sought a transference to the psychic remnants not occupied by the Forec. All three cases finally combine in one issue, so that there is established in the foreconscious a stream of thought which, having been abandoned by the foreconscious occupation, receives occupation from the unconscious wish.

The stream of thought is henceforth subjected to a series of transformations which we no longer recognize as normal psychic processes and which give us a surprising result, viz. a psychopathological formation. Let us emphasize and group the same.

1. The intensities of the individual ideas become capable of discharge in their entirety, and, proceeding from one conception to the other, they thus form single presentations endowed with marked intensity. Through the repeated recurrence of this process the intensity of an entire train of ideas may ultimately be gathered in a single presentation element. This is the principle of *compression or condensation*. It is condensation that is mainly responsible for the strange impression of the dream, for we know of nothing analogous to it in the normal psychic life accessible to consciousness. We find here, also, presentations which possess great psychic significance as junctions or as end-results of whole chains of thought; but this validity does not manifest itself in any character conspicuous enough for internal perception; hence, what has been presented in it does not become in any way more intensive. In the process of condensation the entire psychic connection becomes transformed into the intensity of the presentation content. It is the same as in a book where we space or print in heavy type any word upon which particular stress is laid for the understanding of the text. In speech the same word would be pronounced loudly and deliberately and with emphasis. The first comparison leads us at once to an example taken from the chapter on "The Dream-Work" (trimethylamine in the dream of Irma's injection). Historians of art call our attention to the fact that the most ancient historical sculptures follow a similar principle in expressing the rank of the persons represented by the size of the statue. The king is made two or three times as large as his retinue or the vanquished enemy. A piece of art, however, from the Roman period makes use of more subtle means to accomplish the same

purpose. The figure of the emperor is placed in the center in a firmly erect posture; special care is bestowed on the proper modelling of his figure; his enemies are seen cowering at his feet; but he is no longer represented a giant among dwarfs. However, the bowing of the subordinate to his superior in our own days is only an echo of that ancient principle of representation.

The direction taken by the condensations of the dream is prescribed on the one hand by the true foreconscious relations of the dream thoughts, an the other hand by the attraction of the visual reminiscences in the unconscious. The success of the condensation work produces those intensities which are required for penetration into the perception systems.

2. Through this free transferability of the intensities, moreover, and in the service of condensation, *intermediary presentations*—compromises, as it were—are formed (*cf.* the numerous examples). This, likewise, is something unheard of in the normal presentation course, where it is above all a question of selection and retention of the "proper" presentation element. On the other hand, composite and compromise formations occur with extraordinary frequency when we are trying to find the linguistic expression for foreconscious thoughts; these are considered "slips of the tongue."

3. The presentations which transfer their intensities to one another are *very loosely connected*, and are joined together by such forms of association as are spurned in our serious thought and are utilized in the production of the effect of wit only. Among these we particularly find associations of the sound and consonance types.

4. Contradictory thoughts do not strive to eliminate one another, but remain side by side. They often unite to produce condensation *as if no contradiction* existed, or they form compromises for which we should never forgive our thoughts, but which we frequently approve of in our actions.

These are some of the most conspicuous abnormal processes to which the thoughts which have previously been rationally formed are subjected in the course of the dream-work. As the main feature of these processes we recognize the high importance attached to the fact of rendering the occupation energy mobile and capable of discharge; the content and the actual significance of the psychic elements, to which these energies adhere, become a matter of secondary importance. One might possibly think that the condensation and compromise formation is effected only in the service of regression, when occasion arises for changing thoughts into pictures. But the analysis and—still more distinctly—the synthesis of dreams which lack regression toward pictures, *e.g.* the dream "Autodidasker—Conversation with Court-Councilor N.," present the same processes of displacement and condensation as the others.

Hence we cannot refuse to acknowledge that the two kinds of essentially different psychic processes participate in the formation of the dream; one forms perfectly correct dream thoughts which are equivalent to normal thoughts, while the other treats these ideas in a highly surprising and incorrect manner. The latter process we have already set apart as the dream-work proper. What have we now to advance concerning this latter psychic process?

We should be unable to answer this question here if we had not penetrated considerably into the psychology of the neuroses and especially of hysteria. From this we learn that the same incorrect psychic processes—as well as others that have not been enumerated—control the formation of hysterical symptoms. In hysteria, too, we at once find a series of perfectly correct thoughts equivalent to our conscious thoughts, of whose existence, however, in this form we can learn nothing and which we can only subsequently reconstruct. If they have forced their way anywhere to our perception, we discover from the analysis of the symptom formed that these normal thoughts have been subjected to abnormal treatment and *have been transformed into the symptom by means of condensation and compromise formation, through superficial associations, under cover of contradictions, and eventually over the road of regression.* In view of the complete identity found between the peculiarities of the dream-work and of the psychic activity forming the psychoneurotic symptoms, we shall feel justified in transferring to the dream the conclusions urged upon us by hysteria.

From the theory of hysteria we borrow the proposition that *such an abnormal psychic elaboration of a normal train of thought takes place only when the latter has been used for the transference of an unconscious wish which dates from the infantile life and is in a state of repression.* In accordance with this proposition we have construed the theory of the dream on the assumption that the actuating dream-wish invariably originates in the unconscious, which, as we ourselves have admitted, cannot be universally demonstrated though it cannot be refuted. But in order to explain the real meaning of the term *repression*, which we have employed so freely, we shall be obliged to make some further addition to our psychological construction.

We have above elaborated the fiction of a primitive psychic apparatus, whose work is regulated by the efforts to avoid accumulation of excitement and as far as possible to maintain itself free from excitement. For this reason it was constructed after the plan of a reflex apparatus; the motility, originally the path for the inner bodily change, formed a discharging path standing at its disposal. We subsequently discussed the psychic results of a feeling of gratification, and we might at the same time have introduced the second assumption, viz. that accumulation of excitement—following certain modalities that do not concern us—is perceived as pain and sets the apparatus in motion in order to reproduce a feeling of gratification in which the diminution of the excitement is perceived as pleasure. Such a current in the apparatus which emanates from pain and strives for pleasure we call a wish. We have said that nothing but a wish is capable of setting the apparatus in motion, and that the discharge of excitement in the apparatus is regulated automatically by the perception of pleasure and pain. The first wish must have been an hallucinatory occupation of the memory for gratification. But this hallucination, unless it were

249

maintained to the point of exhaustion, proved incapable of bringing about a cessation of the desire and consequently of securing the pleasure connected with gratification.

Thus there was required a second activity—in our terminology the activity of a second system—which should not permit the memory occupation to advance to perception and therefrom to restrict the psychic forces, but should lead the excitement emanating from the craving stimulus by a devious path over the spontaneous motility which ultimately should so change the outer world as to allow the real perception of the object of gratification to take place. Thus far we have elaborated the plan of the psychic apparatus; these two systems are the germ of the Unc. and Forec, which we include in the fully developed apparatus.

In order to be in a position successfully to change the outer world through the motility, there is required the accumulation of a large sum of experiences in the memory systems as well as a manifold fixation of the relations which are evoked in this memory material by different end-presentations. We now proceed further with our assumption. The manifold activity of the second system, tentatively sending forth and retracting energy, must on the one hand have full command over all memory material, but on the other hand it would be a superfluous expenditure for it to send to the individual mental paths large quantities of energy which would thus flow off to no purpose, diminishing the quantity available for the transformation of the outer world. In the interests of expediency I therefore postulate that the second system succeeds in maintaining the greater part of the occupation energy in a dormant state and in using but a small portion for the purposes of displacement. The mechanism of these processes is entirely unknown to me; any one who wishes to follow up these ideas must try to find the physical analogies and prepare the way for a demonstration of the process of motion in the stimulation of the neuron. I merely hold to the idea that the activity of the first Ψ-system is directed *to the free outflow of the quantities of excitement*, and that the second system brings about an inhibition of this outflow through the energies emanating from it, *i.e.* it produces a *transformation into dormant energy, probably by raising the level.* I therefore assume that under the control of the second system as compared with the first, the course of the excitement is bound to entirely different mechanical conditions. After the second system has finished its tentative mental work, it removes the inhibition and congestion of the excitements and allows these excitements to flow off to the motility.

An interesting train of thought now presents itself if we consider the relations of this inhibition of discharge by the second system to the regulation through the principle of pain. Let us now seek the counterpart of the primary feeling of gratification, namely, the objective feeling of fear. A perceptive stimulus acts on the primitive apparatus, becoming the source of a painful emotion. This will then be followed by irregular motor manifestations until one of these withdraws the apparatus from perception and at the same time from pain, but on the reappearance of the perception this manifestation will immediately repeat itself (perhaps as a movement of flight) until the perception has again disappeared. But there will here remain no tendency again to occupy the perception of the source of pain in the form of an hallucination or in any other form. On the contrary, there will be a tendency in the primary apparatus to abandon the painful memory picture as soon as it is in any way awakened, as the overflow of its excitement would surely produce (more precisely, begin to produce) pain. The deviation from memory, which is but a repetition of the former flight from perception, is facilitated also by the fact that, unlike perception, memory does not possess sufficient quality to excite consciousness and thereby to attract to itself new energy. This easy and regularly occurring deviation of the psychic process from the former painful memory presents to us the model and the first example of *psychic repression.* As is generally known, much of this deviation from the painful, much of the behavior of the ostrich, can be readily demonstrated even in the normal psychic life of adults.

By virtue of the principle of pain the first system is therefore altogether incapable of introducing anything unpleasant into the mental associations. The system cannot do anything but wish. If this remained so the mental activity of the second system, which should have at its disposal all the memories stored up by experiences, would be hindered. But two ways are now opened: the work of the second system either frees itself completely from the principle of pain and continues its course, paying no heed to the painful reminiscence, or it contrives to occupy the painful memory in such a manner as to preclude the liberation of pain. We may reject the first possibility, as the principle of pain also manifests itself as a regulator for the emotional discharge of the second system; we are, therefore, directed to the second possibility, namely, that this system occupies a reminiscence in such a manner as to inhibit its discharge and hence, also, to inhibit the discharge comparable to a motor innervation for the development of pain. Thus from two starting points we are led to the hypothesis that occupation through the second system is at the same time an inhibition for the emotional discharge, viz. from a consideration of the principle of pain and from the principle of the smallest expenditure of innervation. Let us, however, keep to the fact— this is the key to the theory of repression—that the second system is capable of occupying an idea only when it is in position to check the development of pain emanating from it. Whatever withdraws itself from this inhibition also remains inaccessible for the second system and would soon be abandoned by virtue of the principle of pain. The inhibition of pain, however, need not be complete; it must be permitted to begin, as it indicates to the second system the nature of the memory and possibly its defective adaptation for the purpose sought by the mind.

The psychic process which is admitted by the first system only I shall now call the *primary* process; and the one resulting from the inhibition of the second system I shall call the *secondary* process. I show by another point for what purpose the second system is obliged to correct the primary process. The primary process strives for a discharge of the excitement in order to establish a *perception* identity with the sum of excitement thus gathered; the secondary process has abandoned this intention and undertaken instead the task of bringing about a *thought identity*. All thinking is only a circuitous path from the memory of gratification taken as an end-presentation to the identical occupation of the same memory, which is again to be attained on the track of the motor experiences. The state of thinking must take an interest in the connecting paths between the presentations without allowing itself to be misled by their intensities. But it is obvious that condensations and intermediate or compromise formations occurring in the presentations impede the attainment of this end-identity; by substituting one idea for the other they deviate from the path which otherwise would have been continued from the original idea. Such processes are therefore carefully avoided in the secondary thinking. Nor is it difficult to understand that the principle of pain also impedes the progress of the mental stream in its pursuit of the thought identity, though, indeed, it offers to the mental stream the most important points of departure. Hence the tendency of the thinking process must be to free itself more and more from exclusive adjustment by the principle of pain, and through the working of the mind to restrict the affective development to that minimum which is necessary as a signal. This refinement of the activity must have been attained through a recent over-occupation of energy brought about by consciousness. But we are aware that this refinement is seldom completely successful even in the most normal psychic life and that our thoughts ever remain accessible to falsification through the interference of the principle of pain.

This, however, is not the breach in the functional efficiency of our psychic apparatus through which the thoughts forming the material of the secondary mental work are enabled to make their way into the primary psychic process—with which formula we may now describe the work leading to the dream and to the hysterical symptoms. This case of insufficiency results from the union of the two factors from the history of our evolution; one of which belongs solely to the psychic apparatus and has exerted a determining influence on the relation of the two systems, while the other operates fluctuatingly and introduces motive forces of organic origin into the psychic life. Both originate in the infantile life and result from the transformation which our psychic and somatic organism has undergone since the infantile period.

When I termed one of the psychic processes in the psychic apparatus the primary process, I did so not only in consideration of the order of precedence and capability, but also as admitting the temporal relations to a share in the nomenclature. As far as our knowledge goes there is no psychic apparatus possessing only the primary process, and in so far it is a theoretic fiction; but so much is based on fact that the primary processes are present in the apparatus from the beginning, while the secondary processes develop gradually in the course of life, inhibiting and covering the primary ones, and gaining complete mastery over them perhaps only at the height of life. Owing to this retarded appearance of the secondary processes, the essence of our being, consisting in unconscious wish feelings, can neither be seized nor inhibited by the foreconscious, whose part is once for all restricted to the indication of the most suitable paths for the wish feelings originating in the unconscious. These unconscious wishes establish for all subsequent psychic efforts a compulsion to which they have to submit and which they must strive if possible to divert from its course and direct to higher aims. In consequence of this retardation of the foreconscious occupation a large sphere of the memory material remains inaccessible.

Among these indestructible and unincumbered wish feelings originating from the infantile life, there are also some, the fulfillments of which have entered into a relation of contradiction to the end-presentation of the secondary thinking. The fulfillment of these wishes would no longer produce an affect of pleasure but one of pain; *and it is just this transformation of affect that constitutes the nature of what we designate as "repression," in which we recognize the infantile first step of passing adverse sentence or of rejecting through reason.* To investigate in what way and through what motive forces such a transformation can be produced constitutes the problem of repression, which we need here only skim over. It will suffice to remark that such a transformation of affect occurs in the course of development (one may think of the appearance in infantile life of disgust which was originally absent), and that it is connected with the activity of the secondary system. The memories from which the unconscious wish brings about the emotional discharge have never been accessible to the Forec., and for that reason their emotional discharge cannot be inhibited. It is just on account of this affective development that these ideas are not even now accessible to the foreconscious thoughts to which they have transferred their wishing power. On the contrary, the principle of pain comes into play, and causes the Forec. to deviate from these thoughts of transference. The latter, left to themselves, are "repressed," and thus the existence of a store of infantile memories, from the very beginning withdrawn from the Forec., becomes the preliminary condition of repression.

In the most favorable case the development of pain terminates as soon as the energy has been withdrawn from the thoughts of transference in the Forec., and this effect characterizes the intervention of the principle of pain as expedient. It is different, however, if the repressed unconscious wish receives an organic enforcement which it can lend to its thoughts of transference and through which it can enable them to make an effort towards penetration with their excitement, even after they have been abandoned by the occupation of the Forec. A defensive struggle then ensues, inasmuch as the Forec. reinforces the antagonism against the repressed ideas, and subsequently this leads to a penetration by the thoughts of transference (the carriers of the unconscious wish) in some form of compromise through symptom formation. But from the moment that the suppressed thoughts are powerfully occupied by the unconscious wish-feeling and abandoned by the foreconscious occupation, they succumb to the primary psychic process and strive only for motor discharge; or, if the path be free, for hallucinatory revival of the desired perception identity. We have previously found, empirically, that the incorrect processes described are enacted only with thoughts that exist in the repression. We now grasp another part of the connection. These incorrect processes are those that are primary in the psychic apparatus; *they appear wherever thoughts abandoned by the foreconscious occupation are left to themselves, and can fill themselves with the uninhibited energy, striving for discharge from the unconscious.* We may add a few further observations to support the view that these processes designated "incorrect" are really not falsifications of the normal defective thinking, but the modes of activity of the psychic apparatus when freed from inhibition. Thus we see that the transference of the foreconscious excitement to the motility takes place according to the same processes, and that the connection of the foreconscious presentations with words readily manifest the same displacements and mixtures which are ascribed to inattention. Finally, I should like to adduce proof that an increase of work necessarily results from the inhibition of these primary courses from the fact that we gain a *comical effect*, a surplus to be discharged through laughter, *if we allow these streams of thought to come to consciousness.*

The theory of the psychoneuroses asserts with complete certainty that only sexual wish-feelings from the infantile life experience repression (emotional transformation) during the developmental period of childhood. These are capable of returning to activity at a later period of development, and then have the faculty of being revived, either as a consequence of the sexual constitution, which is really formed from the original bisexuality, or in consequence of unfavorable influences of the sexual life; and they thus supply the motive power for all psychoneurotic symptom formations. It is only by the introduction of these sexual forces that the gaps still demonstrable in the theory of repression can be filled. I will leave it undecided whether the postulate of the sexual and infantile may also be asserted for the theory of the dream; I leave this here unfinished because I have already passed a step beyond the demonstrable in assuming that the dream-wish invariably originates from the unconscious.[2] Nor will

I further investigate the difference in the play of the psychic forces in the dream formation and in the formation of the hysterical symptoms, for to do this we ought to possess a more explicit knowledge of one of the members to be compared. But I regard another point as important, and will here confess that it was on account of this very point that I have just undertaken this entire discussion concerning the two psychic systems, their modes of operation, and the repression. For it is now immaterial whether I have conceived the psychological relations in question with approximate correctness, or, as is easily possible in such a difficult matter, in an erroneous and fragmentary manner. Whatever changes may be made in the interpretation of the psychic censor and of the correct and of the abnormal elaboration of the dream content, the fact nevertheless remains that such processes are active in dream formation, and that essentially they show the closest analogy to the processes observed in the formation of the hysterical symptoms. The dream is not a pathological phenomenon, and it does not leave behind an enfeeblement of the mental faculties. The objection that no deduction can be drawn regarding the dreams of healthy persons from my own dreams and from those of neurotic patients may be rejected without comment. Hence, when we draw conclusions from the phenomena as to their motive forces, we recognize that the psychic mechanism made use of by the neuroses is not created by a morbid disturbance of the psychic life, but is found ready in the normal structure of the psychic apparatus. The two psychic systems, the censor crossing between them, the inhibition and the covering of the one activity by the other, the relations of both to consciousness—or whatever may offer a more correct interpretation of the actual conditions in their stead—all these belong to the normal structure of our psychic instrument, and the dream points out for us one of the roads leading to a knowledge of this structure. If, in addition to our knowledge, we wish to be contented with a minimum perfectly established, we shall say that the dream gives us proof that the *suppressed, material continues to exist even in the normal person and remains capable of psychic activity*. The dream itself is one of the manifestations of this suppressed material; theoretically, this is true in *all* cases; according to substantial experience it is true in at least a great number of such as most conspicuously display the prominent characteristics of dream life. The suppressed psychic material, which in the waking state has been prevented from expression and cut off from internal perception *by the antagonistic adjustment of the contradictions*, finds ways and means of obtruding itself on consciousness during the night under the domination of the compromise formations.

"Flectere si nequeo superos, Acheronta movebo."

At any rate the interpretation of dreams is the *via regia* to a knowledge of the unconscious in the psychic life.

In following the analysis of the dream we have made some progress toward an understanding of the composition of this most marvelous and most mysterious of instruments; to be sure, we have not gone very far, but enough of a beginning has been made to allow us to advance from other so-called pathological formations further into the analysis of the unconscious. Disease—at least that which is justly termed functional—is not due to the destruction of this apparatus, and the establishment of new splittings in its interior; it is rather to be explained dynamically through the strengthening and weakening of the components in the play of forces by which so many activities are concealed during the normal function. We have been able to show in another place how the composition of the apparatus from the two systems permits a subtilization even of the normal activity which would be impossible for a single system.

1 *Cf.* the significant observations by J. Bueuer in our *Studies on Hysteria*, 1895, and 2nd ed. 1909.

2 Here, as in other places, there are gaps in the treatment of the subject, which I have left intentionally, because to fill them up would require on the one hand

too great effort, and on the other hand an extensive reference to material that is foreign to the dream. Thus I have avoided stating whether I connect with the word "suppressed" another sense than with the word "repressed." It has been made clear only that the latter emphasizes more than the former the relation to the unconscious. I have not entered into the cognate problem why the dream thoughts also experience distortion by the censor when they abandon the progressive continuation to consciousness and choose the path of regression. I have been above all anxious to awaken an interest in the problems to which the further analysis of the dreamwork leads and to indicate the other themes which meet these on the way. It was not always easy to decide just where the pursuit should be discontinued. That I have not treated exhaustively the part played in the dream by the psychosexual life and have avoided the interpretation of dreams of an obvious sexual content is due to a special reason which may not come up to the reader's expectation. To be sure, it is very far from my ideas and the principles expressed by me in neuropathology to regard the sexual life as a "pudendum" which should be left unconsidered by the physician and the scientific investigator. I also consider ludicrous the moral indignation which prompted the translator of Artemidoros of Daldis to keep from the reader's knowledge the chapter on sexual dreams contained in the *Symbolism of the Dreams*. As for myself, I have been actuated solely by the conviction that in the explanation of sexual dreams I should be bound to entangle myself deeply in the still unexplained problems of perversion and bisexuality; and for that reason I have reserved this material for another connection.

IX

THE UNCONSCIOUS AND CONSCIOUSNESS—REALITY

On closer inspection we find that it is not the existence of two systems near the motor end of the apparatus but of two kinds of processes or modes of emotional discharge, the assumption of which was explained in the psychological discussions of the previous chapter. This can make no difference for us, for we must always be ready to drop our auxiliary ideas whenever we deem ourselves in position to replace them by something else approaching more closely to the unknown reality. Let us now try to correct some views which might be erroneously formed as long as we regarded the two systems in the crudest and most obvious sense as two localities within the psychic apparatus, views which have left their traces in the terms "repression" and "penetration." Thus, when we say that an unconscious idea strives for transference into the foreconscious in order later to penetrate consciousness, we do not mean that a second idea is to be formed situated in a new locality like an interlineation near which the original continues to remain; also, when we speak of penetration into consciousness, we wish carefully to avoid any idea of change of locality. When we say that a foreconscious idea is repressed and subsequently taken up by the unconscious, we might be tempted by these figures, borrowed from the idea of a struggle over a territory, to assume that an arrangement is really broken up in one psychic locality and replaced by a new one in the other locality. For these comparisons we substitute what would seem to correspond better with the real state of affairs by saying that an energy occupation is displaced to or withdrawn from a certain arrangement so that the psychic formation falls under the domination of a system or is withdrawn from the same. Here again we replace a topical mode of presentation by a dynamic; it is not the psychic formation that appears to us as the moving factor but the innervation of the same.

I deem it appropriate and justifiable, however, to apply ourselves still further to the illustrative conception of the two systems. We shall avoid any misapplication of this manner of representation if we remember that presentations, thoughts, and psychic formations should generally not be localized in the organic elements of the nervous system, but, so to speak, between them, where resistances and paths form the correlate corresponding to them. Everything that can become an object of our internal perception is virtual, like the image in the telescope produced by the passage of the rays of light. But we are justified in assuming the existence of the systems, which have nothing psychic in themselves and which never become accessible to our psychic perception, corresponding to the lenses of the telescope which design the image. If we continue this comparison, we may say that the censor between two systems corresponds to the refraction of rays during their passage into a new medium.

Thus far we have made psychology on our own responsibility; it is now time to examine the theoretical opinions governing present-day psychology and to test their relation to our theories. The question of the unconscious, in psychology is, according to the authoritative words of Lipps, less a psychological question than the question of psychology. As long as psychology settled this question with the verbal explanation that the "psychic" is the "conscious" and that "unconscious psychic occurrences" are an obvious contradiction, a psychological estimate of the observations gained by the physician from abnormal mental states was precluded. The physician and the philosopher agree only when both acknowledge that unconscious psychic processes are "the appropriate and well-justified expression for an established fact." The physician cannot but reject with a shrug of his shoulders the assertion that "consciousness is the indispensable quality of the psychic"; he may assume, if his respect for the utterings of the philosophers still be strong enough, that he and they do not treat the same subject and do not pursue the same science. For a single intelligent observation of the psychic life of a neurotic, a single analysis of a dream must force upon him the unalterable conviction that the most complicated and correct mental operations, to which no one will refuse the name of psychic occurrences, may take place without exciting the consciousness of the person. It is true that the physician does not learn of these unconscious processes until they have exerted such an effect on consciousness as to admit communication or observation. But this effect of consciousness may show a psychic character widely differing from the unconscious process, so that the internal perception cannot possibly recognize the one as a substitute for the other. The physician must reserve for himself the right to penetrate, by a process of deduction, from the effect on consciousness to the unconscious psychic process; he learns in this way that the effect on consciousness is only a remote psychic product of the unconscious process and that the latter has not become conscious as such; that it has been in existence and operative without betraying itself in any way to consciousness.

A reaction from the over-estimation of the quality of consciousness becomes the indispensable preliminary condition for any correct insight into the behavior of the psychic. In the words of Lipps, the unconscious must be accepted as the general basis of the psychic life. The unconscious is the larger circle which includes within itself the smaller circle of the conscious; everything conscious has its preliminary step in the unconscious, whereas the unconscious may stop with this step and still claim full value as a psychic activity. Properly speaking, the unconscious is the real psychic; *its inner nature is just as unknown to us as the reality of the external world, and it is just as imperfectly reported to us through the data of consciousness as is the external world through the indications of our sensory organs.*

A series of dream problems which have intensely occupied older authors will be laid aside when the old opposition between conscious life and dream life is abandoned and the unconscious psychic assigned to its proper place. Thus many of the activities whose performances in the dream have excited our admiration are now no longer to be attributed to the dream but to unconscious thinking, which is also active during the day. If, according to Scherner, the dream seems to play with a symboling representation of the body, we know that this is the work of certain unconscious phantasies which have probably given in to sexual emotions, and that these phantasies come to expression not only in dreams but also in hysterical phobias and in other symptoms. If the dream continues and settles activities of the day and even brings to light valuable inspirations, we have only to subtract from it the dream disguise as a feat of dream-work and a mark of assistance from obscure forces in the depth of the mind (cf. the devil in Tartini's sonata dream). The intellectual task as such must be attributed to the same psychic forces which perform all such tasks during the day. We are probably far too much inclined to over-estimate the conscious character even of intellectual and artistic productions. From the communications of some of the most highly productive persons, such as Goethe and Helmholtz, we learn, indeed, that the most essential and original parts in their creations came to them in the form of inspirations and reached their perceptions almost finished. There is nothing strange about the assistance of the conscious activity in other cases where there was a concerted effort of all the psychic forces. But it is a much abused privilege of the conscious activity that it is allowed to hide from us all other activities wherever it participates.

It will hardly be worth while to take up the historical significance of dreams as a special subject. Where, for instance, a chieftain has been urged through a dream to engage in a bold undertaking the success of which has had the effect of changing history, a new problem results only so long as the dream, regarded as a strange power, is contrasted with other more familiar psychic forces; the problem, however, disappears when we regard the dream as a form of expression for feelings which are burdened with resistance during the day and which can receive reinforcements at night from deep emotional sources. But the great respect shown by the ancients for the dream is based on a correct psychological surmise. It is a homage paid to the unsubdued and indestructible in the human mind, and to the demoniacal which furnishes the dream-wish and which we find again in our unconscious.

Not inadvisedly do I use the expression "in our unconscious," for what we so designate does not coincide with the unconscious of the philosophers, nor with the unconscious of Lipps. In the latter uses it is intended to designate only the opposite of conscious. That there are also unconscious psychic processes beside the conscious ones is the hotly contested and energetically defended issue. Lipps gives us the more far-reaching theory that everything psychic exists as unconscious, but that some of it may exist also as conscious. But it was not to prove this theory that we have adduced the phenomena of the dream and of the hysterical symptom formation; the observation of normal life alone suffices to establish its correctness beyond any doubt. The new fact that we have learned from the analysis of the psychopathological formations, and indeed from their first member, viz. dreams, is that the unconscious—hence the psychic—occurs as a function of two separate systems and that it occurs as such even in normal psychic life. Consequently there are two kinds of unconscious, which we do not as yet find distinguished by the psychologists. Both are unconscious in the psychological sense; but in our sense the first, which we call Unc., is likewise incapable of consciousness, whereas the second we term "Forec." because its emotions, after the observance of certain rules, can reach consciousness, perhaps not before they have again undergone censorship, but still regardless of the Unc. system. The fact that in order to attain consciousness the emotions must traverse an unalterable series of events or succession of instances, as is betrayed through their alteration by the censor, has helped us to draw a comparison from spatiality. We described the relations of the two systems

264

to each other and to consciousness by saying that the system Forec. is like a screen between the system Unc. and consciousness. The system Forec. not only bars access to consciousness, but also controls the entrance to voluntary motility and is capable of sending out a sum of mobile energy, a portion of which is familiar to us as attention.

We must also steer clear of the distinctions superconscious and subconscious which have found so much favor in the more recent literature on the psychoneuroses, for just such a distinction seems to emphasize the equivalence of the psychic and the conscious.

What part now remains in our description of the once all-powerful and all-overshadowing consciousness? None other than that of a sensory organ for the perception of psychic qualities. According to the fundamental idea of schematic undertaking we can conceive the conscious perception only as the particular activity of an independent system for which the abbreviated designation "Cons." commends itself. This system we conceive to be similar in its mechanical characteristics to the perception system P, hence excitable by qualities and incapable of retaining the trace of changes, *i.e.* it is devoid of memory. The psychic apparatus which, with the sensory organs of the P-system, is turned to the outer world, is itself the outer world for the sensory organ of Cons.; the teleological justification of which rests on this relationship. We are here once more confronted with the principle of the succession of instances which seems to dominate the structure of the apparatus. The material under excitement flows to the Cons, sensory organ from two sides, firstly from the P-system whose excitement, qualitatively determined, probably experiences a new elaboration until it comes to conscious perception; and, secondly, from the interior of the apparatus itself, the quantitative processes of which are perceived as a qualitative series of pleasure and pain as soon as they have undergone certain changes.

The philosophers, who have learned that correct and highly complicated thought structures are possible even without the coöperation of consciousness, have found it difficult to attribute any function to consciousness; it has appeared to them a superfluous mirroring of the perfected psychic process. The analogy of our Cons. system with the systems of perception relieves us of this embarrassment. We see that perception through our sensory organs results in directing the occupation of attention to those paths on which the incoming sensory excitement is diffused; the qualitative excitement of the P-system serves the mobile quantity of the psychic apparatus as a regulator for its discharge. We may claim the same function for the overlying sensory organ of the Cons. system. By assuming new qualities, it furnishes a new contribution toward the guidance and suitable distribution of the mobile occupation quantities. By means of the perceptions of pleasure and pain, it influences the course of the occupations within the psychic apparatus, which normally operates unconsciously and through the displacement of quantities. It is probable that the principle of pain first regulates the displacements of occupation automatically, but it is quite possible that the consciousness of these qualities adds a second and more subtle regulation which may even oppose the first and perfect the working capacity of the apparatus by placing it in a position contrary to its original design for occupying and developing even that which is connected with the liberation of pain. We learn from neuropsychology that an important part in the functional activity of the apparatus is attributed to such regulations through the qualitative excitation of the sensory organs. The automatic control of the primary principle of pain and the restriction of mental capacity connected with it are broken by the sensible regulations, which in their turn are again automatisms. We learn that the repression which, though originally expedient, terminates nevertheless in a harmful rejection of inhibition and of psychic domination, is so much more easily accomplished with reminiscences than with perceptions, because in the former there is no increase in occupation through the excitement of the psychic sensory organs. When an idea to be rejected has once failed to become conscious because it has succumbed to repression, it can be repressed on other occasions only because it has been withdrawn from conscious perception

266

on other grounds. These are hints employed by therapy in order to bring about a retrogression of accomplished repressions.

The value of the over-occupation which is produced by the regulating influence of the Cons. sensory organ on the mobile quantity, is demonstrated in the teleological connection by nothing more clearly than by the creation of a new series of qualities and consequently a new regulation which constitutes the precedence of man over the animals. For the mental processes are in themselves devoid of quality except for the excitements of pleasure and pain accompanying them, which, as we know, are to be held in check as possible disturbances of thought. In order to endow them with a quality, they are associated in man with verbal memories, the qualitative remnants of which suffice to draw upon them the attention of consciousness which in turn endows thought with a new mobile energy.

The manifold problems of consciousness in their entirety can be examined only through an analysis of the hysterical mental process. From this analysis we receive the impression that the transition from the foreconscious to the occupation of consciousness is also connected with a censorship similar to the one between the Unc. and the Forec. This censorship, too, begins to act only with the reaching of a certain quantitative degree, so that few intense thought formations escape it. Every possible case of detention from consciousness, as well as of penetration to consciousness, under restriction is found included within the picture of the psychoneurotic phenomena; every case points to the intimate and twofold connection between the censor and consciousness. I shall conclude these psychological discussions with the report of two such occurrences.

On the occasion of a consultation a few years ago the subject was an intelligent and innocent-looking girl. Her attire was strange; whereas a woman's garb is usually groomed to the last fold, she had one of her stockings hanging down and two of her waist buttons opened. She complained of pains in one of her legs, and exposed her leg unrequested.

267

Her chief complaint, however, was in her own words as follows: She had a feeling in her body as if something was stuck into it which moved to and fro and made her tremble through and through. This sometimes made her whole body stiff. On hearing this, my colleague in consultation looked at me; the complaint was quite plain to him. To both of us it seemed peculiar that the patient's mother thought nothing of the matter; of course she herself must have been repeatedly in the situation described by her child. As for the girl, she had no idea of the import of her words or she would never have allowed them to pass her lips. Here the censor had been deceived so successfully that under the mask of an innocent complaint a phantasy was admitted to consciousness which otherwise would have remained in the foreconscious.

Another example: I began the psychoanalytic treatment of a boy of fourteen years who was suffering from *tic convulsif*, hysterical vomiting, headache, &c., by assuring him that, after closing his eyes, he would see pictures or have ideas, which I requested him to communicate to me. He answered by describing pictures. The last impression he had received before coming to me was visually revived in his memory. He had played a game of checkers with his uncle, and now saw the checkerboard before him. He commented on various positions that were favorable or unfavorable, on moves that were not safe to make. He then saw a dagger lying on the checker-board, an object belonging to his father, but transferred to the checker-board by his phantasy. Then a sickle was lying on the board; next a scythe was added; and, finally, he beheld the likeness of an old peasant mowing the grass in front of the boy's distant parental home. A few days later I discovered the meaning of this series of pictures. Disagreeable family relations had made the boy nervous. It was the case of a strict and crabbed father who lived unhappily with his mother, and whose educational methods consisted in threats; of the separation of his father from his tender and delicate mother, and the remarrying of his father, who one day brought home a young woman as his new mamma. The illness of the fourteen-year-old boy broke out a few days later. It was the suppressed anger against his father that had composed these pictures into intelligible allusions. The material was furnished by a reminiscence from mythology, The sickle was the one with which Zeus castrated his father; the scythe and the likeness of the peasant represented Kronos, the violent old man who eats his children and upon whom Zeus wreaks vengeance in so unfilial a manner. The marriage of the father gave the boy an opportunity to return the reproaches and threats of his father—which had previously been made because the child played with his genitals (the checkerboard; the prohibitive moves; the dagger with which a person may be killed). We have here long repressed memories and their unconscious remnants which, under the guise of senseless pictures have slipped into consciousness by devious paths left open to them.

I should then expect to find the theoretical value of the study of dreams in its contribution to psychological knowledge and in its preparation for an understanding of neuroses. Who can foresee the importance of a thorough knowledge of the structure and activities of the psychic apparatus when even our present state of knowledge produces a happy therapeutic influence in the curable forms of the psychoneuroses? What about the practical value of such study some one may ask, for psychic knowledge and for the discovering of the secret peculiarities of individual character? Have not the unconscious feelings revealed by the dream the value of real forces in the psychic life? Should we take lightly the ethical significance of the suppressed wishes which, as they now create dreams, may some day create other things?

I do not feel justified in answering these questions. I have not thought further upon this side of the dream problem. I believe, however, that at all events the Roman Emperor was in the wrong who ordered one of his subjects executed because the latter dreamt that he had killed the Emperor. He should first have endeavored to discover the significance of the dream; most probably it was not what it seemed to be. And even if a dream of different content had the significance of this offense against majesty, it would still have been in place to remember the words of Plato, that the virtuous man contents himself with dreaming that which the wicked man does in actual life. I am therefore of the opinion that it is best to accord freedom to dreams. Whether any reality is to be attributed to the unconscious wishes, and in what sense, I am not prepared to say offhand. Reality must naturally be denied to all transition—and intermediate thoughts. If we had before us the unconscious wishes, brought to their last and truest expression, we should still do well to remember that more than one single form of existence must be ascribed to the psychic reality. Action and the conscious expression of thought mostly suffice for the practical need of judging a man's character. Action, above all, merits to be placed in the first rank; for many of the impulses penetrating consciousness are neutralized by real forces of the psychic life before they are converted into action; indeed, the reason why they frequently do not encounter any psychic obstacle on their way is because the unconscious is certain of their meeting with resistances later. In any case it is instructive to become familiar with the much raked-up soil from which our virtues proudly arise. For the complication of human character moving dynamically in all directions very rarely accommodates itself to adjustment through a simple alternative, as our antiquated moral philosophy would have it.

And how about the value of the dream for a knowledge of the future? That, of course, we cannot consider. One feels inclined to substitute: "for a knowledge of the past." For the dream originates from the past in every sense. To be sure the ancient belief that the dream reveals the future is not entirely devoid of truth. By representing to us a wish as fulfilled the dream certainly leads us into the future; but this future, taken by the dreamer as present, has been formed into the likeness of that past by the indestructible wish.

Lightning Source UK Ltd.
Milton Keynes UK
UKHW02f1941060618
323848UK00005B/382/P